IRONIC DRAMA

A STUDY OF EURIPIDES' METHOD AND MEANING

BY THE SAME AUTHOR

PHILIP VELLACOTT

IRONIC DRAMA

*A Study of Euripides' Method
and Meaning*

CAMBRIDGE UNIVERSITY PRESS

Published by the Syndics of the Cambridge University Press
Bentley House, 200 Euston Road, London NW1 2DB
American Branch: 32 East 57th Street, New York, N.Y.10022

© Cambridge University Press 1975

Library of Congress Catalogue Card Number: 74-19522

ISBNs 0 521 20590 5 hard covers
0 521 09896 3 paperback

First published 1975

Photoset and printed in Malta by
St Paul's Press Ltd.

CONTENTS

PREFACE

Herodotus tells, in Book I. 157—60, the story of Pactyes, who came as a suppliant to the city of Cyme. The Cymeans sent to Delphi to ask whether they should hand him over to the king of Persia; and the oracle replied that they should do so. When a leading Cymean called Aristodicus challenged the god's answer, he was told, 'Yes, I bid you give up your suppliant, so that your wickedness may the sooner work your destruction. Never again come to my oracle to ask about handing over suppliants.'

Over the past twenty years, in reading such plays as *The Children of Heracles*, *Andromache*, *The Women of Troy*, *Orestes*, *Iphigenia in Aulis*, and in consulting the available authorities for help in understanding them, I have often felt that same incredulity which sent Aristodicus back to Delphi. He questioned Apollo a second time because he was convinced that the oracle would not plainly command such impiety as the handing over of a suppliant. Pursuing his conviction, he discovered that the oracle given to the first enquirers had been ironic.

Apollo's irony on that occasion may or may not have been characteristic of him. It is not, however, likely to have been a unique instance; and the story makes two things plain: first, that irony of this kind could be recognized as a form of statement with a peculiar force, and was likely to be elicited by an impious question; secondly, that interpretation depended on the will to interpret. The answer given to Erechtheus (see page 194), or the more familiar one given to Orestes (see pages 53—4), may have been of a similar nature. My enquiries into the meaning of Euripides' plays, which eventually led me to undertake this book, were at first based on the hypothesis that this author wrote from a consistent view of the world and of humanity's place in it; and every discovery helped to turn the hypothesis into conviction. It was the crucial case of Helen (expounded in Chapter 5) which first hinted to me that the words of the Euripidean oracle, accepted literally through so many centuries, could in fact be ironic. It is to Helen — Euripides' true Helen — that this book should be dedicated.

Though I have dealt, in varying degrees of fullness, with all the extant plays, this book does not attempt to offer a comprehensive study of the poet. I have kept strictly to that part of the study which I feel qualified to undertake — the author's meaning, and the method by which he expressed it. If in many places I have disagreed with the conclusions of other writers, I none the less acknowledge my infinite indebtedness to the learning, moderation, and enthusiasm of generations of scholars far better equipped than I, whose devotion has made possible the strange fact that in our brash and distracted decade the name of Euripides, and something of the passionate humanity of his created characters, are known to more readers than ever before in two and a half millennia.

I am deeply grateful to Mr Oliver Stallybrass for the devotion, skill, and understanding with which he has prepared the Indexes.

Franksbridge, 1974   P.H.V.

NOTE

When quoting passages from Euripides in translation I have regularly used my own versions from the four volumes of The Penguin Classics, except where it seemed desirable to make a more literal translation to illustrate the argument more clearly.

1

THE CLAIM TO INTERPRET

This book is an attempt to interpret the work of Euripides. Euripides wrote plays; and a play is primarily a work of art. It is also, in the full and proper sense, a popular art; a play does not achieve its life until it has been 'stal'd with the stage' and 'clapper-claw'd with the palmes of the vulgar'.[1] It is not simply created; it is addressed to people, and may invite different inter-pretations from different kinds of people. In the form in which it was first developed in fifth-century Athens it was addressed, not to an élite class or to a chance cross-section of a population, but to a truly national audience whose men would sit a few days later, and had sat a few days earlier, as the sovereign legislative body of the state; an audience comprising a solid core of shrewd and responsible (if often unimaginative) citizens, a growing number of the shallow and vapid whom Aristophanes in *The Frogs* represents by Dionysus, and a small handful of the poet's own peers. In that comedy, which is more about tragedy than anything else, Aristophanes calls dramatic poets 'the teachers of the citizens'. Drama, whatever its origin as a communal religious activity, became in its first vigorous flowering the medium of a message.

There is no need to add to the many descriptive summaries which scholarly writers have given of the 'messages' conveyed by the drama of Aeschylus and of Sophocles. Both poets were revered in their own day, and perhaps not seriously misunderstood in the generations that followed. The case of Euripides is different. Aristophanes' treatment of him suggests that he had the kind of equivocal popularity which could turn, or be turned, against him at short notice. As a poet he was revered; in his function as a 'teacher of the citizens' he was mistrusted. The copious evidence from Aristophanes, and occasional references by writers of the fourth century, indicate that his contemporaries were puzzled to know what it was that he intended to teach them. At one moment he would seem to endorse their favourite prejudice, or indulge their favourite grumble or sentiment, at another to be gratuitously outrageous. In *The Suppliant Women*, for example, how were honest citizens to know whether the dramatist meant them to agree with Theseus, with the chorus, with the Theban Herald, or with Athena in the epilogue? Ordinary people like a message to be clear, and sometimes resent being left to think it out for themselves. Since Athena came last and had divine authority, it was easiest to settle for her, and ignore the contradictions this involved. Euripides' plays were apt to end with a question-mark rather than a full-stop; or the full-stop (as in *Iphigenia in Tauris* and *Orestes*) seemed inconsistent with much that had gone before, and too good to be true. Modern readers of Euripides have found the same difficulty: did he in fact write in order to convey any consistent meaning, any clear moral attitude? Does his work reveal anything which we can recognize as a coherent outlook on human character and human predicament?

There is a tendency among scholars today to answer No. Lloyd-Jones, for example, says,[2] 'we are now chary of trying to extract a general world outlook from the poet's works ... Critical attention has shifted from his supposed views and attitudes to his dramatic technique and methods of construction.' It is true that increased exactness in our understanding of the ancient world has led us to question the similarities between that world and ours and made the differences more evident. Yet when these differences have been fully acknowledged, the reader who still believes that Euripides' plays have reference and meaning for us must search for a principle of interpretation. I believe that to decline this search is to abandon a central obligation of criticism, as well as to miss much of the fire and fascination of the plays, whether in the study or on the modern stage. For the poet's personal character we have almost no evidence; but we do need to understand his character as a writer. For example, the commonly accepted view of *Andromache* as an expression of national antipathy to Sparta involves the assumption that Euripides was the sort of writer who used his craft to encourage such feeling, or who exploited war-time sentiment to gain popularity.[3] The critic who writes about Euripides must make up his mind whether he can accept such an assumption or not, and must search the plays until he finds solid grounds for a decision.

From the first twenty-four years of Euripides' productive life only one play survives complete, out of nearly twenty that he is known to have composed; and that one, *Alcestis* (438), shows a sophisticated accomplishment in design and execution, and a depth of emotional and psychological insight, fully comparable with those of the later dramas. This fact encourages us to consider the main body of his extant work (including the more substantial fragments, which all belong to the later part of his life) as theatrically mature, morally serious, and, while not uniform, yet generally consistent in quality. In pursuing the enquiry I shall decline to dismiss *Iphigenia in Aulis* as 'a thoroughly second-rate play'.[4] or *The Children of Heracles* as 'a thoroughly bad play',[5] or to accept the apologetic phrases sometimes used about *Andromache*.[6] I shall remember instead that *Iphigenia in Aulis* was written within a few months of the completion of *The Bacchae*, and the other two plays a few years after *Medea* and

Hippolytus; and that the deficiency may lie in our understanding rather than in the poet. I appreciate, of course, the reluctance to interpret Euripides in terms of 'a general world outlook', but I hope to offer in reply a sober alliance of reason with imagination based on a strictly objective view of what is in the text. Imagination is a dangerous word; lack of knowledge in one small area of the field may lead to serious or absurd error; but lack of imagination leads to even more distorting results. Since many of the interpretations which I shall put forward in this book differ radically from those usually accepted, I begin by stating two of the reasons which may be held to justify a new attempt to understand this author.

First, the nature of the work we are to study: it is drama. More than that, it is work which the response of modern culture has almost universally acclaimed as great drama. In drama of lesser quality the exact significance of a character, a situation, a sentence, might elude us because there was some detail of custom or circumstance we were not aware of. In great drama it is broadly true that the effect of custom or circumstance is limited and dispensable; when the critical moment comes, the voice and the gesture are those of plain man or woman, of 'the thing itself', the 'forked animal' naked and alone in the tempest, stripped of place and time. If not alone, he is confronting a second such elemental being, and the whole of which the two are factors is still further from the nature of a mere literary entity, still closer to our personal experience of the complexity of life. Most Greek plays include in their design an *agōn*, a matching of strength. Even when, as often, this takes the form of a forensic debate, the true dramatic interest lies less in the balancing of arguments than in what each speaker reveals of himself and of his function in the drama. In an *agōn* the topical, the transient, furthers the plot; what moves the listener is timeless. In the *Oresteia* Clytemnestra's purple drape and Agamemnon's unsandalled feet are Homeric; the confrontation of man's resolve with woman's is as much of our age as of the poet's. The distance between ourselves and these beings is discounted by another feature of drama which, speaking directly to the sense of sight, unites us with them as not even epic narrative can. One figure kneels, clinging to an altar; near by stands the carved image of a god. The god and the altar are what terrified flesh appeals to in extremity. Opposite the altar a hand grasps a weapon; a sharpened edge, now as then, means the pain of dying. Behind the group is a door, whose opening or closing can supersede all language. Waiting down stage stands a Messenger holding an urn or a battered shield. All these symbols are timeless; they give to drama a dimension denied to other forms of literature, and utter without speech the unchanging passion of mortality. The poet's lines may sometimes be hard to understand, but his stage-properties need no translator.

A second reason for attempting a new interpretation of Euripides is the nature of his dramatic method. It has long been recognized that his writing is sometimes ironic; but the recognition has been arbitrarily limited. The purpose of irony in the theatre is to allow those who can to penetrate it and find a further meaning, while others take words at their face value. I hope to show that Euripides' use of irony is much more extensive and systematic than has yet been acknowledged. At the beginning of this century A. W. Verrall began to explore this aspect of Euripides; but the dubious nature of some of his conclusions obscured the value of his important insights,[7] so that his work has not been followed up. It is only in recent years that a few writers on Euripides[8] have felt bold enough to renew the suggestion that dramatists whose audience contained an entire population, from the lowest intellectual level to the highest, may well have made it their art to communicate to each level what was appropriate or acceptable. This is probably true of Aeschylus; of Sophocles at least in *Oedipus Tyrannus*;[9] and I believe it is the key to the most important areas of Euripides' thought and art. It would seem too that Euripides over-estimated the number of his contemporaries whose response to irony could match his use of it; the lack of discernment which we find reflected in Aristophanes' characters was followed a few generations later by the obtuseness of Lycurgus[10] (see pages 194–5). Our present generation responds readily to irony, revels in it; therefore we should have the better chance of understanding Euripides. The interpretation of a writer whose meaning lies near the surface neither needs nor allows testing; the interpretation of irony is tested by each new example. If as we read Euripides our recognition of irony as his habitual method yields intelligible and coherent results in play after play, our claim to understand his method and his meaning will be a strong one.

The limits of what is undertaken in this book must be made clear at the outset. A play in performance is a complex organism today, and was little less complex in the time of Euripides. The Athenian citizen who sat in the March sun to watch these plays had his attention claimed by many different sounds, sights, and thoughts. The design of costumes and masks; the stage setting; unexpected treatment of familiar stories; the music, vocal and instrumental; the choreography, styles of acting or singing, the performance of known individuals — all these were matter for recall and comparison, judgement and dispute. And enveloping all these partial preoccupations was the deep communal experience of springtime festival and pageant, sobered by the opening of a new military and naval campaigning season. The degree of attention that could be spared for the actual words spoken, whether in the play as a whole or in a particular speech or dialogue, will in some cases have been small. The author directed the production, composed the music, and trained the chorus; and when the festival was over, the only element of the play that was available to the ordinary person for subsequent study was the text, more or less as we possess it today.

In this book, then, I shall study the text of Euripides' plays, recognizing that it represents only one of many elements comprised in that original public performance for the sake of which the whole composition was undertaken. But I shall recognize also that the nature of this text, at every point in every play, so far from suggesting a mere framework on which music, dance, decor, and the telling of a plain tale could be deployed, invites the reader to the fullest exercise of his theatrical and humane imagination. We must also acknowledge that it is difficult to understand how words spoken through a mask on the stage of a vast open-air theatre could convey the kind of subtlety we shall be studying — the innuendo of falseness beneath acceptable eloquence, the ironic pathos of nonsense spoken in good faith by an innocent victim. How could such subtleties possibly be perceived? The broad answer is that, in the theatre, they could not; but the complete answer must add that, none the less, the subtleties are there in the text.

But I am not only looking for subtleties; I am attempting a kind of simplicity which many gifted scholars seem to me to have neglected. Critics of Shakespeare would be in general agreement, for example, that *King Henry IV*, 1 and 2, and *King Henry V*, are plays about the idea of kingship, that *Hamlet* is about death and man's contemplation of it, that *Macbeth* is about the nature of evil. To ask, What is the play about? is a simple approach, but a valid and valuable one. In the study of Euripides this question has been too little considered. I shall attempt to answer it in the case of at least ten plays; and in doing so I shall, as far as I am able, ignore received assumptions and look strictly at what is in the text.

George Steiner, in the fourth of his Eliot Memorial lectures,[11] speculating on the prospect for European culture, says:

Already a dominant proportion of poetry, of religious thought, of art, has receded from personal immediacy into the keeping of the specialist. There it leads a kind of bizarre pseudo-life, proliferating its own inert environment of criticism . . . Never have the meta-languages of the custodians flourished more, or with more arrogant jargon, around the silence of live meaning.

My object in this book is to encourage both the sense of 'personal immediacy' in reading Euripides and the sense that a 'live meaning' lies under the silence of centuries. The student of an ancient Greek dramatist is confronted both by historical puzzles and by complex technical structures; he should regard the study of these as chiefly the means to an end beyond them, an end which is found in the living issues and human realities which are the matter of the plays. (I believe that on this principle, at a risk of error which can be guarded against, a valuable degree of understanding can be attained also by a reader of translations.) I know no meta-language, and hope to avoid jargon; but I do claim that we can continue to progress in interpreting Euripides. I shall offer new interpretations of a dozen or more of the plays, and these will be based on a consistent view of the author's ironic method. In each separate instance a case can be stated more or less plausibly for the traditional interpretation; but this tradition always leaves us with what is sometimes referred to as this poet's 'notorious unevenness', or with conclusions that tempt critics to use phrases such as those quoted on page 2. What I hope to offer is an interpretation enabling us to see the whole of the extant work as the creation of a serious and competent dramatist, as an artistic statement relevant to timeless human issues, consistent and comprehensible.

The present general view of Euripides has been largely influenced by reaction to views which were popular in the first decades of this century. Lloyd-Jones[12] describes the position in a stimulating passage on Euripides. Speaking of the generation of Gilbert Murray he says: 'Their Euripides was what would be called in modern jargon a 'committed' poet, an enemy of traditional religion, a pioneer of female emancipation and a protester against the brutalities of his own country's imperialism.' My own view is that in regard to men's attitude to women Euripides was a more radical critic of his society than Murray conceived him to be: not 'a pioneer of female emancipation' or of any other programme, but a prophet who knew that he was and would remain unheeded. As to being 'committed', the word now designates someone who makes his conviction clear by overt action. Much of Euripides' conviction, especially in the matter of women, was for most of his fellow-citizens too radical to be comprehensible, and to the rest he presented it in a fabric of irony which in his day was penetrated by few. Lloyd-Jones continues in the next paragraph: 'That conception of Euripides is now no longer popular. It now seems harder to extract from the many different opinions and attitudes voiced by Euripidean characters and choruses those which can safely be regarded as the poet's own.' Perhaps no constructive criticism is ever 'safe'; but equally no criticism which seeks first to be safe is likely to be constructive. Unfortunately the conception of Euripides which now seems to be 'popular' is that of an able dramatist and poet who could not decide whether his object in writing was to produce works of art, to present a comprehensive tragic view of life, to gain popularity, to shock and to mystify, or to propagate certain political and social views. In the course of this book I shall consider many attitudes and opinions voiced by Euripidean characters; and I hope to show that we can in fact sift the genuine from the false, the direct from the ironic, and establish a principle of interpretation. I shall not attempt to 'extract' opinions (the term is a loaded one) from dialogue or lyric to fasten on the author. On the two great controversial moral issues which are as painfully unsolved in our own day as they were in his — the position of woman in society, and man's behaviour in war — on these issues the material is abundant; and if one play seems to contradict another in a vital point, we must be sensitive to the complexities within each which may, at a profounder level, yield a consistent understanding.

Was Euripides a 'protester'? Did he hold, or wish to propagate, particular views on such matters? Lloyd-Jones in the passage referred to says that 'the case for women' (a curious phrase, itself inviting interpretation) 'is sometimes argued with all the resources of the poet's eloquence, but so is the case against them'. This is true; but it is naïve to conclude from this that the author himself did not know where he stood on such an issue. Each passage of this kind must be interpreted in its own context; the key to meaning will often be the role which the speaker holds in the moral pattern of the play — and to discover this will demand both reflection and comparison. Lloyd-Jones writes, in the same passage, 'That Euripides ... in describing the cruelties of the Greeks towards the Trojans ... wished to protest against the cruelties of the Athenians towards their subjects remains a matter of conjecture.' It depends on what we understand by 'protest against'. One thing is certain: whatever moral opinions Euripides held, he knew the futility of trying to impose them on anyone who was not ready to accept them. Instead, his characters by word and act hold up a mirror to contemporary patterns of behaviour on which he tacitly invites his audience to venture their judgement. How far he is from forcing his own opinion on spectator or reader is shown by the judgements on various characters recorded in both ancient and modern times, which show that critics have declined to look for a further meaning below the surface. Aristotle calls Menelaus (in *Orestes*) a bad character — for which the only obvious ground is that Orestes takes that view; and Orestes in this play is a mentally unbalanced criminal. Modern scholars in general regard Demophon (in *The Children of Heracles*) and Peleus (in *Andromache*) as heroes, even if faintly embarrassing ones; are ready to be sympathetic towards Agamemnon (in *Iphigenia in Aulis*);[13] and never question that Helen, in *The Women of Troy* and *Orestes*, is presented as a despicable and worthless person; they admit the motive of piety as some justification for human sacrifice in *The Children of Heracles* and *The Phoenician Women*, and even in *Iphigenia in Aulis*. I suspect that many Athenians in watching these plays felt uneasy because they knew they were being invited to make moral judgements which they preferred to evade.

'A matter of conjecture'? The truth is, that conjecture in such matters is of the essence of the proper study of Euripides. If no inference of personal attitude can be made connecting the words he wrote with our knowledge of human life and of the history of his time, his integrity as an author is under question and the whole study may prove a barren exercise. Without such inference, Euripides remains a name in the index of a textbook. And if his method includes irony, it is only by accepting the risk of error in interpretation that we can claim the possibility of perception. If a scholar whose intuitive knowledge of a Greek author's style is fine enough to restore lost lines in a faulty manuscript shrinks from venturing his judgement in interpretation of the author's mind, he is surely in danger of perpetuating for his chosen field of literature that 'bizarre pseudo-life' of which Steiner writes in the passage quoted above. And it is on important questions of this kind that the qualified student of English or European literature, even if he depends on translations for his knowledge of Greek drama, may on occasion claim to hold opinions worth the attention of the Greek scholar.

The most important comments on Euripides by ancient Greek writers were those of Aristophanes in *Thesmophoriazusae* and *The Frogs* (with more incidental reference in a few other plays) and of Aristotle in the *Poetics*. Aristophanes, in both these comedies, presents Euripides in person and constantly quotes and parodies his writings; but the general tone is not at all hostile. A clear impression remains that these plays were offered to an audience which contained both admirers and haters of Euripides, as well as others who were sometimes the one and sometimes the other, or who mistrusted him or mistrusted their own ability to understand him. Aristophanes himself probably disagreed with Euripides' more radical and critical attitudes, but agreed with him on a central political issue, namely that the war ought to be ended. Agreement or disagreement, however, were less important to Aristophanes than success and perfection as a composer of comedies; so that we can read these plays as providing some reflection or indication of the moods and opinions of the audience.

From *Thesmophoriazusae* it becomes clear that the man in the street thought of Euripides primarily as a playwright who filled his plays with wicked women and with eloquent male attacks on the whole female sex; next, as one who persuaded people to believe that gods do not exist; and thirdly as a contriver of lively and adventurous scenes. The women of Athens, assembled to celebrate the Thesmophoria, indict the poet chiefly on the first of these counts (the second is not followed up); but in the end the women and Euripides make a bargain and part on good terms. The whole piece is light-hearted caricature; it gives us the poet's public image, but in fact tells us very little about the man or his work. The treatment of the poet in *The Frogs* is more general and more significant and must be described here in full.

A further six years of the war have passed since *Thesmophoriazusae*; the

year is 405, and final defeat lies fifteen months ahead. Aristophanes' first
aim is still entertainment, and the comedy here is as rich as he ever wrote;
but serious advice to the Athenians takes at least as important a place. They
must forget internal quarrels and restore disfranchised citizens; and they
must make peace with the Spartans, who six months earlier, after the
Athenian victory at Arginusae, had yet again offered to evacuate Decelea and
bring hostilities to a close. And while himself offering this kind of advice to
those who have come to see his comedy, Aristophanes makes it clear that
the role of the tragic poet in giving moral and political guidance (for in a
city-state the two were much less separable than with us) was even more
important than his own. The plot of *The Frogs*, Dionysus' journey to Hades to
bring back his favourite playwright, evidently reflects the keen sense of
loss the Athenians felt when in 408 Euripides went to Macedon, and still
more when he died there eighteen months later. He had given a voice to all
those who questioned national, social, and religious assumptions; just
as Aeschylus, dead a generation before the war with Sparta began, still
provided (ironically, since he himself had been a questioner) a voice for
nostalgic spirits who found it dangerous to question. In part the division
was between generations. Euripides had presented this division, with its
painful contradictions, as early as 421 in *The Suppliant Women*. Now in the
comic contest between the two poets the arguments Aristophanes gives
to both sides are the popular ones, full of frivolous misunderstanding and
topical allusion; and the 'trial-by-weight' of the rivals' lines makes a crescendo
of laughter without ever revealing a clear bias toward either poet as an
instructor of citizens, until at last the moment of decision comes, and Dionysus
says,[14]

Well, now, listen, you two. I came down here for a poet.
EURIPIDES :   What do you want a poet for?
DIONYSUS :   To save the city, of course.

Suddenly the tone is serious. Pluto has promised Dionysus that he can take
one of them back with him to Athens, and Dionysus has responded with:

Whichever of you can think of the best piece of advice to give the Athenians at this
juncture, he's the one I shall take back with me.

He poses two test questions to the two poets. The first is, What should be
done about Alcibiades? The citizens, Dionysus indicates, are divided in
their opinions, and constantly change their minds about the man who has
done more harm to the Athenian cause than any other man, yet is still felt
by many to be indispensable. What answer to this question did Aristophanes
himself think of as a good answer? He has been careful through nine-tenths
of the play not to name Alcibiades, though he has named a dozen other

notable politicians. He makes Euripides answer, in effect, that Alcibiades is not to be trusted; and he makes Aeschylus say that Athens cannot afford not to trust him (1427–33). It would be possible to argue that Aeschylus' advice to 'tolerate Alcibiades' peculiarities' was better than Euripides' counsel to have nothing to do with him; but if Aristophanes intended this test-question to be decisive, one would expect him to make the point clearer. The second test-question is, How can the City be saved? To this Euripides replies first with a characteristically antithetic and allusive couplet, a parody of his own style:

> Believe the unsafe safe, the safe unsure;
> Mistrust what now you trust, and fear no more.[14]

Dionysus, who all through the play has represented the average or sub-average feather-pated citizen, finds this couplet a strain on his intellect, whereupon Euripides paraphrases it with incisive clarity (1446–50):

Our present rulers are not saving the City; therefore to save the City we must change our rulers.

When this question is put to Aeschylus, he first says he is at a loss to know, since the citizens have not enough strength of mind either to choose good rulers or to resist bad ones (1458–9). Finally he pronounces thus (1463–5):

[The Athenians will prosper] when they regard their enemies' land as their own, and their own as belonging to their enemies; reckoning that their real wealth (income) is their ships, and that the wealth they now have is poverty.

Stripped of its oracular garb this means, 'Abandon Attica, invade the Peloponnese. Your ships are your only wealth.' Such advice recalls, first, the policy of Pericles in the opening stages of the war twenty-six years earlier; secondly, the famous Delphic oracle of 480, 'Trust in your wooden walls.' In the desperate situation of 405 it sounds like mockery. Thereupon Dionysus, who undertook his journey to Hades in order to bring back Euripides, chooses Aeschylus; and the chorus sing a song to express their satisfaction that

> A man with a shrewd and intelligent mind
> (A man with a sense of proportion)
> Is returning to earth, as this comedy ends,
> To the joy of his colleagues, relations, and friends . . .
> To save the city . . .

In the delighted excitement of the performance all those spectators who had ever been irritated or made uneasy by Euripides would feel that Dionysus had made the choice they wanted, that they had been right all along. They would certainly not weigh up the answers upon which the choice had been based; and Aristophanes, who was not simple-minded or unsophisticated, knew they would not. There is nothing in his text to support the assumption that he intended to show Euripides as being inferior to Aeschylus in the value of the guidance he offered to the citizens; the reverse, if anything, is nearer to the truth. It seems to me that at this point in the scene Aristophanes himself is not deciding for either Aeschylus or Euripides, but is demonstrating the illogical, even preposterous behaviour of the Athenian people in choosing their advisers. Dionysus at every point is the average Athenian: he misses Euripides, but has not the courage to choose him for an adviser. He is frivolous where he should be serious, ready to make his slave his master, unable to keep his attention fixed on anything for more than half a minute, or to tell good advice from bad. The irony of choosing Aeschylus is further pointed by the chorus in their closing lines, which plead for peace and condemn the war-mongers; for the only serious claim to authority that Aeschylus has made in the trial-scene is his inculcation of military virtues. Perhaps the chorus hoped that his dislike of Cleophon, if nothing else, would inspire him to offer counsels of peace. The comedy seems to end with a happy victory for tradition and good sense; but the spectator who saw it in this light equated himself intellectually with Dionysus. Thoughtful Athenians walking home may have felt that, for once, they had heard from Aristophanes a note of final despair.

More than this, some few of them would perhaps recognize in the subtlety with which the message of the comedy had been conveyed to those who would receive it, and concealed from those who would not, precisely the kind of irony which they had learnt to interpret in Euripides' tragedies. Those citizens who responded to the chorus's line about 'a man with a shrewd and intelligent mind' by observing that Aeschylus, in his reply to the final test-question, had shown himself a hesitant, out-of-date bumbler, surely found themselves in as small a minority as the child in Hans Andersen's tale who called out, 'But the Emperor has no clothes on!', and recalled the same experience from productions of Euripides' plays. The two last they had seen (of those known to us) were *The Phoenician Women* and *Orestes*; and they would remember Eteocles, or Pylades, standing forward to address in rousing tones a war-sated audience which had lost its capacity to criticize or question. And when Aristophanes makes Dionysus reject Euripides with the famous quotation, 'My tongue swore . . .', we should do him the credit of assuming that this line is of a piece with the whole passage; that his true irony is pointed, not at the tragedian, but at those who slandered him and quoted him out of context.[15]

We turn now to Aristotle. The phrase most often quoted from Aristotle's remarks on Euripides is that he was 'the most tragic of the poets'. The context of this phrase indicates that by 'most tragic' the writer means 'most powerful in arousing pity and fear'; and though in other parts of the *Poetics* Aristotle says that a good tragedy may have a happy ending, in this central part of his argument he emphasizes that the play which ends in misery is the 'most tragic', that this 'is the right ending', and that Euripides, though to be criticized in other points, is supreme in this vital quality of the 'tragic'.[16] In a useful discussion of this subject John Jones[17] suggests that none the less Aristotle felt a decadent element in Euripides: 'The pathetic self, the solitary and inward self, was cultivated at the expense of that godlike impersonal vitality which Aristotle had at the forefront of his mind when he wrote: "Tragedy is an imitation not of human beings but of action and life".' This is true; but it seems to me to be an incomplete statement; and the other half of the truth is something that Aristotle too failed to perceive. We today recognize, as the fifth-century admirers of tragedy recognized, the aesthetic and the human value of that 'godlike impersonal vitality' which speaks to us every time our eye falls on a sixth-century *Kouros*, or from many pages of *Agamemnon*; and certainly Euripides recognized it to the full. But Euripides saw too that this same vitality was 'godlike' in an exact sense – that it contained a large element of mere cruelty, barbarism, and insensitiveness to the suffering of others, especially of women. As Jones says:[18] 'Euripides appears with a new interest in, and new reverence for, the humanity of mere consciousness ... He is holding to a new apprehension of the human self.' In fact Euripides was concerned to say that to be godlike was a less laudable aim than to be human; that action and life which ignored human beings corrupted its own vitality. We find this well illustrated when we compare the story of *Agamemnon* with the story of *Iphigenia in Aulis*, and consider the two pictures of the king of Argos.[19]

In the *Poetics* Aristotle mentions only four of the seventeen plays of Euripides now extant: *Medea*, *Iphigenia in Tauris*, *Orestes*, and *Iphigenia in Aulis*; and three known to us from fragments, *Cresphontes*, *Melanippe*, and *Peleus*.[20] These references, together with a speech of Lycurgus which we shall consider in Chapter 7, are our chief evidence about the reactions of educated men to the work of Euripides three generations after his death. We shall now briefly consider each of the five comments that Aristotle makes upon Euripides' plays.

In his first reference,[21] speaking of appropriateness in dramatic characters, Aristotle says: 'As an example of unnecessary badness of character, there is Menelaus in *Orestes*.' The fact is that in *Orestes* Menelaus is violently abused by Orestes after he has promised to do his best to help him;[22] when, in view of this attitude, and of the obstinately stupid line of defence which Orestes adopts at his trial, Menelaus changes his mind – Euripides leaves him

hardly any alternative — and does not plead for Orestes' life, Orestes and
Electra join in branding him as a cowardly self-seeking traitor (1056—9). In
the whole play there is not a line to suggest that this judgement is not as
perverted and sick as the murderous and suicidal exploits which follow. Yet
Orestes' judgement on Menelaus was accepted by Aristotle, as it is accepted
by most modern readers of Euripides,[23] partly because Orestes is the central
character in this play, and partly because in earlier plays such as Sophocles'
Aias and Euripides' *The Women of Troy* Menelaus' character had been established as bad.

The second reference[24] is to *Iphigenia in Aulis*. Aristotle criticizes the
character of Iphigenia as inconsistent because 'as a suppliant she is quite
unlike what she is later'. The action of this play confronts Iphigenia first
with a situation in which her father proposes to commit a crime against her
(the chorus have no doubt that it is a crime of the worst kind — see 1089—97);
but at first there is still a hope that the crime may be prevented. The action
proceeds, the situation changes, and the hope vanishes; Iphigenia faces
the new situation with a new resolve. Her character can only be called inconsistent if it is assumed that the proposed sacrifice is a pious and acceptable act — as the audience may well assume in Aeschylus' *Agamemnon*,
though there too room is left for a different view. In *Iphigenia in Aulis*, as we
shall see in Chapter 2, Euripides from the beginning presents the sacrifice as
an outrage. Therefore the charge of inconsistency in the character of Iphigenia
is groundless.

The third reference[25] is to *Medea*: 'It is obvious that the unravelling of the
plot should arise from the circumstances of the plot itself, and not be brought
about *ex machina*, as is done in *Medea*.' By 'the unravelling of the plot'
Aristotle appears to mean Medea's escape from Jason's vengeance. When
he says 'it is obvious' that this should have been brought about through 'the
circumstances of the plot itself', he is clearly thinking of certain plays,
perhaps of Sophocles, whose principle of construction he prefers to what he
finds in *Medea*. He assumes that what seems to be new or unusual must be
faulty or inferior, when it would be reasonable to assume instead that it was
designed for a new or unusual purpose. In this play Euripides has presented
a situation in which no 'unravelling' is possible. To have Jason kill Medea
would be bathetic, meaningless, and artistically false. The first audience
may have included few who could perceive a metaphysical significance in
the chariot of the Sun; but that does not excuse Aristotle, or us, from searching for it. And such significances are discerned through experience and
understanding, not of the theory of dramatic structure, but of the agonizing
dilemmas of human passion.

The fourth comment concerns the value of 'discovery' as an element in
tragic plots. Aristotle rightly says that the most effective kind is that which

occurs naturally in the course of the action, like Orestes' discovery of his sister (in *Iphigenia in Tauris*) from her recital of the letter she wishes to send.[26] But he then goes on to criticize Iphigenia's discovery of Orestes as being 'manufactured' and therefore 'inartistic', because Orestes himself proves his identity by showing knowledge of certain facts not generally known. This Aristotle calls a 'fault', and suggests that Orestes 'might have brought some tokens as well'. It seems not to occur to him that, since two related discoveries are to be made successively, the emotional atmosphere in which the second occurs will necessarily differ from that of the first, so that a different method will be appropriate. Euripides knew that his plays would be read; but in matters of this nature he surely thought first of performance in the theatre. It may perhaps seem arrogant to dispute in this way with Aristotle; but a revealing comment on his kind of criticism is his own statement on the last page of the *Poetics* that 'the effect is as vivid when a play is read as when it is acted'. One had suspected he thought that.

Finally, Aristotle gives a rule for the chorus:[27] 'The chorus should be regarded as one of the actors; it should be a part of the whole, and should assume a share in the action, as happens in Sophocles, but not in Euripides.' This is a curious statement because, of the seven surviving plays of Sophocles, *Oedipus at Colonus* is the only one where the part of the chorus involves anything more than sympathy, mourning, or advice; while of the seventeen surviving plays of Euripides there are six where the action of the chorus affects the development of the plot. It is possible that knowledge of the lost plays of both poets would reverse the picture; but it is equally possible that this statement of Aristotle betrays either a prejudice against Euripides' method or an imperfect knowledge of his work. It is hard to believe that he was unaware that in *The Bacchae* and *The Suppliant Women* the chorus is central to the action; or that he had not observed the part taken by the chorus in the ethical pattern of *The Children of Heracles*, *Ion*, and *Iphigenia in Tauris*; though it is possible that the exceptional significance of the chorus in *Orestes* escaped him as it has escaped most modern commentators.

To summarize: it seems clear, first, that Aristotle's interest in Euripides was limited to the more technical aspects of his plays, and did not extend to any general ideas or philosophy which Euripides might have embodied in his writings; secondly, that Aristotle was unaware of any ironic element in either plot or dialogue. In venturing to disagree with him on this last point we may be encouraged by the evident inaccuracy of some of his specific comments.

It begins to be apparent that Euripides, while retaining the fascinated and puzzled interest of most Athenians, was nevertheless in his central thoughts isolated both from the masses who enjoyed or laughed at his technical and verbal innovations and from the educated who suspected dangerous or disagreeable tendencies in his meaning. To some traditional minds he must have seemed as subversive an influence as Socrates (though looking in a different direction), and been regarded with the same apprehensive reserve as that encountered in our own generation by the radical critic who soberly describes a 'normal' education as conditioning for an insane society.[28] We shall see in later chapters how frequently Euripides takes familiar heroic characters, identifies them with his fellow-Athenians in contemporary situations, and presents them acting in embarrassing or disgraceful ways, at the same time showing that these are the accepted ways of his own society. For those who could follow his meaning there was the suggestion that the whole life of Hellas was built on a false and self-destructive pattern, in which slavery divided more than one-half of the human race from those called free, while the subjection of all women in a less absolute form of slavery left the world in the possession of 'free' males — a minority who assumed that privilege and power were theirs by native right. With this despairing analysis the poet offered, as comfort, the rare but indestructible goodness of individual men and women, the zest of physical and mental life, and the visible beauty of a heartless universe. It was inevitable that a man burdened with such a prophecy should be isolated.

But to recognize this is to see something important for our present study. It is said that the differences, in modes of thought and feeling, between the fifth and fourth centuries B.C. and our own times make it difficult to understand Euripides or to ascribe to him either a clear moral outlook on the world or even a coherent dramatic purpose. These differences are undeniably great. But I would suggest that, in connexion with the kind of ideas we are considering, they are less relevant than the differences which divided Euripides from his contemporaries, and which similarly in our day separate the radical thinker not only from the masses but from many of the more traditional minds among his fellow-intellectuals; that the more significant gulf lies not between the ancient world and ours, but between the lonely critic of society and the average member of society in any century. It may well be the unique comprehensiveness of Euripides' thought, fenced by his ironic method, that has baffled modern attempts to interpret him, as it bewildered readers of his own time. The critical approach needed for understanding his work may be much the same now as it was then. His very isolation from his contemporaries brings him close to the kind of perception which ought to be attainable for us today, after four centuries of European literature and philosophy, several generations of psychology, and the ferment of current sociological thought.

In offering what I believe is a substantially new interpretation of the poet's work as a whole, I shall attempt to do two things. The first will be to distinguish between what is ironic and what is direct. The second, to relate situations, speeches, actions, and moral attitudes found in the plays more directly to the life of the Athenians who formed the first audience than is usually thought to be critically valid. These two aspects of the study are of course closely related, and their relation constitutes a principle of study which will become apparent as the argument proceeds. That is to say, when a statement or a speech seems incredible in the direct sense, we shall consider the possibility that it is ironic, and then apply and test this as a hypothesis elsewhere. A hypothesis is not an article of faith but a basis for study; and it will be necessary to avoid the assumption that Euripides' work is nowhere inconsistent or obscure. Such a process of reasoning is not circular but spiral, or rather escalatory. The results reached can have no 'proof' other than their own self-evidence. Understanding is not arrival at established façts, but an increasing perception of coherence.

I have already mentioned (pages 7—8) my belief that 'conjecture' is a proper and necessary part of our attempt to interpret Euripides. E. R. Dodds, in his edition of *The Bacchae* (Oxford 1960) p. xlvi, writes:

In many of his plays [Euripides] sought to inject new life into traditional myths by filling them with a new contemporary content — recognizing in the heroes of old stories the counterparts of fifth-century types, and re-stating mythical situations in terms of fifth-century conflicts ... In his best plays Euripides used these conflicts not to make propaganda but as a dramatist should, to make tragedy out of their tension. There was never a writer who more conspicuously lacked the propagandist's faith in easy and complete solutions.

The principle of interpretation contained in this statement is of central importance, and the argument of this book is based on it. The tension out of which tragedy is made in *The Women of Troy*, culminating in Hecabe's lament over Astyanax, is the tension experienced by the audience of 415 B.C.; Thucydides recorded this kind of tension not only in the Melian Dialogue, but earlier in the debate between Cleon and Diodotus about the sentence passed on Mytilene (III.36—50).[29] No single instance of this kind is of much value in itself; but that similar connexions should be studied in the whole of this poet's work is indicated by Aristophanes in those passages of *The Frogs* which I have already discussed on pages 9—11. It will not be out of place, then, in our study of *The Children of Heracles* to consider the importance of the Athenians' experiences connected with Plataea; to seek an immediate relevance in the recurring theme of human sacrifice; to find in *Orestes* as powerful a statement about the war as in *The Phoenician Women*; most of all, to try to get past the impregnable assumptions of Euripides' society and the imperviousness of his fellow-citizens to pathos and irony alike — and past the similar obstacles embedded in modern European social structure, to discover what it was that Euripides had to say about woman.

The place of woman in the world and in society, and as a central factor in the life of every man, was the theme which more than any other occupied Euripides during his half-century of creative work. Webster's thorough survey of the plays and fragments in *The Tragedies of Euripides* (1967) has clarified the overall picture; and I shall refer, with grateful acknowledgement, to many of his findings as conclusive, though sometimes disagreeing with his interpretation. He shows in his second chapter that from as early as 455 Euripides produced a long series of plays about women, some of whom were noted for their misdeeds, others for the cruelties they suffered. He finds it probable that Euripides wrote, over a period of twenty-five years, nine sets of three tragedies, in each of which one play dealt with a 'wicked' woman and one with an 'unhappy' woman. Whatever the details, it is evident that during the first half of his career (from which we possess only three complete plays, two of them written at the very end of that period), the theme of woman was his main preoccupation. Of the seventeen extant plays there is only one, *Heracles*, in which no role of first importance is given to a woman — or to women, as in the chorus of *The Bacchae*. What connexion the dramatist finds between woman's wickedness and woman's misery, is a point we shall examine in Chapter 4; for the present we shall note, in anticipation, that he draws a clear picture of male cruelty and contempt as a constant factor in the fate of women. He presents a world in which society, organized and dominated by men, assumes without question that the life of woman is always at man's disposal; and in which most women, under the pressure of society, make the same assumption. Most of the men in Euripides' plays either express or imply the view that the human race consists essentially of free males, with women and slaves as second- and third-class members.[30]

A constant and all-pervading feature of this man-dominated society was, of course, war. This was a topic which Euripides for the most part avoided during his first twenty-five years of play-writing; then the war began, with the long-drawn-out and distressing saga of Plataea — daily visible in the persons of the refugees — which Thucydides describes more fully than any other comparable incident except the last days of the Sicilian expedition; and Euripides wrote *The Children of Heracles*. In this play we see against a background of war two women: one a mere girl, facing with authority and quiet despair a singularly painful example of man's attitude to woman; the other old, rendered savage by a lifetime spent as the victim of a dynastic quarrel. *The Children of Heracles* was followed in the next twenty years by seven more plays about war still extant, plus at least two known to us in fragments. The theme of woman was not abandoned; in six of these war-plays it is prominent; but the audience was a nation at war, and Thebes and Troy now provided a topical theme. The words which Thucydides gives to Pericles in the Funeral Speech early in Book II, when the war was a year old, celebrate the glory of selfless courage and a man's gift of his life in battle, with a truth in which there is no irony. The irony is felt later in the History, as the total pattern shows itself, when the subsequent narrative invites an ironic glance back to the Funeral Speech, by describing an incessant routine of slaughter both military and civilian, spreading and intensifying over the whole of Hellas for the next twenty years. The account includes episodes of glory and of disaster, words of courage and words of hatred; but that early note of sublime moral confidence is not heard again. In its place come the acid rationalism of the Melian Dialogue and the brave despair of Nicias retreating from Syracuse — both being preludes to frantic massacre. The sense of blood-guiltiness tacitly reflected in the prose of history finds a clear voice in poetic drama. It is touched on in *The Children of Heracles*; wept over in *Andromache* and *Hecabe*; grows to bitter pessimism in *The Suppliant Women*; becomes a symphony of indignation in *The Women of Troy*; while in *The Phoenician Women*, *Orestes*, and *Iphigenia in Aulis* the nature and consequences of war are exposed in a forceful and penetrating statement which is unique in the literature of the ancient world.

A third theme, linking the two just outlined, now comes into view. That both Thucydides and Euripides felt the inhumanities of war as a miasma of guilt affecting the whole Hellenic race can probably not be questioned; but what of the inhumanity of man to woman? There is not, so far as I know, any suggestion of guilt, even unconscious guilt, on this account in other writings of the fifth or the fourth century, until we come to the later plays of Menander. We shall consider the evidence for such a feeling in a number of Euripides' plays including *Alcestis*, *The Women of Troy*, *Orestes*, and *Iphigenia in Aulis*; and in the question of the poet's treatment of the figure of Helen (Chapter 5) and of the theme of sacrifice (Chapter 7). I shall not attempt to prove any thesis on the matter; but the possibility, I think, emerges that Euripides saw *the guilt of man* as the central idea of his life's work. In the plays there is no lack of scenes and of descriptions arousing pity and fear; but if that were all, the work would stop short just at the point where the more creative half of the dramatist's art was ready to begin. Perhaps no one is quite sure what Aristotle meant by 'the purging of the emotions'; the feeling of pity presumably cannot be a healthful experience unless it leads either to action or to a conscious change of attitude. Cruelty, or suffering, like anger, is in itself no more and no less interesting than disease; what demands the vision of a tragic poet is the articulation of guilt, something on which the hope of a cure can rest. Euripides was too realistic to think of any change in the two great sources of human misery as possible in his own day or in any foreseeable future; in our twentieth century both the subjection of woman and the addiction to war remain strongly entrenched. But his vision discerned the root of the disease in the universal condition of anger; his message on this topic is clear, and we shall study it in the last chapter.

It is obvious that such themes were unpopular, and that the better they were understood, the deeper the offence they would give. A dramatist in submitting his play had to convince the board of selectors that it was worthy to be 'granted a chorus', and in presenting it to win the applause of the populace. No unperformed play could survive. This helps us to see a possible reason why Euripides presented his most telling truths in ways which carried illumination to the sympathetic instructed spirit, and roused anger in the shrewd and suspicious reactionary; but which made it easy for the average obtuse listener or reader to be unaware that anything harsh or disturbing had been said. The enquiries conducted by Sophists were often radical, and Athenians were doubtless prepared to discuss the equality or inequality of the sexes, or the moral contradictions of warfare, in an emancipated atmosphere of male intellectualism. But drama is not academic; it is personal and immediate. Euripides' unpopularity, which is clear enough from Aristophanes, would have increased to the point where it silenced him altogether, if the majority of citizens who so failed to understand him had begun to glean some notion of what he was really saying about their treatment of their wives and daughters. The second truth Euripides offered in his later work, that the present war was a symptom of insanity,[31] was no less uncomfortable. The average citizen was prepared to be told, in a democratic spirit, that the better policy would be to make peace with Sparta, and to praise examples of moderation and mercy in others; even in the late years of the war he could applaud *Lysistratē* or the chorus's exhortations in *The Frogs*; but he still voted with Cleophon in the Assembly and did not want to hear his conduct or attitude called insane. The prophecy in the epilogue of *The Suppliant Women* proved all too true.

Euripides, then, was not merely alone, a solitary voice in his own world; he was destined to have no true successor. Menander, eighty years later, admired and echoed him, and may well have understood at least part of his radicalism; but though Menander's comedies are serious in the same way as Shakespeare's comedies are serious, they are not tragedies; their judgements are made on the level of the practical and possible, and do not attempt any fundamental challenge.

In our day radical criticism of the position accorded to women by society, and the description of war as liable to develop into a self-propagating insanity — this kind of view is familiar; but it is certainly not general and is often not popular. It is safe to say that, in the two hundred years before the last war, one place where resistance to this kind of outlook was likely to be strongest was in the Classical Faculty of an ancient university. The monastic life, the academic ambience, the exclusion of women, the mistrust of all politics but the safest and all emotions but the most conventional, produced successive generations of devoted and brilliant scholars of the Greek language, literature, philosophy and history; and their erudition seemed then to be unaffected by the fact that many, perhaps most, of them were men of precisely the habit of mind which Euripides observed and criticized in his fellow-citizens; defenders of tradition, suspicious of questioners; towards women, polite but rigid; towards religion, formal; embarrassed by moral criticism of accepted practice, especially in public matters. It is not surprising that perception of the irony of Euripides has emerged so slowly from the naïve conventionality of nineteenth-century exposition.

APPENDIX TO CHAPTER 1:
THE GODS IN EURIPIDEAN DRAMA

The greater part of this book is given to studying what is done and said by mortal men and women in the plays, to discovering the immediate and the universal significance of each dramatic pattern. But every play also offers for our interpretation a timeless, cosmic setting; the presence, power, or command of a god is always an essential part of the human crisis. Euripides uses the extra dimension thus created, and the shift between the mundane and the supernatural worlds, as a further vehicle for ironic comment on human behaviour and the nature of Necessity. The immortal beings, greater and lesser, who peopled the imaginative world of Homeric heroes appear again in the fifth-century Attic theatre substantially unchanged in name and nature, and in their formal relation to human society. Euripides' dramas outline a universe in which gods indeed exist, and exercise irresistible power, but where man, though always at their mercy, nevertheless claims a power of survival whose value is different but absolute, and a moral sovereignty which gods by their nature cannot share. To attempt to describe Euripides' religious views is outside the scope of this book; but it is well to give here a very brief summary — which will be particularized as we examine each play more closely — of the *functions* which Euripides assigns to gods in his plays, without assuming that these functions define his view of the *nature* of gods.

In seven of the plays the god concerned is Apollo, though only in two, *Alcestis* and *Orestes*, does he appear in person. In more than half of the plays a god appears in the epilogue and speaks *ex machina*; in five plays the prologue is spoken by a god or gods, and in *Heracles* two gods appear in the middle of the action.

Let us look first at those epilogues where gods claim that their intervention in human affairs is at least partly disinterested, or that they represent the principle of *dikē*, the ultimate balancing of fortune and misfortune, of crime and retribution, for which Zeus is responsible; whose function is to announce a divine purpose or destiny for one or more of the mortals who have figured in the action, to give explanation and instruction to human blindness, or to institute some custom or festival and relate ceremony to the significant past. The surviving plays give five examples.

In *The Suppliant Women* Athena, by inciting the younger generation to war and revenge, contradicts everything which in the course of the action has claimed the sympathy of all spectators capable of making liberal and morally sensitive judgements — the moderate and disciplined action of Theseus, the common sense of the Herald, the direct pleading and irrefutable reason of the chorus. The irony of her address goes further. The exceptional humanity of Theseus as described by the Messenger (720–30, 758–68) has presented with deep conviction a moral attitude whose authority transcends both law and custom. The legalistic tutoring in political behaviour which occupies the first two-thirds of Athena's speech is in plain contrast to this moral authority; and Theseus' speech of submission offers a bitter comment on the usual fate of idealist leadership. In *Ion* Athena offers, as a solution of the dilemma, the very explanation which Ion's honesty has just rejected as contemptible. In *Iphigenia in Tauris* Athena's appearance, if taken as a serious ending, exposes the Messenger's long narrative as an artificial device for causing suspense, and shows that, if the gods have any wider purpose, its fulfilment is precarious and haphazard; and indeed the Messenger's factual account carries more conviction than Athena's remote command. In *Andromache* the comfort offered to Peleus by Thetis is so cold and ambiguous as to be derisory (this will be discussed in detail in Chapter 2). Finally all these more gentle ironies are crowned by the cruel and withering parody of an epilogue in which Apollo speaks at the end of *Orestes*, in words which mock the agonies witnessed in the play.[32]

There are three epilogues where the message is direct and irony absent; two of them are spoken by the Dioscori. In *Helen* the Twin Gods have little to do beyond calming the rage of Theoclymenus. In *Electra* their condemnation of the crime, and their sympathy for weak and deluded mortals, ends with dignity an action in which there is nothing to be explained, where there is room only for shame and sorrow. At the close of *The Bacchae* Dionysus states unequivocally that Fate and the universe know neither pity nor pardon; Cadmus, pleading for pardon, speaks of a moral world to which gods are blind. The implied lesson is the same as that offered at the close of *Hippolytus*, that such qualities and attitudes are the pre-rogative of mortals, a spiritual power which enables the transient to challenge the eternal. In none of these epilogues is there any hint[33] that gods overrule humans for their own good, or direct events to fulfil a wider justice beyond man's vision.

In *The Women of Troy* we find a prologue in which Poseidon begins by talking in sorrowful tones of the fall of Troy and the temples running with blood. Then enters Athena, who had favoured the victors; and at her request he agrees to raise a storm and drown the Greeks by thousands on their way home. Lest we should imagine that this project belongs to a broad concept of cosmic justice, Athena explains that her motive is personal resentment and nothing else; Poseidon accepts this without demur. In *Hippolytus* Aphrodite opens the prologue with a long speech, and Artemis dominates the first part of the epilogue, leaving the final passages to the mortals. These two goddesses are not concerned either with the past crimes of the House of Minos (though characters and chorus are fearfully aware of them) or with the future of the Athenian dynasty. Aphrodite's divine purpose is to get her own back on Hippolytus for his neglect of her; that of Artemis is to get her own back on Aphrodite, since she cannot thwart her. Humans contemplating present or past misfortune have always been apt to comfort their misery or calm their guilt by seeing a divine purpose in events, as Orestes does in *Iphigenia in Tauris* 1012–16 (compare also Peleus in *Andromache* 1283); but Orestes' trust is a third time betrayed by Apollo, and the whole tenor of Euripides' work seems to me to deprecate such an attitude as groundless, harmful, and undignified. This interpretation of the poet's mind is supported by the one other theophany occurring in the extant plays, that of Iris and Lyssa (Madness) in *Heracles* 822—74. Here the visible malice of divine forces provides the background against which, in the last scene, Heracles in his distress holds fast his belief in the moral nature of gods — echoing the irony in *The Women of Troy* mentioned above. In the course of this book I shall study numerous examples of the way in which Euripides encourages his listeners to reject old, incomprehensible notions of divine 'justice' (which include, of course, the whole 'logic' of human sacrifice) and to look instead to their own moral sense, however fallible it may be. We shall also see how, when a god speaks *ex machina*, his unfolding of an inscrutable 'divine purpose' may come as revealed truth to those in the audience, and those characters on stage, for whom irony was intended as a veil; while to those for whom it is a mirror it will show — as a mirror should — a reflection to be interpreted by contraries.

This brief summary of the function which Euripides allots to gods in his dramas should not be taken as suggesting that Euripides taught his listeners not to believe in the existence of gods. He was popularly accused of doing this,[34] and it is clear that his Apollo, Artemis, Aphrodite and the rest do not in any way endear themselves. But they represent realities in human experience. The often-quoted line, 'If gods do evil, they are not gods', expresses the opinion of an unknown character in a lost play, *Bellerophon* (Fragment 294), and certainly not the opinion of the dramatist. The charge of irreligion may be countered by observing that his references to Zeus are serious even when sceptical,[35] and seldom ironic.[36] It must also be said now that the account given above of divine appearances in Euripides' plays may seem to orthodox scholars merely tendentious. Editors usually regard the epilogues of *Andromache, Ion, Iphigenia in Tauris*, as providing in some sense, even if perfunctorily, happy endings with an acceptance of divine purpose.[37] Such a reading of the plays is not to be called incorrect, only incomplete; it was, I surmise, the view which the poet expected most of his audience to accept. More than that, it seems that he was at times concerned to show the rich and sensitive features of a world in which the presence and activity of gods was for men and women still a living reality. That world had by no means vanished from fifth-century Athens; it lived side by side with realism and the denial of imagination. To say that Euripides himself did not believe in the presence of gods is beside the point; he was concerned with the way believers and unbelievers met and spoke to each other, with the way two worlds mingled in human crises. The tenderness and truth of the last scene in *Alcestis* belongs to the world of belief. So does the warmth of humanity which in the recognition-scene near the end of *Ion* suddenly floods in to drown the hatred, violence and deceit which have coloured the preceding scenes; and here the lasting freshness of this imaginative world is symbolized by the wreath of olive-leaves, still green after sixteen years. This picture is probably not cynical; though clearly it may be read as ironic by those who will.[38] The critical temper of our own generation is one which Euripides would have welcomed. If in interpreting the human characters, and the plots which comprise their actions and sufferings, we insist that these plays are the coherent work of a single creative mind, and so reject as unsatisfying those conclusions which seem contradictory or absurd, I hope that a no less consistent picture of the gods as Euripides presented them will incidentally emerge.

2

THE IRONIC METHOD 1

Divine powers show themselves in many forms,
And gods bring about many things unexpectedly.

This statement in Euripides' familiar tailpiece expresses one frequent element
in tragedy: the contrast between expectation and fulfilment. This contrast
exercises its power upon the audience because at critical points in the unfolding of a plot the audience can see the imminent outcome, and can see that the
hero cannot or will not see it. The more elated, the more poetically expressed,
the hero's confidence becomes, the more poignant is the audience's awareness that his hope is groundless and his reason blind. So Heracles walks
happily with Megara and his two sons into the palace where Iris and Madness wait for him. This is 'dramatic irony'. D. A. Raeburn, in an unpublished
paper, 'Dramatic Irony', says that dramatic irony presupposes 'a vital
relationship between actors and audience. What is being performed is not
independent of the spectators but depends on their involvement as witnesses.'
Irony of this nature has been generally recognized as characteristic of all three
dramatists; it can be understood at once by an audience of average intelligence.
This 'dramatic irony' was not called 'irony' in the ancient world; Raeburn in
the paper just quoted points out that 'Irony is not mentioned in the *Poetics*
and its use as a technical literary term seems to be entirely modern.' The word
eirōneia became familiar as the term used by Plato to describe Socrates' pretence of ignorance in philosophical discussion. The kind of irony which
Euripides employs as his most frequent and powerful weapon was something
different from this, and different also from 'dramatic irony'. It appears never
to have been given a name in the ancient world; but 'irony' is the only name
we can give to it today.

   I have selected for exposition in this chapter three plays, *The Suppliant
Women, Andromache,* and *Iphigenia in Aulis.* Of these, *Andromache* will be
studied again in Chapter 4, all three in Chapter 6, and *Iphigenia in Aulis* in
Chapters 7 and 8. But there will in fact be hardly any repetition; and none of
these three plays, relevant though they are to those chapters, can be studied as
a whole under any of those separate topics, while together they provide a con-
spectus of the poet's ironic method which we should consider at the outset,
before becoming involved with particular themes. I have added a few para-

graphs on an ironic element in *Electra*, partly because it does not belong to any of the main themes I shall discuss later, partly because it may alert the reader's perception to the possibility of irony in unexpected places.

It is unfortunate that some modern writers on Greek drama tend to become suspicious at the first mention of a 'hidden meaning' or 'two levels of understanding', of one message for the common hearer and another for the discerning.[1] The necessity for such distinctions is in fact inherent in the nature of these plays and of their audience. There are successive levels at which this distinction between the direct and the ironic is found. In *Agamemnon* the Watchman says that the beacon will bring

> Great news for Clytemnestra, in whose woman's heart
> A man's will nurses hope.

And before leaving the stage he adds

> I speak to those
> Who understand me; to the rest — my door is shut.

Later Clytemnestra speaks ironically first to the Herald, then to the King. The Elders say that they 'interpret' her (616); but after the King has entered the palace they cannot interpret Cassandra. In *Agamemnon* the author takes the audience with him and shows them irony at work between his characters; but in *Eumenides* he leads them out of their depth. Orestes, on trial, is unable to continue his defence, and commits it to Apollo, whose dubious, barely honest arguments are in contrast to the genuine perplexity of Orestes. To attempt to interpret this situation is to face the central moral problem of the trilogy; and this task is not incumbent on the rapt spectator, but in due course, in the written text, presents itself to the reader's thought.

Irony is a filter which separates different meanings for their appropriate recipients. Besides the distinction between spectator and reader, there are distinctions between listeners of different capacity. The capacity to respond to lyric poetry, to dramatic pathos, to social criticism, to visible pageantry, would not necessarily correspond to any scale of intellectual acumen. The audience included conservatives and progressives in aesthetic values, as in morals and politics. Some would be stupider than the citizen who voted to ostracize Aristeides, others coarser than the Boor described by Theophrastus. The poet's national and religious duty was to speak to them all — surely a task to baffle invention; since what pleased one man must irritate another. It was not only his duty; it was necessary to his existence as a poet: to be given a stage, he must find favour. Public judgements are nearly always conservative; so this meant that a play must commend itself as acceptable to religion, to morality, and to the state. The critical activity of Socrates, whose influence was that of a private person, was held to be so inimical to all three that it led eventually to the draught of hemlock. A poet presenting a play at the Spring Dionysia was not a private person; he was the nation's chosen spiritual instructor. Most of the plays of Euripides are capable of appearing inoffensive to accepted standards; and both the ancient and the modern worlds have in general so interpreted them. But our study will reveal below their orthodox surface a criticism so fundamental that, had its full purport been grasped, its implications followed, by a substantial number of citizens, he would have run the risk of being arraigned as a subverter of society, and denied the only audience which could give life to the fruits of his genius. The intensity of feeling for which his work is famous is not merely the product of an exceptional facility in expression. It springs from his vision of Hellenic society corrupt and sick; honouring the family as its bond of strength, yet infecting the love of man and woman with injustice and resentment; honouring freedom above all, yet turning free men into slaves; honouring the life of the city-state, yet destroying it with the insanity of mutual slaughter. His contemporaries praised him as a creator of lyric beauty and tragic pathos; but the quality of truth, which finds not a single acknowledgement in any recorded voice from his own or following centuries is, above all, the treasure which rewards those who, two and a half millennia after him, search his works for light on the unchanging mystery of humanity.

We will now begin a general survey of Euripides' method. The first example studied will be the portrait of Theseus found in *The Suppliant Women*. This portrait is one of two main themes in the play; the other is the difference between justified and unjustified war, and this will be examined in Chapter 6.

The chorus are the mothers of the seven chiefs who made war against Thebes, were defeated, and all died on the battlefield except Adrastus who had led the expedition. Creon king of Thebes refused the customary permission to recover for burial the bodies of the dead. Adrastus has now come with the bereaved women to the temple of Demeter at Eleusis to beg Theseus, and Athens, for their help. They have spoken first with Aethra, Theseus' mother, and she has sent a herald to summon Theseus. 'For women,' she says, 'the part of wisdom is to act through men.' (The latter half of this scene, 246– 365, throws back an ironic shadow on this line.) Theseus arrives, questions Adrastus about the circumstances of the expedition, and listens to his appeal on behalf of the mothers of the dead men. Then in reply he makes a lengthy speech (195–249) which demands detailed study. Theseus, in the generation before the Trojan War, had united for the first time the scattered communities of Attica in a single state. He is the Athenian national hero and, like his father Aegeus in *Medea*, he represents especially a role which Athens still claimed to fill, as protector of the outcast and helpless.

Theseus begins with a philosophical sermon (195–218), the drift of which is: By the kindness of gods, the blessings of human life outweigh its evils; therefore men ought to be content, and not let pride lead them to war. The first noticeable thing about this sermon is that, serious and practical though it may be, as a reply to the immediate question — the plight of these mothers whose sons lie unburied — its piety is irrelevant and its smugness offensive. Further, the audience who watch the play have been at war for ten years, have seen their farms plundered repeatedly, and are not likely to be impressed with such arguments as

> I praise whatever
> Immortal power took man's life from its primal chaos
> And brutishness, disposed it in an ordered state,
> Endowed it first with understanding, then bestowed
> The tongue to convey meaning through articulate speech;
> Gave us earth's fruit for food, and, lest supply should fail,
> Sends rain to nourish growing plants, and fertilize
> The womb of earth . . .
> Then, since God makes such rich provision for our life,
> Are we not wanton, showing discontent?

There is irony beneath irony here. When he turns to apply the homily to the case of Adrastus, he censures him for being 'enslaved to Apollo's riddle, as though [you believed that] gods live'. The phrase is puzzling; but on any interpretation it seems incongruous with what he said only three lines earlier, when he spoke of men's 'truculent hearts claiming a wisdom higher than divinity's'. When we turn back to the dialogue which precedes the sermon, we find the puzzle still harder. For there Theseus first criticized Adrastus for taking heed of 'an obscure oracle of Apollo' which told him to 'marry his daughters to a lion and a boar'; then blamed him for not 'consulting prophets and observing altar-flames' before he set out on the expedition, and for not heeding the warning of the prophet Amphiaraus. What is the meaning of this contradiction? Either the author has been careless in writing a speech for a revered hero, or he is using the hero's words to offer a comment on politicians who make ambiguous and random use of oracles to serve the argument of the moment. Adrastus made two unwise alliances, Theseus continues, and then

> You led the entire army of Argos out to war . . .
> Misled by young men, who love popularity
> Above all else, multiply wars unscrupulously,
> And corrupt our citizens — one, to obtain a generalship,
> Another to gain office and use it for his pleasure;
> A third, for money, heedless of what injury
> His act may cause to the whole people. Citizens

Are of three orders: first, the rich; they are useless, and
Insatiable for more wealth. Next, the very poor,
The starving — these are dangerous; their chief motive is
Envy; they shoot their malice at those better off,
Swallowing the vicious lies of so-called champions.
The middle order is the city's life and health;
They guard the frame and system which the state ordains.
    Shall I then form alliance with you? What sensible
Reason for this could I offer to my citizens?
Go, then; farewell; and since you chose an imprudent course,
Fight with your fate yourself, and do not trouble us.

What are we to make of this whole speech? The first part of it showed Theseus as pompous, irrelevant, insensitive; then came the confused remarks about oracles and omens; and the last part is another sermon, this time on a political theme — a tirade against 'young men' and a eulogy of the 'middle class', uttered by a king who has himself been praised as a 'young man', but is also about to demonstrate how greatly he is influenced by his mother. And the conclusion reached has little bearing on the problem in hand; what Adrastus requested was not 'alliance' for himself but action on behalf of the chorus of suppliants. It seems clear that in the passage beginning 'Citizens are of three orders . . .' the speaker's eloquence has carried him on his hobby-horse so far away from the matter under discussion that he has suddenly to return to it with a 'most lame and impotent conclusion'. There is certainly nothing here which could be the intended 'message' of such a writer as Euripides. In short, the speech as a whole is caricature. Of what, or of whom? Perhaps of leading middle-class citizens, regularly elected to office, eloquent on the subject of young men, muddle-headed as politicians, but on a rare occasion capable of efficient action and a noble gesture; or perhaps of some particular person or speech — it is impossible to say. The important thing is, that we should be confident enough in our general judgement of the author to know that its contradictions and irrelevancies, and above all its 'party' attitude, while likely to draw applause from the many, invites the few to ironic interpretation. This view is confirmed by the unexpected dignity of Adrastus' reply, 253–62.

Aethra next urges Theseus to change his mind and help the suppliants. She says little that he has not already heard from Adrastus and from the women; but she recalls him to the point at issue, and epitomizes the duty of Athens in a memorable phrase (312–13):

    This one bond makes all cities one:
Free, honourable respect for universal rights —

and her arguments convince him. In his reply to her (334–58) we have first the laudable claim of Athens 'to be always the punisher of injustice', and a proper confidence in her ability to perform this role. Then follows the democratic principle of consultation before engaging in a war; and it is announced in these terms:

> I desire that all my citizens
> Shall give their free assent; they will uphold my wish,
> But their hearts will be stronger in this cause, if I
> Have given them reason. When first I assumed leadership,
> I gave my people freedom and the equal vote,
> And on this basis instituted monarchy.

If this is not a quiet ironic comment on the kind of political freedom enjoyed by Athenians under the leadership of Pericles or of Cleon, then Euripides was a dull writer.[2] Lines 354—5 show again the patronizing attitude to Adrastus, and the assurance of monarchic authority in a democratic framework.

We now come to the encounter between Theseus and the Theban Herald. The democratic decision has been announced (393—4):

> With warm goodwill the Athenian people, when they saw
> That I desired it, undertook this enterprise.

Five lines later the Herald enters with

> Who is king absolute here?

This need not be felt as a sneer either at Theseus or at the necessary place of authority in a democracy; the tone is objective, perhaps cautionary — though irony cannot be ruled out. Theseus' reply begins with a fair statement:

> This . . . is a free city.

The same statement was made some years earlier by Demophon in *The Children of Heracles*, and there events proved it a dubious claim (see Chapter 7, pages 187—8). Theseus continues (407—8):

> We give no special power to wealth;
> The poor man's voice commands equal authority.

Another political sermon, on an unimpeachable text. But, whatever truth such an assertion may have had fifty years earlier, it surely carried less conviction in 421, in a community harassed and regimented by the exigencies of war, dislocated by the increase of population, and bemused by able demagogues. The unrealism of it provokes the Herald to interrupt — which he does, mingling the wisdom of Thucydides with that of Socrates to powerful effect.

The plain truth of his broadside knocks Theseus a little off balance; but he recovers at once, realizing that this is the moment when, if ever, he must state
convincingly the established doctrine of democracy. There are two alternative directions in which his thoughts can turn to seek for the inspired word
or phrase. They may look at the realities of the immediate present – which
here include the group of anguished suppliants before him and the loyal
citizens he has just been addressing, together with the fact that he has already
today changed his mind completely on a vital issue and could presumably
have carried the popular vote for either decision. Or, if that direction offers
formidable problems, his thoughts may turn instead to what he learnt at
school, to theories he remembers hearing powerfully expounded, when he
was a boy, by some great national leader. It is not hard to see from which
direction Theseus draws his inspiration for this speech (429–41):

> A state has no worse enemy than an absolute king.
> First, under such a ruler there is no common law.
> One man holds the whole law in his own grasp; that means
> An end to equality. When laws are written down,
> Both poor and rich possess their equal right; the weak,
> Threatened or insulted by a prosperous neighbour, can
> Retort in the same terms; the humble man's just cause
> Defeats the great. Freedom lives in this formula:
> 'Who has good counsel which he would offer to the city?'
> He who desires to speak wins fame; he who does not
> Is silent. Where could greater equity be found?

Such a picture of the ideal Athens had its usefulness as a recognized standard
for legislation or for judicial practice; but Aristophanes' Dicaeopolis, in
The Acharnians a few years earlier, would have commented with ribald
aptness upon its relation to the ordinary citizen's life. Theseus passes to his
next point, 'young men'. The contrast between young and old has become a
refrain. Aethra and the chorus are old; Theseus and Adrastus are young, as
were the dead chiefs. Adrastus has confessed that it was young men's folly
that led him to ruin (160); Theseus has enlarged (232–7) on the bad
influence of young men in politics; the chorus and Adrastus have praised
Theseus because he is young, and begged him to excuse the errors of other
young men. But now in the second scene Theseus, as it were, changes sides,
and says that

> the people, vested with authority,
> Values its young men as the city's great resource . . .
> How can a city grow in strength, when all its young
> And bold spirits are mown down like fresh stalks in spring?

The first and obvious point here is, that 'the people, vested with authority', had refused to take the chance offered by the victory at Pylos a few years earlier to end the war by which all its young and bold spirits were being mown down. The second point is, that Theseus' argument about 'young men', whether or not it alludes to current politics, is improvised casuistry. His final assertion confirms the general picture of his mental position: 'An absolute monarch,' he says, 'rapes the daughters of the citizens.' We may remember, first, that these lines (452—5) were written by the author of *Medea*, whose heroine tells a group of sympathetic Corinthian ladies that marriage was often indistinguishable from legalised rape (*Medea* 230—51, especially 236—7). We may recall, next, the lines in *Iphigenia in Aulis* (1274—5) where Agamemnon explains to his daughter that the sacrifice is necessary because Greek wives must be saved from being raped by Phrygians (see below, p. 176). Theseus concludes

> Thus much in answer to the points you aimed at me.

But those who had learnt how to listen to Euripides in his ironic vein will have observed that not one of the Herald's indictments — which were aimed at the practice, not the theory, of democracy — has received any direct answer.

On the other hand, the speech in which Theseus states his resolve to go to Thebes and bring back the dead for burial (517—63) is a clear, courageous, and noble utterance:

> You fought your foes with glory to yourselves, and shame
> To them. That done, the score is paid. Permit their bodies
> To hide below ground, and each part to return there
> Whence first it came into this light; breath to the sky,
> Flesh to the soil. For we have in our own bodies
> But a life-tenancy, not lasting ownership;
> At death, the earth that bred us must receive us back.

The portrait of Theseus is composite; and it may well be offered as a portrait of Athens in the first decade of the war. In one aspect we see courage, generosity, and reverence for principle; in the other, complacency, self-worship, self-deception, and a readiness to evade the issue. The poet addresses to his mother-city words to 'cleave her heart in twain', as if he would plead with her to 'throw away the worser part of it'. It was unlikely that his plea would reach any ear that needed to hear it; but a prophet must unburden himself.

The portrait is continued in the Messenger's narrative. Theseus' leadership amidst the carnage of battle — whose horrors are detailed without zest and without sparing — is praised without irony. His men win the battle, and then (720ff.):

> they were making for the gates.
> All over Thebes there was shouting, wailing of young and old;
> Terrified thousands filled the temples. But Theseus,
> With the way clear before him, would not enter the walls.
> 'I have not marched from Athens to destroy this town,'
> He said, 'but to demand the dead for burial.'
> There is a general! He is the kind of man to choose —
> Hardy in danger, an enemy to arrogant states . . .

The humanity of refusing to sack Thebes can hardly have been expected to appeal to more than a certain proportion of a citizen body which six years earlier had with difficulty been persuaded to rescind the sentence of massacre on Mytilene. The Messenger carefully refers his enthusiasm, and that of the audience in the theatre, not to the victor's forbearance but to his military success. This, however, cannot alter the fact that, for the author as for the reader, Theseus' civilized behaviour in the moment of victory is the peak of his achievement; if this were not so, there is no conceivable reason why Euripides should have made the point here, for Athena to contradict in the epilogue. It is the most radically novel event that has occurred so far in the play; and its importance as an element in Theseus' character is underlined when the Messenger tells, 758—68, how Theseus with his own hands raised the putrid corpses and washed their wounds. No one in the play comments on the sparing of the city; what will be done with this uncomfortable rebuke to standard military practice? We wait for an answer through Adrastus' funeral speech, a choral ode, and the episode of Evadne and Iphis. Then enter in procession the Sons of the dead chiefs, carrying urns which hold their fathers' ashes. As Theseus at his first appearance ignored the pleading of the bereaved mothers, so now their grandsons ignore them (1143—52):

> SONS: Father, your son mourns for you:
>   Do you hear? Shall I one day,
>   Shield in hand, avenge your death? God grant it!
>   Justice for my father's blood —
>   It will yet come, with the favour of heaven.
> CHORUS: This evil sleeps not yet.
>   Why must we always weep?
>   I have had enough of disasters and of misery.
> SONS: The day will come when . . . I march bronze-clad
>   At the head of a Danaid army
>   To avenge my father's death.

Theseus makes no protest. He presents the urns as a gift to the boys, that Argos may remember the kindness of Athens. Suddenly Athena appears, unannounced.

She comes to do two things. First she deals with the pact which Theseus has just made with the Argive boys. It was a pact of generosity with the hope of gratitude, sealed with Athenian blood at the funeral of Argive dead. Athena lifts this ceremony out of its heroic and solemn simplicity, and dresses it in the pedantic bargaining and religious officialdom of fifth-century diplomacy. Then she addresses the Sons (1213–26):

> When you reach manhood you shall sack the city of Thebes
> In vengeance for your fathers' blood . . .
>   Once your beards darken your cheeks,
> Lose no time . . . You shall lay their city in the dust.
> This is the inescapable truth.

And Theseus replies:

> I will obey you, Queen Athena; by your voice
> Alone I am saved from error, led in the right path . . .
> Guide my decisions; while your favour rests on us,
> Athens will live henceforward in security.

This foolish faith has been contradicted by all the reason and eloquence of the play — by the piety of Theseus, the experience of Adrastus, the logic of the Herald, and the intuition of the chorus. But what can a mortal king say, when a god first ignores, then by implication rebukes, that one admirable act by which chiefly we should wish to remember him? Which is right, Theseus or Athena? Every citizen must answer for himself; for both are Athens. Theseus is the Athenian tradition of nobility and generosity, unable to shed its accompanying flaws; Athena is the contemporary Athenian Assembly. The poet leaves us no doubt of his own belief; but his pessimism has no illusions. Theseus' renunciation of his ideal of humanity is the tragedy of the Athenian people.

Andromache is a play about the status and fate of woman, set against a background of war and political intrigue. I shall therefore refer to it at some length in Chapter 4, and briefly in Chapter 6. But it is also one of the most zestfully and ingeniously ironic of all Euripides' dramas; and here I shall examine two scenes where the dramatist's method can be clearly observed.

The play has most often been described as a piece of anti-Spartan propaganda; this view I believe to be mistaken.[3] It is usually based partly on the long speech (590–641) in which Peleus, having discovered Menelaus apparently about to kill Andromache and her child, abuses him and Spartans in general at great length. Before looking at Peleus' speech, let us describe the situation. It is a strange one; it would be hard to find in all Euripides' plays a situation whose details are, on the surface, less convincing.

Andromache has been Neoptolemus' concubine for some years and has given him a son. Neoptolemus' wife Hermione, being childless, believes that Andromache uses witchcraft to make her barren. Neoptolemus has been away for about twelve days on a visit to Delphi. Menelaus has come, on his own initiative, from Sparta —a much longer journey; and by coincidence has reached Phthia during Neoptolemus' absence. Neoptolemus is expected back any day; so Menelaus, in order to 'take his daughter's part' and ensure that Neoptolemus treats Hermione properly as his wife, arranges to kill Andromache and her —and Neoptolemus' —son. It is clear that this perverse proposal is emotionally disturbing to Hermione, and at the same time gratifying to her violently excited jealousy; and she believes that what Menelaus is doing will help her. Andromache points out the absurdity of it all, but to no effect. Menelaus prepares a tableau of sacrifice. When Peleus appears and stops the proceedings, there is a show of wordy resistance; then three long speeches; and Menelaus smoothly abandons the whole project and decamps at once. What is the meaning of it all? The audience is in the same position of ignorance as Andromache herself. It is hard not to believe that her life has been in real danger. Menelaus' words have been cool and confident, while even Andromache must almost have laughed at Peleus' absurdities. Both men leave her bound and kneeling while they pursue their lengthy recriminations. The sudden surrender of Menelaus strikes Andromache as suspicious; and she begs Peleus to guard against trickery (752—6). Like the audience, she has to accept Peleus' reassurance because there is no alternative; but her apprehension at Menelaus' inexplicable behaviour is rational enough. When the fourth episode and the exodus at last lift the disguise from the purpose of the two villains, the excitement and pathos of what is happening on stage prevent anyone from asking how it is connected with what went before. A few might work it out as they recalled the play later; we have no means of knowing how many readers subsequently perceived the whole ironic design. Yet if study of the text in our day can reveal a complete and logical structure, it is rash to deny that this was the work of the author, or that it contains a meaning he wished to convey to those who could find it; rash too to assume that what appears on the surface to be faulty, absurd, pointless, is to be ascribed to the author's deficiency. I believe, on the contrary, that Euripides often had things to say in criticism of his fellow-Athenians which, for his own reasons, he preferred not to express directly; that in any case he did not grudge them their traditional entertainment; but that for his own satisfaction, and to encourage those few who shared his radical spirit, he embedded in his plays what he felt to be truths urgently needed by the society of which he was a member.

In the case of *Andromache*, I do not think we can be sure why he chose to construct a play where the mysteries and absurdities of earlier scenes are to be solved only by those who later, in recollection or in reading, piece together the details of a vicious and heartless intrigue. He had already, so far as we can tell from fragments of earlier plays (see Chapter 4, pp. 92–5), shown repeatedly the arrogance of men who dispose of women's lives as if they were articles of property. The caricature which Peleus offers of a vapid, fire-eating 'patriot', who finds any stick good enough to beat the Spartans with, was not one to cause serious offence, even if (as is conceivable) it mirrored some well-known personage. The fact remains that, as we shall see, under the anomalous surface of melodrama lies a coherent and tragic complex of villainy which reveals itself, not to the general audience, but to the reader who has learnt to trust the seriousness of the author's intention and the competence of his art. Now let us examine the encounter between Menelaus and Peleus.

Peleus arrives to be confronted with the tableau of 'sacrifice'. Andromache tells him that Menelaus is about to kill her and her son. The two men exchange a number of undignified defiances. Peleus has threatened to break Menelaus' head with his stick; but when invited to try it, prefers to use his tongue. At this moment Menelaus shows no fear of Peleus; he has at least two men with him, and Peleus is apparently unattended. Why, then, after listening to Peleus' speeches and delivering one himself, does he suddenly give in and go off home? In 730–1 he tells Peleus:

> For my own part, as a stranger here I don't intend
> Either to commit violence or submit to it.

He is speaking the truth — however violent his gestures have been. He is not such a fool as to imagine that killing Neoptolemus' son would make Neoptolemus feel more kindly towards Hermione. What object, then, has been served by the elaborately prepared sacrifice-scene? Its result (and a result may sometimes point to an object) becomes apparent immediately after the next choral ode, in the frantic and guilty despair of Hermione, which makes her ready to escape with Orestes at a few minutes' notice. Orestes in that scene will explain how this rearrangement benefits himself, and it is easy to see how it benefits Menelaus. But the 'sacrifice' has not only driven Hermione to suicidal terror of her husband; it has induced Peleus to tell Menelaus twice (639, 708–9), and before witnesses, to take Hermione out of the house. Without the 'sacrifice' (which Hermione irrationally insists on regarding as her own crime more than her father's (912), being supported in this (836) by the

Nurse), it might have been difficult to induce Hermione to fall in so obligingly with the scheme of the two men.[4]

Let us now look in more detail at the earlier scene. To entice Andromache from sanctuary, Menelaus says that he will spare her son's life if she gives herself up. When she does this, he says that he will hand her son over to Hermione to dispose of. This cynical quibble inspires Andromache's outburst against Spartans in general (445–53):

> Spartans! The whole world hates you above all other men!
> Lies are your policy, treachery your accomplishment,
> Your craft is crime and cruelty; your hearts warped and sly,
> Your minds diseased, you lord it over the Hellene world;
> Justice lies dead! What wickedness is not in you?
> You add murder to murder, you make gold your god;
> The whole world knows your speech is one thing, your intent
> Another. My curse on you!

The words undoubtedly expressed for the audience their anger at such actions as the Spartan massacre of the defenders of Plataea a year or two before this play was produced. In these eight lines there is no irony; they are too tragic even for applause. But when Peleus arrives to find Andromache bound and kneeling, anger assumes an altogether different tone (590ff.):

> You blackguard, son of a blackguard! Are you called a man?
> What claim have you to count as a man? A man from Troy
> Made you a cuckold when you left your house unlocked,
> Unguarded, as if your wife were chaste —though the truth is,
> A wickeder woman never lived. No Spartan girl
> Could grow up modest, even if she wanted to.
> You never find them staying at home; no, they go out
> With bare thighs and loose clothes, to wrestle and run races
> Along with the young men. I call it intolerable.
> Then can you wonder that your women don't grow up
> Modest? You should ask Helen about that —Helen,
> Who left your home, all sacred ties, and cheerfully
> Went gadding off with her young man to foreign parts.
> Then what do you do? For her sake you collect that vast
> Army of Greeks and march them off to Troy. You ought
> To have spat her out, not stirred a single spear for her,
> Once you had learnt what kind of woman she was; you ought
> To have let her stay in Troy, you ought to have paid her money
> Never to ask to be taken back. But oh, no! You
> Never thought of that; the wind was blowing the other way.

These are only the first twenty lines out of fifty-one; and for good measure

Peleus later gives us another thirty-three in a similar vein. Is this the tragic poet Euripides seriously exhorting his fellow-citizens to indignation against the Spartans? The notion is as absurd as the hero himself. Did the grotesque fertility of Peleus' vituperation make men rock with laughter? Perhaps; but it is more likely that speeches of this nature were to be heard daily in the Agora and in the Assembly; and that those who applauded Peleus because they agreed with every word he spoke far outnumbered those who found him ridiculous and who would have laughed, had not the applause made them inclined to weep, as they reflected that this was the level of patriotic emotion on which Athens was fighting a war to the death with Sparta. In the last scene of the play the old man suddenly becomes tragic as he kneels by the body of his grandson. The hush of genuine feeling lasts for a few minutes; but Euripides will not let us off with a sentimental 'after all'. Stupidity, though briefly shaken by true sorrow, soon recovers. Thetis has only to recite the most perfunctory fairy-tale comfort,[5] and all is well again: 'At your bidding, goddess, I will end my grief.' The shallowness of sorrow matches the shallowness of hatred.

All this is clearly an ironic comment — but upon what? It was written, as far as can be judged, between 427 and 425.[6] It was not until many years later that Thucydides, writing of the Corcyrean revolution which occurred in 427, and which he saw as the beginning of a sharp deterioration in standards of behaviour all over Hellas, described (III.82—4) the passion of revenge as one which thenceforth governed all others, using party conflict as its vehicle and excuse. Those chapters reflect the memory of a vivid and disturbing personal experience; and this play was written during those years, on a theme of revenge, by a poet who shared the historian's view of this prevalent passion. The pathetic Peleus storms at the pretence of revenge which he sees before him, unaware that the victim of a true revenge, his grandson, will soon be laid at his feet. His garrulity rages on, while Andromache kneels with her wrists tightly corded (719—20). Both method and meaning here recall the scene in *Alcestis* where Admetus and Pheres hurl insults at each other across the coffin of the woman who saved their lives. Disregarded and expendable woman represents the world of ordered, peaceable civilian life whose preservation is supposed to be the object of the wars which men make their perpetual occupation. Probably the point of this irony was felt by some few of Euripides' contemporaries; but no record of any such perception has survived, and it rarely appears in modern criticism.

We now come to the end of the third episode and the beginning of the fourth; both are passages where the logic of the action appears strangely unconvincing on the usual interpretation. In performance logic is secondary, visual and emotional impact is dominant. In *Andromache* this impact has to dominate an unusually strong logical network of circumstance which, though unlikely to invalidate the theatrical experience of a good production, offers the careful reader a fascinating experience of an alternative kind. That Euripides wrote for readers as well as for spectators is too well established to need proving here; and this play illustrates this aspect of his art better than most.

We have already looked at the part played by Peleus earlier in the third episode. Now in 715 he orders Menelaus' guards out of his way. Menelaus does not resist, or tell his men to resist, but allows Peleus to untie Andromache and Molossus, while the chorus comment —admiringly, one would suppose —

> Old men are liable to be so uncontrolled
> That once they are in a rage there is no resisting them.

Menelaus then delivers himself thus:

> You fly too easily into mere abusiveness.
> For my own part, as a stranger here I don't intend
> Either to commit violence or submit to it.
> For the present, since I've not unlimited time to spare,
> I am going home. Not far from Sparta a certain city
> Which once was friendly has turned hostile. I must now
> Lead out a force to attack them and regain control.[7]
> When I have arranged that matter to my satisfaction
> I shall return here . . .

This speech is in every line so plainly an improvised pretence that Andromache is understandably alarmed, and warns Peleus to be on his guard; but he is confident (757—63):

> Now do stop talking like a terrified woman . . .
> I only need to look a man like that in the eye
> To make him run, for all my white hair . . .

Modern audiences, readers, and scholars have in general shared his simple confidence;[8] but such innocence is hardly invited by the harsh tone of this play, and we should look more closely.

Menelaus, as I have said, is speaking the truth when he denies any intention to commit violence; but his actions have suggested the opposite. He has captured the escaping child, used him as a bait to lure his mother from sanctuary, tied them both up, and brought them on stage ostensibly to kill them. To do this he has left his palace in Sparta for a period which cannot be much less than a month; and he now says he is going back, having ap-

parently accomplished nothing, but will return again soon to have a talk
with his son-in-law. The mention of 'a certain city not far from Sparta' is as
thin a pretext as anyone could invent. What, then, has happened since the
beginning of the previous scene to change Menelaus' mind? Two things: first,
enough time has passed to enable Peleus to come over from Pharsalus, and
the sacrificial tableau was in order when he arrived. Since Menelaus had
intercepted the slave who tried to take Molossus away, he could have intercepted the messenger who went to summon Peleus; but he did not. The
simple conclusion is that he wanted Peleus to see the sacrificial tableau.[9]
Only one other significant thing has taken place: Peleus has ordered
Hermione out of Neoptolemus' house. Menelaus' speech quoted above
indicates that he is going home because his purpose here is accomplished;
the outrageous 'sacrifice' has induced Peleus to dismiss Hermione. We find
at the beginning of the next scene that Menelaus has gone away without a
word to his daughter, leaving her distracted with fear, and with the guilt
which he has led her to incur, and ready to fall into the arms of anyone who
will escort her out of reach of her husband's indignation. Her guilty terror
is so clearly the necessary result of Menelaus' actions that it is natural to
assume he had intended it; the rest of his intention becomes equally clear
early in the fourth episode.

When Orestes arrives he says that he is on his way to Dodona. Phthia is
many days' journey from Sparta. From Argos or Delphi to Dodona is somewhat further, and the natural route does not lie through Phthia, for that
would mean an unnecessary crossing of the Pindus range as well as a good
deal of extra mileage. One would be more likely to take ship from Corinth to
the Ambracian Gulf and then travel north up the valley of the Arachthus.
However, no one will work this out while watching the scene. Orestes has
arrived —a little hot and breathless, as the chorus notice (880). He has surely
not been hurrying like that all the way from Delphi; perhaps, then, for a
quarter of a mile or so, from his rendezvous with Menelaus, where they
have been on the alert for the party bringing Neoptolemus' body. Or are we
to suppose, after a scene like the last, that Euripides would expect a reflective
listener or reader to be naïve enough to regard as pure chance the presence
of an uncle and a nephew from the same district of Peloponnese in the same
little town of Thessaly on the same day? This is what most modern scholars
have supposed; and the attempt to probe a little beneath this rickety surface
has seldom been made. Orestes introduces himself (884ff.):

> I am the son of Agamemnon and Clytemnestra;
> My name is Orestes. I am travelling to Dodona,
> To Zeus's oracle; and since Phthia lies on my way
> I would like to enquire about my cousin, Hermione
> Of Sparta, if she is well and all goes happily

With her. She lives at a great distance from us now,
But we at home still think of her affectionately.

If we are right in assuming some degree of subtlety here, Orestes has
(like Menelaus, 732) 'not unlimited time to spare', since other travellers are
on their way northward to Phthia, only a mile down the road. So he directs
the dialogue with Hermione somewhat firmly:

> OR.:   What has gone wrong? You have no children yet; the source
>   Of trouble, then, can only be one thing: your marriage.
> HER.: You have said the words for me. It is that very thing . . .

It is clearly shown how Menelaus had succeeded in convincing his daughter
that the initiative in the attack on Andromache had been hers, not his, and
how Orestes plays up to this (906—16):

> OR.:   That's a bad thing —for a man to live with two women.
> HER.: That's how it is. I took steps to defend myself.
> OR.:   One woman against another —you contrived some plot?
> HER.: I did; I meant to kill her and her bastard son.
> OR.:   Did you kill her? Or were you stopped by some mischance?
> HER.: Yes, Peleus stopped me. He supported the guilty cause.
> OR.:   Was anyone helping you in this plot to murder them?
> HER.: My father came from Sparta for this very purpose.

This is almost a case of guilt implanted by hypnosis. Hermione has laid
no plot. The Nurse too has been brainwashed and has twice referred to
Hermione's 'plot' (807, 836). The plotting and the execution were Menelaus'; yet here Hermione claims the 'plot' for hers, and Menelaus is
mentioned as an afterthought; Orestes drives the point home (919):

> I understand;
> You are terrified of your husband, after what you have done.

The primary dramatic purpose of Hermione's speech 920—53 is to allow
Hermione to recover from her hysteria and to allow the audience to establish
emotional contact with her as a pitiable woman who has some excuse for
her terror. It contains also a series of ironies which should help us to forgive
Hermione for her earlier behaviour. She appeals to Orestes 'in the name of
Zeus and family love' to take her away 'as far as possible from here, or to
my father's house'. She has not grasped the incredible fact that her father
has deliberately abandoned her to her present despair, and she still believes
in 'family love' and wants to go to him. 'If my husband comes back before I
can escape' is the most direct kind of dramatic irony because Neoptolemus
is in fact dead; it is ironic in a second sense because everything we have

heard of Neoptolemus tells us he would have been kinder to Hermione than her father has been; but it is also the last of a whole series of lines which should have progressively made some at least of the audience realize that Neoptolemus was dead before the play began. Then come twenty-one lines about the poisonous influence of gossiping women who asked her why she allowed Andromache to 'share her house and share her husband'. We wonder what can be the reason for this circumstantial tirade aimed either at the women of the chorus or at others like them. At last comes the sentence (947), 'One of them will have taken a bribe to upset her marriage'; and our sudden reversion of thought to that competent organizer Menelaus may well explain the whole passage.

Orestes now has all the cards in his hand and can proceed rapidly. There is a good deal of exposition to be done, so his speech sounds like a formal prologue. His summary of the recent history of the House of Atreus makes it at last clear why it was an advantage to Menelaus to use his daughter to gain him a profitable alliance with the power of Argos in exchange for his present distant alliance with the insignificant city of Phthia —especially since Neoptolemus was out of favour with Delphi. 'I knew affairs had reached a crisis here ... so I watched the situation' (959—61). Orestes does not say how he knew, or whether he watched from Argos or from Delphi or from some lurking-place in Phthia near the palace. If we are sitting in the theatre we have little time to consider the matter. But if we are reading the play at leisure, we find that Orestes' plausible concern has confirmed suspicions already awakened by Menelaus; and the suggestion that the two men have been collaborating on the spot is not far behind. Hermione works nothing out, since she has now only one thought, to get Orestes to take her away immediately. Once he has promised to do this, and she has committed herself to him, there is no going back. He holds Hermione by her guilt about Andromache, but that can be improved upon: he will make her guilty also of her husband's death. Gripping her by one wrist and looking into her face, he promises that he will kill Neoptolemus; under those terrifying eyes she dares not speak a word of protest. Whether it was possible in an ancient production to show during Orestes' last speech the dawning of awareness in Hermione and in the chorus that Orestes, though using the future tense, is proclaiming his already accomplished murder, we do not know. It can certainly be done on the modern stage; and it is a theatrical effect unique in ancient drama.

Those who deny that an ironic pattern underlies the events of this play commit themselves to supposing that, after a scene-ending of this intensity, the dramatist could ask a thoughtful spectator to imagine an interval of twelve days passing while the fourth stasimon is performed. The notion makes dramatic nonsense. The orthodox view also includes the supposition that Neoptolemus on reaching Delphi spent not three days, as the Messenger says, in sight-seeing, but at least fourteen. During performance an audience does not think arithmetically; but the arithmetic is there for the reader, and was put there by the author.

If doubts still remain that the essence of *Andromache* is found in its ironic implications, the epilogue should dissolve them. We have laughed at the valiant Peleus, and forgotten him in watching Orestes hypnotize Hermione. Now Peleus has reappeared, to kneel weeping beside his grandson's murdered body. He had wept too when news came of Achilles' death; and now he re-members, from a long time ago, the happy period of his youth; and he calls upon Thetis, who for a few years had been his adored wife, to return and comfort him. She appears above her shrine (1231ff.):

> Peleus! In remembrance of our marriage in days past
> I have left my father's house to visit you — I am
> Thetis. My first advice to you is: Do not let
> Today's calamities cause you undue distress.
> I too had hoped to be happy in my children; yet
> I lost the son I bore you, Achilles fleet of foot,
> The hero of Hellas. Now, listen to what I came
> To tell you . . .

Thetis is an immortal; and immortal eyes (as Artemis says, *Hippolytus* 1396) 'are forbidden to shed tears'. She makes it plain that today's calamities do not cause her undue distress; her sorrow for Achilles is as graceful and as two-dimensional as that of Artemis for Hippolytus. She continues:

> Carry the body of Achilles' son
> To Apollo's temple at Delphi, and there bury him
> For a reproach to the Delphians, that his tomb may bear
> Witness to his violent murder at Orestes' hands.

Neoptolemus had once made a journey to Delphi (52—3) to reproach Apollo, and this had led to today's tragedy. His body has just been carried three days' journey to rest in Phthia; and now Thetis commands his grandfather to carry him all the way back, to perpetuate the family feud with Apollo and the Delphians. (We have already noted the similar irony of Athena's advice in the epilogue of *The Suppliant Women*.) The comfort Thetis offers to Andro-mache (see Chapter 4, page 120) is as insensitive as her command to Peleus; and her statement that the future prosperity of Molossus will be a mark of divine concern for Troy (1251—2) is crueller than anything Hermione said in the first scene. Her promises to Peleus would be an even sharper mockery, if Peleus were vulnerable. She foretells 'divine, unfading immortality', and a life shared with herself; when he has buried his dead in Delphi, he is to go to a certain sea-cave and there 'sit down and wait until I come out of the sea with fifty dancing nymphs to escort you home'. But she closes her speech with:

> Now end your grief
> Over the dead; for this decree the gods have fixed
> For ever: death is a debt which every man must pay.

Peleus is unaware —perhaps a large part of the audience is too —that her last lines, verbally at least, cancel her earlier promise. His banal profession of faith in noble blood and in the gods (in that order) mocks neither the legend nor the supernatural world, only the shallowness of dull heroes.

The full force of this powerful play can only be felt when the plot is understood as presenting the first of the poet's two great themes, injustice to women, against the background of the second, the cruelty of war. This aspect of *Andromache* will be studied in Chapter 4. Meanwhile it is interesting to note how complete an answer is given, by the 'ironic' approach here outlined, to the traditional complaint that this play falls into two barely connected halves. The closely timed collaboration of Menelaus and Orestes follows as a necessary conclusion from a study of the text based on the assumption that Euripides was not naïve, but an accomplished artist who knew what he was doing in every line; within this perception is contained the key to the coherent structure of the whole piece.

I turn now to another play which illustrates in detail Euripides' particular use of irony: *Iphigenia in Aulis*.[10] I shall not attempt a complete exposition, but examine first the role of Achilles in his two scenes, and then the crucial speech of Clytemnestra to Agamemnon, 1146—1208.

In the *Iliad* Achilles is the fighting man *par excellence*, reputedly invincible; accepting some degree of authority from the commander-in-chief, and asserting a more definite degree of independence; combining mental capacity with physical in pursuit of the aristocratic ideal —'to be a speaker of words and a doer of deeds' (*Iliad* IX.443). In this play, where realistic dialogue links the 'heroic' action with the feeling of the contemporary scene, Achilles is indeed a soldier; but like Demophon, Eteocles, Orestes, he is a hero's degenerate son; he conforms to the pattern of his fellow-chiefs, and their reciprocal intrigues at the outset of the Trojan War may be taken as reflecting the corrupt and cruel irrationality of military behaviour near the end of the Peloponnesian war — this play was written in 406. Cruelty and corruption were the poet's theme; he found both in the legend of the sacrifice of Iphigenia and the lie Agamemnon told his wife to enable him to carry it out. He added a further point to illustrate the irrationality which so often lies behind both these vices. Probably the best known version of the legend of Aulis was that given in Aeschylus' *Agamemnon*, where the fleet was harbour-bound by stormy north-east winds. (This seems to be the version Euripides accepts in *Iphigenia in Tauris* 15, though there is some uncertainty in the manuscripts.) A sacrifice to change an adverse wind is surely irrational enough (at Syracuse in 413 comparable folly had cost thousands of Athenian lives); but at Aulis in this play there is not even an adverse wind. This is established first by Agamemnon in the prologue (9—11):

> No cry of a bird, no sound from the sea,
> The winds are silent, Euripus hushed

and again by Achilles when he first appears (813—18):

> And now, stuck here, with barely a breeze over the strait,
> I have to keep the Myrmidons quiet. They're always at me:
> 'What are we waiting for, Achilles? How much longer
> Must we keep counting days till we set sail for Troy?
> Have you plans? If so, tell us; if not, let's all go home.
> Why waste time waiting for those two to make up their minds?'

The Myrmidons, with their question, What are we waiting for? are an important part of the play's ironic pattern. In the fifth century, as in Homer, the usual nautical practice was to row a ship out of harbour, and after a mile or two hoist sail if the wind was suitable. In cases of urgency oars could be used for greater distances unless there was a gale blowing against them. The entire fleet bound for Sicily in 415 raced from Peiraeus as far as Aegina, from sheer high spirits; and in 427 the ship bearing reprieve for Mytilene rowed at top speed for over a hundred miles. At Aulis a state of near-mutiny among the troops, alluded to several times in the course of the play, was certainly a matter of urgency. If rowing had not been the obvious course, the Myrmidons would have had nothing to complain of.[11] Why then was the sacrifice ever mooted? The question is left entirely obscure here; but the reason given in Aeschylus' *Agamemnon* by the chorus (803—4) is surely the deep anthropological basis of all such occasions: Agamemnon sacrificed his daughter *tharsos hekousion andrasi thnēiskousi komizōn* — trying to put willing boldness into men who were going to their death. This is part of the general *mania*, irrational excitement, referred to in Euripides' play by both Agamemnon and Achilles (1264, 808—9) as the driving force of the expedition.

Achilles the 'doer of deeds' has been described to us already (206—30) by the chorus, who watched him running in full armour beside his horses. When he meets Clytemnestra his performance as a 'speaker of words' is more than disappointing. He is uncouth, tasteless, rude, and above all totally self-centered; but once he hears that he has been treated with disrespect, he at least turns serious; and when Clytemnestra appeals to him to help her and save Iphigenia, he becomes entranced with the picture of himself which is taking shape in this exciting situation, and regales Clytemnestra with a speech of fifty-five lines on his favourite topic. He begins by reviewing the principles of his early education; continues on the theme of his own and his family's honour; gives his oath that Iphigenia shall not die, staking his own life for it; points out what a prize he is as a prospective son-in-law; explains that if his permission for using his name as a decoy had been properly sought he would have granted it — 'But, as it is, these generals treat me with contempt'; again promises deliverance; and ends with his own apotheosis. His own honesty is what most impresses him (926—7):

> I was brought up by Cheiron, a good man; from him
> I learnt simple straightforward ways;

and later (1005—7):

> One thing I've said, be sure of: I won't tell you lies.
> If I do — if I trifle with you, may I die!

But even if he means what he says, intelligence ought to tell him that unless he initiates some decisive action immediately he is promising the impossible. Intelligence is not his strong point; and the chorus, young as they are, see through him, and in the next stasimon speak of the sacrifice as certain. The best they can say as a non-committal comment on his speech is,

> Son of Peleus, your words are worthy of yourself . . .

Why do they not say, 'Of your father'? The next stasimon will offer an answer.

When Clytemnestra has welcomed his readiness to help, and they begin to consider what action is necessary, Achilles proposes that words should come before action (1011ff.):

> ACH.: Let us first urge her father to a better mind . . .
> CLYT.: That's a cold hope; still, what do you think I ought to do?
> ACH.: First kneel and beg him not to kill his child; and then,
> If he resists you, you must come to me. Suppose
> You win him over: then I need not stir, your cause
> Is saved. I'll be in better standing with a friend;
> And the army won't accuse me, if I've won my point
> By reason, not by force. If this works, everything
> Will turn out well, without me, both for you and her.

Clytemnestra's comment, 'How wise you are', says much in few words.

But what if her appeal fails? 'Where shall I see you? ... Where shall I come?' Achilles answers,

> I'll be on the look-out for you, in the right place;
> You had better not be seen rushing distracted through
> The soldiers' quarters. Family dignity must be
> Preserved ...

The sense of falsity recalls Demophon's second appearance in *The Children of Heracles* —the posture of a man preparing to break a promise (see Chapter 7, page 187). When Achilles has gone, the chorus sing of the marriage of Peleus. The gods and the Muses came to that wedding-feast, and Cheiron prophesied the greatness of the son Thetis would bear. But nowadays, as Iolaus said, 'You'd hardly find one in a score who's not a worse man than his father' (*Children of Heracles* 327—8); and this Achilles is no more to be compared with the hero Peleus than Athens in 406 is to be compared with the Athens of the miraculous 'fifty years'. After speaking of Thetis's son, the chorus say

> Your wedding-day, Iphigenia, will be different ...

They know that Achilles will not make good his promise. The imminent sacrifice awakes in them no sense of piety, of divine will, of a great cause heroically served. In their clarity of judgement they lump together Agamemnon, Menelaus, Calchas, Odysseus, Achilles, in one total condemnation (1089—97):

> Where now can the clear face of goodness,
> Where can virtue itself live by its own strength?
> When ruthless disregard holds power,
> When men, forgetting they are mortal,
> Tread down goodness and ignore it,
> When lawlessness overrules law,
> When the terror of God no longer draws men together
> Trembling at the reward of wickedness?

Yet, just as in *The Children of Heracles* hope was left for Demophon's honour, so here even for Achilles shame is not total. When his Myrmidons mutiny and attack him, though he has lost authority he has not lost all sense of what is due to his name and parentage. He comes, attended only by two men who bear his armour, to Agamemnon's tent to find Iphigenia. Even if he could have carried out a rescue when the danger was first known, it is now certainly too late; but his wish to be thought honourable (not an entirely base motive) works with his mediocre intelligence to produce, apparently, a hope that some miracle may cut the knot. Even at the last moment he is still asserting his resolve to fight for Iphigenia; and if this were void of any sincerity, why should he have come? Iphigenia speaks (1368ff.) in time to save him from the last disgrace. He has a fighter's courage; and now he recognizes courage where he did not expect to find it. He is gripped by an unfamiliar, because unselfish, emotion; and it shocks him at last into genuineness of feeling. Would this have steeled him to fight the Myrmidons? Euripides leaves the question unasked.

This play contains also two passionately ironic sequences which I omit here because they belong respectively to the two themes of war and sacrifice and will therefore be considered in Chapter 6, pages 173–6 and Chapter 7, pages 201–3. But this is the place to examine the speech (1146–1208) in which Clytemnestra appeals to Agamemnon not to sacrifice Iphigenia. Again it is necessary, if we are to feel the true force of what is said, to describe exactly the situation. Agamemnon's repentant letter, being sent too late and intercepted by Menelaus, has failed to prevent Iphigenia from arriving, accompanied by her mother, in the Greek camp. The two have met Agamemnon and exchanged greetings, and Agamemnon has made an inept attempt to induce Clytemnestra to leave Iphigenia with him and go back immediately to Argos. Clytemnestra has replied roundly that she will stay and take her proper part in the wedding. She has also met Achilles, and the Old Slave has disclosed to them both Agamemnon's duplicity. Achilles has promised that he will save Iphigenia's life, but his speech and manner do not inspire confidence. At last Agamemnon and Clytemnestra face each other. Agamemnon confesses the truth; and Clytemnestra addresses to him the speech which is her one last chance of saving her daughter from the knife. We should try to imagine 'the most tragic of the poets' preparing to write this speech. With what kind of reasoning or appeal shall she move Agamemnon, and the audience, to tears? A little later in the same scene Iphigenia herself pleads with her obdurate father – let us look at this speech first. The child (everything points to Iphigenia being, in this play, aged about thirteen) uses with delicacy and truth every kind of pathos – the pathos of youth, of family love, of bodily tenderness, of early memories, of tears, of the love of life and light. When Agamemnon has listened, he says (1255)

I am well aware what's pitiable and what is not –

words which can only refer to the contrast between the two appeals he has heard. Euripides could write, when he wished, an utterance to wring the heart. What did he write, at the opening of this scene, for Clytemnestra? The forty lines of dialogue preceding her speech give some presentiment of its tone. 'Of all *my* wrongs . . .' (1124); 'I've heard all you plan to do *to me*' (1141). Then the speech begins:

                    First — to make this the first shame
I charge you with — you married me against my will,
Took me by force, killing my first husband Tantalus;
You grabbed my baby from my breast, and broke its head
On the hard ground. My brothers, the two sons of Zeus,
Mounted their gleaming horses and made war on you.
You knelt as suppliant to my old father Tyndareos;
He saved your life, and you became my next husband.
I was reconciled to you; and you will testify
That I was, both to you and to your family,
A perfect wife; chaste in my person, prosperous
In ordering your household; joy attended you
On entering, and good fortune blessed your going out.
A man with such a wife is the possessor of
A rarity; bad wives are plentiful enough.
I bore you three girls first, and then this boy, your son;
Now you are taking one girl from me heartlessly.

In these eighteen lines Clytemnestra refers fifteen times to herself,
fifteen times to Agamemnon; once, and last, to 'one of her daughters'. Every
sentence is framed either to accuse Agamemnon or to commend herself. Two-
thirds of the speech are still to come, but Agamemnon has already been
reminded of everything that ever made him regret marrying his wife.
Clytemnestra continues, after a brief and scathing reference to Helen, with
thirteen lines describing the grief she will suffer if she is deprived of her
daughter; then twelve lines describing the disgrace Agamemnon will incur,
the remorse he will feel — this is the most hopeful part of the speech, but it
relapses quickly into scolding:

                    Or is your sole imperative
Your secure sceptre and your military command?

She then suggests that it would be fairer to kill Menelaus' daughter Hermione:

                    I am your chaste and faithful wife;
Yet I must lose my daughter, while the whore Helen
Can keep hers . . .

She speaks no word appealing to his pity, to his fatherly love, his decency,
his courage; and is so unconscious of her unconscionable perversity that she
can add:

                    Now if anything I've said
Is untrue or irrelevant, tell me.

Euripides has not delineated for us a bad woman; at other times we can
feel sympathy with her; but in this speech he shows the misery of a wretched
marriage suddenly erupting like poison at the one urgent moment when
balm was needed to save a life. Part of the drama is, that the clear-eyed
Iphigenia must stand by and see and hear what is happening, and know that
her last hope has gone, except for what she herself can say to unsay her
mother's words. But the main force of this unhappy speech lies in its revelation of how the fact of being a woman and a wife without love has
destroyed a person and a mother. For in this final play the poet's two great
themes, the enslavement of woman and the tyranny of war, carry equal
weight; and the chorus, who begin with wide-eyed adoration of the heroic
warriors, by the third stasimon utterly condemn their cruel and irreligious
acts. As in other plays man's moral sense passes outraged judgement on the
actions of gods, so here woman passes judgement on man – the chorus by
their blazing words, Iphigenia by her natural innocence, and Clytemnestra
by the impotence of her own moral collapse in the face of man's cruelty.

It is well to define again, after studying this example, what is meant by
calling such a speech ironic. The speaker is of course unconscious of irony.
The author composed the speech to come just, but only just, within the
bounds of acceptability as a speech made by an indignant mother pleading
for her daughter's life. It contains several obvious features of the *dikanikos
logos*, the lawyer's harangue familiar to all citizens from their jury-service;
and this interest may cover some of the selfish insensitivity, the festering
resentment, which we recognize as colouring almost every sentence. It
ends with

> Change your purpose; do not kill
> Your child and mine. This is the way of sanity –

and that ending of the speech is as it should be, and helps listeners to forget
the odious beginning and prepare their hearts to melt at Iphigenia's genuine
pathos. But neither of these points excuses Euripides for giving Clytemnestra
so repellent, so self-defeating a speech, unless he had a further meaning. If
Agamemnon 'knows what is pitiable and what is not', so did Euripides and
so should we. Here Euripides is seeking, as often before, some answer to the
question: Since war is made by ordinary citizens, and ordinary citizens are
decent people, where does the senseless cruelty of war come from? Aeschylus'
treatment of this story in *Agamemnon*, which Euripides probably knew by
heart, may guide us. There, in the *parodos*, 122–55, the readiness of Agamemnon to sacrifice his daughter is presented as his qualification for undertaking similar wickedness, but on a vast scale, in the destruction of Troy
despite the opposition of the gods made evident in the stormy north-east
winds.[12] Here the chorus of girls from Chalcis, thinking of the distant day
when Troy will be captured, say (776):

There will be heads forced back, throats cut . . .

being not yet aware that this is to happen today, in the very grove of Artemis they passed on their way to the camp (185—6). Men who will do the one will do the other. The sacrifice is to Artemis; but in this play Euripides wastes no time in that condemnation of Artemis which was of some importance in the earlier play (*Iphigenia in Tauris* 380—91). Here the supernatural is treated equivocally, there is no stormy wind, the responsibility is man's alone. The father who will perform the crime and the mother who had a chance to prevent it confront each other; and we see — an all too recognizable marriage, its realities for the first time openly displayed and put into words. We know that Iphigenia was lost before she began to speak.

It may be that what I am calling irony is simply the gap which must exist in the work of every profound and creative dramatist between what he knows he has put into a scene and what he knows most of his audience will receive from it. When Shakespeare created Ariel and Caliban he was intensely concerned with his own meaning, and somewhat casually, I surmise, with what the Londoners would make of his fantasies. An artist may have rich things to say to his own people and world; but people must take the message as he wants to give it. He still writes first for himself.

Before ending this preliminary survey of Euripides' ironic method with some examples of lines spoken by the chorus, I should like to notice one passage, *Electra* 349—407, whose interest has a peculiarly modern flavour. In this play Euripides, by presenting Electra as married to a peasant, sets his story in an atmosphere which is sharply conscious of social distinctions. Electra shows from the outset that she is deficient in that quality which her peasant husband recognizes as belonging to noble blood (406—7) —

> If they're as noble as they look, they'll be
> Equally at home in a cottage or anywhere else.

She is never at home in her cottage; she exaggerates her debasement to feed her anger. When her brother and Pylades arrive, saying they bring news of Orestes, the Peasant welcomes them. Then follows (364—85):

> OR.: By the gods! Is this the man whose loyalty has made
>   Your marriage no marriage, to save Orestes' honour?
> EL.: This is the man who is known as 'poor Electra's husband'.
> OR.: Well! There's no clear sign to tell the quality of a man.
>   Nature and place turn vice and virtue upside down.
>   I've seen a noble father breed a worthless son,
>   And good sons come of evil parents; a starved soul
>   Housed in a rich man's palace, a great heart dressed in rags . . .

This man is not a leading Argive citizen;
He's not a well-known member of a famous house;
He's one of the many; yet he's a true nobleman . . .

Is Orestes here 'pondering the mysterious separation of personal merit and
exalted status' (Jones, *On Aristotle and Greek Tragedy*, 244)? I think not, for
two reasons. First, this play was staged about 413 B.C. Athens had been at war
for some eighteen years; the increase in population, the ruthless mobilizing
of manpower, the endless state of emergency, must have done for the entire
Athenian community what Sophists, and the familiar discussions about
nomos and *physis*, 'law' and 'nature', had done for the educated. Some kept
their station in life, others changed it; but the notion that a poor man could be
generous, and a rich and powerful man despicable, was surely no longer a
startling notion, however rare examples of it might be. In the second place,
the significance of Orestes' words must be gathered from what we already
know of Orestes. When Electra first tells him about her marriage, he twice
(at least) imputes unworthy feelings to the Peasant (256–60); and when
Electra at last convinces him that her husband is 'by nature virtuous', Orestes
immediately says, 'We must reward him', *eu drasteon*. The point is subtle; but
that upper-class thought, 'we reward the honest poor', rankles; for we are not
in Homeric Mycenae, but in hard-pressed democratic Athens. Judgements of
this kind cannot be taken as certain; but the remarkable correspondence of
feeling between that age and ours which is shown in e.g. 406–7 (see above)
makes the comparison here worth considering. One other hint of the contrast
between the delicacy of feeling shown by the Peasant and the ill-adjusted
nature of Orestes comes in 553–4. Orestes comes out with Pylades to meet the
Old Man who long ago had smuggled him out of the palace to safety after the
murder of Agamemnon.

> OLD MAN (*aside*).   They have nobility; but it may be counterfeit.
>   Many who are nobly born belie it. None the less —
>   (*To* Or. *and* Pyl.) My courteous greeting to our guests.
> ORESTES: Greeting, old man.
>   — Electra, whose friend is this antique relic here?
> ELECTRA: This man, sir, was my father's guardian when a child.
> ORESTES: What? the same man who got your brother safely away?
> ELECTRA: Yes; if Orestes lives, he owes his life to him.

To have answered courtesy with gross discourtesy, and discover too late who
it is that he has scorned — this is Orestes' role. It is congruous with the fruitless
passion of remorse in the final scene; it confirms the unpleasant impression
made by 256–60; and it gives significance to the Old Man's reflection about
counterfeit nobility. The speech 367–85 comes when our suspicion of

Orestes' true nature has barely been aroused, and is there for those listeners to enjoy who feel most at ease with the platitudes of an earlier generation; who will not notice the callow patronage and naïve insolence of mediocrity airily praising virtue. For those who reflect on the play as a whole its character is painfully different, and its lesson far more radical than the trite lesson which Orestes labours with such banality. Except for the entertaining catechism of noble connexions which Clytemnestra pursues with her husband in *Iphigenia in Aulis* 695 — 712, this speech of Orestes is, I believe, the only exact picture of snobbery in fifth-century drama.

Lastly we should look at the way Euripides uses irony in a chorus. The sentiments uttered by a chorus are usually direct and candid, and offer our emotions a rest after the deceptions or perversions of heroic characters. In fact these lines from *Medea* may be the only clear instance of conscious irony in a choral ode (1081 — 9):

> I have often engaged in arguments,
> And become more subtle, and perhaps more heated,
> Than is suitable for women;
> Though in fact women too have intelligence,
> Which forms part of our nature and instructs us —
> Not all of us, I admit; but a certain few
> You might perhaps find, in a large number of women —
> A few not incapable of reflection . . .

The chorus here are modestly putting forward their opinion that childless people are happier than parents. Their modesty can perhaps be genuine; but these lines occur in a play whose heroine is far more intelligent than her male opposite, and is none the happier for her mental distinction; this makes irony probable. Many plays show examples of brief ironic comment by a chorus after some ill-advised speech. A notable example of this is *Orestes* 605 — 6. Orestes, confronted by Tyndareos, has excused his matricide on the ground of Clytemnestra's wickedness, the necessity of deterring other women from imitating her, and the baneful effect of unhappy marriages; and before Tyndareos replies the Women of Argos put in this observation:

> It's always women who prove natural obstacles
> Placed in the path of men, to spoil their happiness.

Sometimes, however, Euripides uses his chorus as an ironic mirror of human reaction to events, to invite the criticism of those 'not incapable of reflection'. The first stasimon of *Andromache* begins with the story of the Judgement of Paris, thought of as the cause of the Trojan war; and continues with a passionately expressed wish that Hecabe had, as Cassandra urged her, killed Paris at birth. Lines 293 — 300 include a sort of refrain of 'Kill that child!' spoken by good-hearted women to whom the war at Troy, which ended perhaps seven years ago, is already an unreal legend from a remote world — although there in front of them, before the altar of Thetis, sits Andromache, whose infant son Astyanax was murdered at Troy by the victorious Greek army in which their king was a leading hero. In the scene which is about to open, Andromache's other son Molossus will be threatened with death by Menelaus, and these same women will then say (491):

> This killing is a godless, barbarous business;
> It is revolting.

A closely parallel case is *Iphigenia in Tauris* 438—46. In this play the killing of Clytemnestra, who murdered her husband, is spoken of with appalled horror, yet when the chorus speak of Helen, who left her husband, they express a longing to see her throat cut. The irony in both these passages is an appeal to people to make proper use of their imagination. Finally, the chorus in *Orestes* is a special case of elaborate irony, which will be fully studied in the next chapter.

We have now considered the working of irony in several plays, and in later chapters we shall examine many more examples. It is perhaps not possible to prove in any single case that irony was intended. These first passages taken together should appear more convincing; but it is not until the poet's work has been surveyed as a whole, and a comprehensive concept formed of the two great themes which inspired the bulk of his life's work (in so far as we can judge from what remains of it) that we can hope to form a clear acquaintance with the ironic tone which is never far away, even in the most heartfelt passages. It will also have begun to be evident that the study we have embarked upon is not merely a matter of analysing and setting in order perceptions which are familiar to readers of this author, but involves the tracing of an unsuspected and at times disturbing range of ideas. These ideas, as we pursue their expression in successive studies, will be found to be consistent, radical, and subtly humane, and to cohere in a world outlook and a view of the human scene which is almost as relevant to the modern world as to the ancient. The remaining chapters, while not claiming to be a comprehensive study of Euripides' thought, will examine the development of his principal themes in a substantial number of plays, in an attempt to reach a general understanding and a detailed perception of his ironic method. As the next step in this study, Chapter 3 will be devoted to a fairly complete exposition of one play, *Orestes*.

THE IRONIC METHOD 2 –
Orestes

Orestes was produced in 408 B.C.; later in the same year Euripides left Athens for Macedon. There is no evidence, apart from unreliable personal anecdotes, to show why, at the age of about seventy-three, he should have done this. The exposition of *Orestes* given in this chapter will offer a suggestion; and the whole study of Euripides' ironic method, by showing how radical, how likely to cause offence, were his implied criticisms of social behaviour, will point to the conclusion that his exile may have arisen from the same unpopularity which necessitated his constant use of irony. In Macedon, as the guest of King Archelaus, he wrote *The Bacchae, Iphigenia in Aulis*, and a play called *Archelaus* of which fragments amounting to about ninety lines remain; and died when he had been there a year and a half. Thus *Orestes* was the poet's last personal address to the Athenians;[1] and we may assume it was written with this in mind, since the momentous decision to leave Athens was likely to have been contemplated for some time.

The play is about the consequences which Orestes' crime of matricide brought upon him. In any discussion of the play's meaning we must decide whether we should regard this murder as a terrible but necessary and divinely-ordered act of justice, or as a crime beyond pardon and redemption[2]. We are not left long in doubt of the author's intention; the tone of the prologue is ominous from the opening sentence. The best that Electra can say of Apollo's command is that it was 'not contrary to justice' (28); and here the attached particle *men* implies a following 'but . . .'. The desperate sickness of Orestes and the indignation of the citizens at the pollution brought upon Argos, with the likelihood of a death-sentence for both murderers, point to the horror of the crime. The only excuse seriously put forward (as distinct from the various arguments recounted in the Messenger's speech) is that of 'obedience to a god' (31); but the god of healing has not healed his obedient servant Orestes. Electra hopes that Menelaus will save her and her brother from the Argive sentence; but the thoughtful listener will realize that that sentence is no less just, and can no more be set aside, than Apollo's command. When the chorus enter they concede that the matricide was just, but Electra herself replies that it was wrong (194). Orestes at the end of his first scene, when he is more sane than at any other time, blames Apollo for commanding 'a most unholy deed', and is sure that his father himself would have forbid-

den the murder (285—93). He makes virtually the same admission to
Menelaus (396). The chorus in the first stasimon express pity for Orestes without condoning his crime; in the second they make their condemnation
explicit (819—24):

> That noble deed was not noble . . .
> 'Crime in a just cause' is an impious sophistry,
> An insanity breeding in evil hearts.

They have no hope that such a crime can ever be atoned or redeemed. Orestes'
statement in the epilogue that Apollo's oracles 'were not deceptive after all,
but sound and true' (1666—7) is immediately followed by perhaps the most
unmistakably ironic two lines to be found in any play:

> Yet, I confess, I felt uneasy, lest the voice
> I heard, and took for your voice, was in truth the voice
> Of some accursed fiend.

The poet has made it evident that his play is about a crime beyond pardon, a
sickness without cure.

Once this fact is grasped, we have at least some provisional guidance on
two important points. First, why did Euripides choose this theme for his last
play before quitting Athens? What did he wish to say to his audience? W. D.
Smith[3] has shown that the imagery of disease is elaborated consistently
throughout the play, which begins with 'hope of moral health' for Orestes
and Electra but continues with the disappointment of this hope. Disease, he
says, is 'a metaphor for the moral condition which is the play's subject'.
Similarly Arrowsmith[4] finds the unifying motif of the play in 'the gradual
exposure of the real criminal depravity of Orestes and his accomplices'; and
other analyses reach comparable conclusions. But, as in so many scholarly
enquiries, only the first and less important question has been asked. Since
Euripides wrote for an audience which he knew and which knew him, we
must ask next, Why should he want to talk to them about disease and
depravity in 408 B.C.? The reason is at hand: Because the city was mortally
sick after twenty-three years of desperate war, and in spite of some temporary
successes only the most sanguine could hope for more than two or three years'
postponement of the sentence of death. We shall in due course note many
details of the text which corroborate this general line of interpretation; but
first we should observe another point which is clarified for us once we realize
that Euripides is presenting Orestes' act of vengeance on Clytemnestra as a
culpable and fatal error which neither divine nor human impulse could
excuse.

This second point is the place of Menelaus in the drama. Most scholars,
including those just quoted, hold that Euripides meant us to picture Menelaus

more or less as Orestes pictures him — as a cowardly and ambitious opportunist who 'means to see Orestes and Electra put to death by the city's
command, and then ... to take the palace, the throne, and the land for
himself (1058—9)'.[5] But the line-reference given here is to words spoken by
Orestes in desperate resentment, words as unfounded as the abuse he hurled
at his uncle (717—19) in return for his offer of prudent help (704—5, 709—13).
We should judge Menelaus by the situation in which the dramatist has placed
him, not by the opinion of another character who is presented as a mentally
disturbed murderer. This situation is, that Menelaus has been asked, on the
moment of his return from seventeen years' absence from Hellas, to save the
life of a man lawfully arraigned before a democratic assembly for a polluting
crime — and the man is his nephew. In addition to this, Argos is not Menelaus'
city. Menelaus' brother Agamemnon, king of Argos, had been murdered there
seven years before, and the citizens had by this time evidently accepted
Clytemnestra as *de facto* queen, while the Messenger mentions (894) a faction
which supported Aegisthus. As Tyndareos points out, if the Argive court
could condemn Orestes, Orestes could have lawfully accused his mother
before the same court (500—3). As it is, the act of matricide is condemned as
unpardonable not only by the Argive citizens, by the chorus, and by Tyndareos,
but even by the two remorseful murderers in their opening scene, before the
visible process of their degradation has begun. Orestes' request for help therefore puts Menelaus in an impossible position, in which he behaves with pru-
dence and decency; his reply is wordy, but reasonable. Are we to insist that
Menelaus is lying when he says that the ships and men he has left in the
harbour are not a force strong enough to succeed in an armed attack on the
city of Argos? Yet this is the outrageous action which Orestes demands of
him. Since Menelaus' reasonable and (in the circumstances) generous offer
to try persuasion with Tyndareos and with the Assembly (704—5) is met
with shouts of vituperation, are we to be surprised at finding that the offer
has been withdrawn, or are we justified in denying, with Orestes, that it was
an honest offer?[6] The fact that Aristotle made this mistake (see above,
pages 12—13) does not excuse us from exercising careful judgement based
on the text. Our view of what Euripides intended to be the character of
Menelaus vitally affects the import of every scene from his first entry to the
epilogue.

Seven years earlier Euripides had produced *Electra*, with Orestes playing
a part equal in importance to his sister's. The chief point of connexion
between the two plays is the remorse and self-abhorrence which fills both
murderers when their act is accomplished; but *Orestes* is not a sequel. In
Electra the psychological interest is paramount; in *Orestes* there is psychological interest in abundance, but the intention underlying the whole drama
is political. In the previous year, 409, *The Phoenician Women* had shown the

words and deeds of soldiers fighting a war; *Orestes* contains no fighting, but its drama symbolizes the inward sickness of which bloodthirsty violence is the outward expression. It is usual to call this play a melodrama; if we are to call it a tragedy we shall need to decide what the significance of the epilogue is, and whose fate is meant to move us to pity, and what sort of moral world the poet is adopting as a basis for his dramatic thought — that is to say, whether the matricide was an act of pious obedience or a crime. Kitto notes that the contrast between the loyal affection which in the opening scene unites brother and sister, and the folly and criminality of their later behaviour, 'derives a tragic quality from one suggestion in the play, that these two are the last tainted offspring of a tainted house'.[7] This, I think, is true, and makes a sound starting-point for the interpretation of the play. We can however go further, and say that if the reference of the drama is political, then as the action progresses at least a few Athenians in the audience will have identified themselves and their city, sick and insane from a generation of war, with the desperate, floundering, condemned man they are watching. For them at least this makes the piece not melodrama, but tragedy uniting audience with actors in one purgative experience.

But interpretation, with which we are mainly concerned in this study, grew from subsequent reading, discussion, and pondering; it was not the preoccupation of the greater part of the first audience. What most of them saw on the stage, in the spring of 408, was not a pattern of symbols demanding interpretation, but two well-known figures from a familiar story. The prologue soon indicated to them at what stage of events the action was to begin: Orestes has killed his mother and is now stricken by the Furies with madness. The prologue also states that Menelaus and Helen have come home; so there is no surprise when presently Helen enters. The audience know how they should regard Helen; they recall *The Women of Troy* and at least four other plays where speakers have been unanimous about Helen's character and the treatment she deserved. Menelaus too they know as a villain fit to be cuckolded. For these, the majority of spectators, there will be great variety of entertainment: a 'mad scene', a violent quarrel, a splendid *aria* by Electra, an amusing and perhaps topical Messenger, a blood-curdling murder, a gloriously comic Phrygian, and real fireworks at the end (1541–4, 1618). This is the play which ever since has been commented on, classified, praised, or excused, and on the whole not much liked by modern readers, thought it was popular in antiquity. Let us take Kitto's hint, and begin by looking for its tragic quality.

The spectators who first looked for tragic quality in *Orestes* would be those who expected Euripides at each spring festival to give them his own unique tragic vision of their world as they faced it in that year and month. In the previous year (or it may possibly have been in 410) he had given them *The*

Phoenician Women, where in the first scene Antigone, spotting the enemy chiefs from the Theban battlements, had reminded citizens that Spartan troops, now permanently based sixteen miles away at Decelea, were likely to be seen at any time from the walls of Athens; and the play had proceeded to invite an identification of Thebes, and the House of Oedipus, with the imperilled fortunes of the Athenian Empire, and the mutual deaths of Eteocles and Polyneices with the mortal struggle between Athens and Sparta.[8] Its final tableau as described by the last Messenger, of Iocasta lying dead over the bodies of her two sons, could already in 409 symbolize the prostration of Hellas, the mother-country, by the murderous opposition of her two chief cities. So it needed no stretch of imagination, when Electra in the prologue of *Orestes* recounted the successive crimes and disasters of the House of Tantalus, to see in her picture of doom the decline of Athenian greatness. In 408, though total defeat was still four years off, the situation was already desperate; but even those who most expected truth rather than comfort from this poet can hardly have been prepared for the disturbing lines with which this play begins. To feel their force we need to direct carefully the opening sequence.

From the central doors Electra must enter first; then come slaves bearing a couch on which Orestes lies; they place it on the stage. Electra tends him, ascertains that he still sleeps, covers him with his cloak, and then, since what she has to say does not concern Orestes for the first twenty-eight lines, she comes down stage to speak directly to the audience:

> There is no fate so terrifying to describe,
> No bodily pain or heaven-sent cruelty so sharp,
> Which human flesh may not be destined to endure.[9]

For many in the audience, perhaps for most, this was merely a fair description of the suffering which afflicted Orestes and Electra as a consequence of obedience to Apollo; and indeed the lines may have been spoken beside the unconscious figure on the couch. But, for those who remembered Antigone staring from the battlements, or for those who already saw awaiting their city and their families the fate which Athens had prescribed for Mytilene, Scione, Melos, this opening may well have seemed to overstep the bounds of what is tolerable in a national theatre even in the name of truth. The meaning of the words would be confirmed by what followed – a picture of Tantalus, son of Zeus, made the equal of gods, and now punished for *hybris* by terror of 'the rock that leans and lours above his head' (6). The ancestral saga continues. Tantalus' grandson was Atreus, 'whom the Fates doomed to make war on his own brother Thyestes' – an echo of Eteocles and Polyneices.[10] The curse descended through Agamemnon to Orestes, who 'in obedience to Apollo' killed his mother; and Electra adds

And in the killing I took what part a woman could.

The whole picture is recalled, in a more personal tone, at the end of the first stasimon (339–47):

What other house should I weep for
Than the House of Tantalus?

Electra describes Orestes' insanity. In Chapter 6 we shall see how Euripides develops the imagery of insanity as applied to war, particularly in *The Phoenician Women*, *Orestes*, and *Iphigenia in Aulis*. In the first episode of *Orestes* we see insanity, roused and fed by reciprocal revenges, in contrast with the sanity still preserved in him by affection and loyalty; thereafter ingrained folly strengthens insanity, which soon affects both Electra and the chorus. For the present, Electra explains that Menelaus reached the harbour last night and is expected at the palace today; and that he sent Helen on ahead under cover of darkness, 'knowing that, if she came by day, she would be stoned by those whose sons were killed at Troy'. Helen will be on stage in a moment; she will speak only thirty-six lines. If we are to understand what is going on, we must know how Euripides thought of Helen, and what he intended by her part in this play.

Although it is true that Euripides sometimes presents the same person in different characters in two different plays, yet the question of Helen cannot be properly discussed in relation to this play alone. In Chapter 5 I shall examine the part which the poet allots to Helen in his work as a whole. In dealing with *Orestes* I shall now consider as exactly as possible the material the author has provided. When Helen was last in Hellas her home was not Argos but Sparta; and she has been away for about seventeen years. She and Menelaus are reconciled; she is content to be home again, and Menelaus is as devoted to her as ever. She has been in the palace (after a night without sleep) for only a few hours, and is reunited with her daughter Hermione; but she has certainly not spoken with Orestes, and only briefly with Electra, before she enters at line 71. Her ship reached Nauplia at night, and she came ahead to the palace immediately; only after she had set out did Menelaus learn of the murder of Clytemnestra (369–74). So Helen reached the palace a few hours ago knowing that the citizens of Argos were ready to stone her on sight; having recently heard that her sister Clytemnestra, on whom she had counted for a welcome, had murdered Agamemnon; and on entering the palace she learnt that Clytemnestra herself had been killed six days before. Little of this would occur to an audience during performance; but anyone who has written plays knows that details of this sort, and many more, must be clear and coherent in the playwright's mind before he begins to compose dialogue or design a scene. Helen is nearing forty.[11] She comes out of the palace door and sees before her Electra, who 'took what part a woman could' in killing her sister. Her cry, 'How could you do it?' is both natural and sympathetic, and accords with the tone of her enquiries (88, 90) about the motionless figure on the couch.

The orthodox view of this scene, however, insists that Helen is here (and everywhere else except in *Helen*) an unpleasant and despicable character. Reasons for this view are not usually given, since it is taken to be self-evident; but several reasons can be seen. One is that Electra in 126—31, and Orestes, Tyndareos, and Pylades later, express detestation of Helen; another — and probably most influential —reason is that Hecabe in *The Women of Troy* does the same; another, that characters and choruses in five other plays, where Helen is not even a *dramatis persona*, abuse her at every opportunity. These curious facts will be examined in Chapter 5; at present we will say simply that our view of Helen in *Orestes* must be founded only on the text of *Orestes*, and that anything else is unsound criticism. The facts of the text are as follows.

Electra in the prologue refers twice to Helen. First, 19—20:

Menelaus married Helen, the woman the gods hate.

Then, 56—66:

> And his wife
> Helen, source of all sorrow, he has sent on ahead
> To our house —last night; he knew that, if she came by day,
> She would be stoned by those whose sons were killed at Troy.
> She is indoors, weeping for her sister Clytemnestra
> And all the misery of our house . . . Now Hermione
> Is a joy to Helen and helps her to forget her troubles.

Then follows (71—125) Helen's single scene on stage. This scene has almost always been interpreted solely from Electra's point of view. I shall attempt an objective study of it presently; but the survey of Helen's role in succeeding scenes must first be completed.

In the first episode, as soon as Orestes is ready to listen, Electra tells him that Menelaus and Helen have returned (245—6). Orestes replies with a bitter comment on Helen, and the upsurge of anger brings on his insane fit. In the second episode Tyndareos couples Helen with Clytemnestra in his general condemnation of wicked women (520—2); and after Tyndareos has gone Orestes, kneeling before Menelaus, begs him to help him 'for Helen's sake' — and in the same breath expresses self-disgust at stooping low enough to use Helen's name as his plea (669—72). Menelaus has the dignity to ignore this. When Pylades arrives, on the first mention of Menelaus, before he has been on stage for thirty seconds, he abuses Helen (737); and again four

lines after, when Orestes responds with a contemptuous gibe at her. Pylades
then adds that Helen is responsible for the deaths of the Greeks who fell
at Troy (743). There is another gibe at 750. Neither of these young men has
ever met Helen.

The third episode begins with the Messenger, whose function has no connexion with Helen; but after Electra's monody comes the dialogue between
Orestes, Electra, and Pylades, which reaches its apex with Pylades' proposal
(1105–14):

PYLADES: Let's kill Helen — that hurts Menelaus most of all.
ORESTES: How can we do it? I'm ready, if the plan will work.
PYLADES: Why, with a sword. She's here now, hiding in your house.
ORESTES: She is, yes — making a list of all the valuables.
PYLADES: When she gets Hades for a lover, she'll stop that.
ORESTES: How shall we manage? She has a Phrygian bodyguard.
PYLADES: What bodyguard? I'm not afraid of Phrygians.
ORESTES: True — chaps who polish her mirrors and put out her scents.
PYLADES: Has she brought all her Trojan frills and trinkets here?
ORESTES: Hellas falls far below her standard for a home.

Another imaginative gibe at 1122; and then 1130–50, a concentrated paean
of hate against Helen. The chorus, who in their first two stasima when they
were morally serious made no reference to Helen, now carried away by
Pylades' eloquence endorse the project of murder (1153–4), and presently
cooperate by keeping watch to prevent the plan being frustrated (1246–95).
Helen, unseen, remains the centre of interest until her death-cry (1296–1301),
when Electra's ferocious lines convey a frenzy of hate unparalleled in
Euripides. The arrival of Helen's daughter Hermione brings the invisible
victim more vividly before us, while the chorus of respectable wives express
their hope of 'seeing with their own eyes the dead body of Helen bleeding on
the palace floor', and ascribe the horrible act to 'divine justice' (1357–62).
Next the Phrygian keeps all thought focused on Helen for a further hundred
and sixty lines; in fact, for well over four hundred lines Helen has replaced
Orestes at the centre of the tragedy. Menelaus appears, and Orestes from the
fortress wall disputes with him about Helen. Finally she appears, mute, with
Apollo in the epilogue, which is as much concerned with Helen as with
Orestes; her presence — like that of the restored Alcestis, except that Helen
is not restored — achieves eloquence through silence.

This rapid survey exhibits the curious but undeniable fact that the role
of Helen in this play, so far from being irrelevantly dragged in, is from beginning to end at the centre of the drama — just as Alcestis, though absent for
fully half of the action, is at the centre of hers. The three murderers and the
chorus characterize themselves by what they say of Helen as well as by
their acts; the attitude of the Phrygian (who is by no means to be dismissed

as an abject, merely comic, or insignificant person) and that of Menelaus give a different view of the elusive figure; the audience or reader has to exercise free judgement. The part played by Helen in later scenes will be examined in due course; for the present we must look in detail at the prologue scene.

Helen's opening address to her niece, 'Electra, maiden for so long a time' (72), is often said to be a sneer at Electra's unmarried state. However, to sneer at 'old maids' was, as far as is known, not a usual habit of unpleasant people in Euripides' time, perhaps because the competition for husbands was more a matter of fathers bargaining with dowries for sons-in-law. In fact, in 663 Orestes uses the same phrase about his sister. Electra had suffered cruel wrongs since Agamemnon's death, and one of them was that she had been kept unmarried. Greeks were not reticent about such matters. Enforced virginity was as openly referred to, as naturally pitied, as bereavement; Electra (whose name itself means 'unmarried') would be unlikely to resent the phrase. Helen continues (75—6):

> Speaking with you, I catch no taint from what you did;
> The blame for that I lay on Phoebus.

The Argive Assembly had forbidden any citizen to speak with the matricides (47); and Tyndareos is surprised (481) to find Menelaus in conversation with the polluted Orestes. Helen's attitude is more humane and charitable and, since Apollo commanded the murder, consistent with piety; though line 76 has encouraged some commentators, whose censorious ardour matches that of Orestes, to point at the hypocrisy of blaming gods for human errors. Three lines later Helen claims for herself the same charity that she extends to Electra ('by a destiny of god-sent madness', 79); though we may note that, in practical human experience, there is some difference between the command of an oracle (which Orestes knows he could have, and ought to have, disobeyed — see 288—93) and the inner compulsion of Aphrodite which in Greek drama is universally recognized as irresistible and, in men, pardonable (see e.g. in Sophocles' *Trachiniae* the love of Heracles for Iole). 'I weep,' says Helen, 'because Clytemnestra was my sister, and I had not seen her since I sailed to Troy. Now I feel alone.'

Electra's reply is, that Helen and her husband 'have come home crowned with happiness and success, to find her and her brother crushed by misfortune'. The only kind answer to such a statement is to turn to something else; this Helen does:

> HELEN: How many days has he been lying on this bed?
> ELECTRA: Ever since the day he shed the blood that gave him life.
> HELEN: Pitiful son! Pitiful mother, to die so!

There is nothing here to suggest that Helen's attitude is heartless or shallow, or anything but sympathetic and generous.

Helen has come out early because the one urgent thing she must do is to lay her offering on her sister's grave. But it is already light. How is she to find her way through unknown, hostile streets to where Clytemnestra's ashes lie? Electra's words have already hinted (89) what will later be explicit (161–5, 191–4) – that she laments Clytemnestra's death as bitterly as Helen does; and Helen feels a bond with Electra's misery. She says (92–6):

> Will you go for me to my sister's grave . . .
> To pour out wine, and lay an offering of my hair?

She is innocently unaware of Electra's hatred.

ELECTRA: But what prevents *you* visiting your sister's grave?
HELEN: I shrink from being seen in the streets of Argos.
ELECTRA: Good; it's time you felt some shame for your disgraceful conduct.
HELEN: What you say is just, Electra, but not kind.
ELECTRA: What makes you afraid to face the citizens?
HELEN: I fear the fathers of those who died in the war.
ELECTRA: You well may. Your name is execrated here.
HELEN: Then save me from this fear. Do what I ask.

Helen three times replies to harshness with gentleness; but she knows now that Electra hates her, and she sends Hermione to carry her gifts to the grave. She says to her daughter:

> Now take this jar
> For a libation, and these locks cut from my hair,
> And go to Clytemnestra's tomb . . .
> Beg her to have kindly thoughts
> For me, and you, and for my husband, and for these
> Two unhappy children, whom Apollo has destroyed.

Hermione goes out carrying the gifts, and Helen returns indoors. What qualities has Helen shown? Warmth, sensitiveness, sympathy, a need for friendship, a mature graciousness. What Euripides has given us here, with infinite poignancy, is a picture of two women, each aware of the prospect of standing as the solitary target for angry men throwing stones. (The stoning scene from Cacoyannis's film *A Girl in Black* is relevant.) There is nothing that the two have in common except the fate of being women, and being hated.

When Helen goes indoors, Electra's own hatred bursts (126–7):

> What potent evil lives in native quality!
> While sound and noble natures possess enduring strength.

This can only mean that she alludes to her own nature as sound, noble, and strong, and to Helen's as evil. Almost all scholars and translators have

accepted Electra's judgement as being the view of the dramatist, and put a
forced interpretation on the preceding scene to reflect this view. It is better
criticism to read the scene first, interpret it in its own terms, and then ask
whether lines 126–7 are the author's judgement on Helen or on Electra.
Electra continues:

> You saw how she had cut her hair off near the ends[12]
> So as not to spoil her beauty? She's the same woman
> She always was. — May the gods hate you, for the ruin
> You've brought on me, and on Orestes, and on all Hellas!
> Oh, miserable life!

By this time, however, Helen has left the stage, and it is too late for the
audience (or the critic) to take a careful look at the coiffure which the author,
as director, had prescribed for Helen. It is generally assumed that the unbalanced and guilty Electra was correct both in her observation of Helen's
hair and in her ascription of her own misery to Helen rather than to other
more obvious causes. Of this there will be more to say in Chapter 5; for the
present we note that in *Orestes* the two women are set side by side so that we
may compare their crimes, their excuses, and the impression of good or evil
which each gives when on the stage. There is no mystery about Electra. She is
as different as possible from the steadfast heroine of Aeschylus or Sophocles;
though she shows the same devoted loyalty to her brother. At this point she is
distracted with remorse and guilt; later in the play she is a homicidal maniac.
This alone should guide us in assessing her judgement of Helen. If Euripides
had wished to show Helen as worthless, he would have done so subtly, but
unmistakably. He presents her as withdrawn, veiled; as one whom men and
women unite in vilifying, but whose presence gives no ground whatever for
this attitude.

But there is also a more positive reason for rejecting the usually accepted
image of Helen; a more positive aspect of her role in *Orestes*. Helen is a touch-
stone, a person to whom each character in turn establishes his or her relationship. The only character who has no connexion with her is the Messenger.
There are three characters whose moral judgement the poet allows us to
respect: Menelaus, Hermione, and the Phrygian; and all three love and
honour Helen. The other four characters, and the chorus in their later, corrupt
phase, abuse and hate her. Electra first mentions her (19) as 'the woman
the gods hate'. But Electra is mistaken; for at the end of the play, when human
hatred has done its worst, the gods receive Helen to 'the folds of the sky';
and there the woman whom the Elders in *Agamemnon* called '*Helenaus*',
'destroyer of ships', becomes 'the goddess who saves sailors', *nautilois sōtērios*
(1637), sharing the function of her brothers the Dioscori.

We now return to the entry of the chorus. Electra's annoyance at their
coming has sometimes been thought to reflect a feeling on the author's part

that in a play of this kind a chorus is superfluous; but the subsequent significance of their behaviour refutes this. These women of Argos have an important dramatic function which depends partly on the sympathetic character established for them in the *parodos* and maintained until in 1153–4 they give a sign of their sinister change. In the present scene their dialogue with Electra shows their gentle forbearance towards the overwrought princess, their affection and concern for the unconscious Orestes. Their condemnation of the matricide and of the oracle, clearly stated in the second stasimon, only echoes what Electra herself says in this scene.

Now Orestes wakes, in his right mind; and the talk between brother and sister is touchingly realistic. When Orestes feels strong enough to stand, Electra tells him first that Menelaus has come; then she adds that he has brought Helen with him; and since we have seen (130–1) what feelings she bears for Helen, we can also see how the hatred in her voice wakes hatred in Orestes, who replies (247)

If he had come alone, he'd be a happier man . . .

to which Electra responds with

Oh, what a vicious pair of daughters Tyndareos
Fathered – two names of infamy throughout Hellas!

The sudden flaring of hate at once shatters Orestes' precarious sanity, and for several minutes the scene reels with his raving violence. He lets fly with a bow and arrows at the Furies he sees in the air – a macabre echo of the entertaining ballet-movement in *Ion* 154–81, where Ion points his arrows at the birds. When Orestes recovers, we are shown for a few minutes the anguished remnants of nobility and goodness in this ruined life (288–303):

I believe my father, had I asked him face to face
Whether I ought to kill her, would have gripped my hand
And begged, implored me not to lift a sword against
My mother, since that could not bring him back to life,
While it doomed me to the agonies I now endure.
    Come, then, dear sister, uncover your head, and don't
Cry any more, however desperate things are.
And when you see me losing heart, support me, and
Comfort me in the horror of my insanity;
And when you weep, I will be at your side, and speak
Loving encouragement. This is the kind of help
We ought to give in time of need to those we love.
    So come, Electra, go indoors now and lie down
And give your weary eyes the sleep they sadly miss . . .

Electra replies

> I will not fail you; I will die or live with you;

and she goes indoors, while Orestes lies down exhausted on his couch, and the chorus gather round to perform the first stasimon and pray for his deliverance.

They have already done what they could to comfort Electra in her despair; though she knows the truth (194):

> CHORUS.   Just it may have been.
> ELECTRA.   Right it was not.

Now as they stand by Orestes' couch they plead with the 'black-visaged Eumenides for mercy on the son of Agamemnon in his madness'. Their attitude here is one of pity rather than condemnation; a move towards sternness will be felt when in the second stasimon they adopt an authoritative tone which uncompromisingly condemns both Apollo's command and Orestes' obedience, and which establishes this as the moral standpoint from which every subsequent development is to be viewed. The antistrophe of that ode, 819ff. (see above, page 54), is the basis of the tragic element in this play. It will be important to remember this when, later, the chorus succumb to corrupting influence, and when Apollo in the epilogue ignores both truth and ethics. The Argive women now mourn for Apollo's instrument (316ff.):

> O unhappy Orestes,
> For the hideous task appointed you,
> For the obedience that destroyed you . . .

and proceed to connect their thought with Electra's prologue-narrative:

> The greatest happiness is not permanent
> In the world of men;
> But the storms of God rise against it,
> Like a light sailing-ship they shatter it,
> Terrors and disasters roll around it,
> Till crashing waves close over death.
>   And this was the House of Tantalus,
> Born from the marriage of gods—
> A house that claimed my reverence
> More than any house I have known.

Whether in these lines the poet, having resolved to leave Athens, is bidding farewell to his native city, is a matter of conjecture; as is the similar question whether Shakespeare in *The Tempest* said farewell to the London theatre.

It is hard to believe that such a conjecture did not occur to some members of this play's first audience.

Now the chorus turn to greet a newcomer (348—55):

See! Menelaus comes, adorned with magnificent robes, which proclaim his descent from the House of Tantalus.[13]

For a few lines only, the air of foreboding is dispelled; the return of a king after many years is, the chorus feel, a moment when unpleasant truth should be disguised rather than faced. But Menelaus, looking at his ancestral palace, blunders straight into reality (356ff.):

My home! In one sense I am glad to see you on my return; yet at the same time I weep. Never have I seen another house more miserably encircled on every side with disasters.

(The same picture was given in *The Phoenician Women* 250—1:

All around this city
Gleaming shields mass like a dense cloud.)

Menelaus quickly puts aside the ominous thought with a more superficial tone; and after this the symbolism of the doomed house is left to explain itself.

I have already referred (above, pages 12—13) to Aristotle's judgement of Menelaus as 'an unnecessarily bad character'; and earlier in this chapter (54f.) I outlined the embarassing situation in which Menelaus finds himself when confronted with Orestes. He has reason for the caution which characterizes his opening speech. He has no means of knowing whether he himself is welcome or unpopular in Argos — where it is unsafe for his wife to move about in daylight. He has some ships, but their crews are not an army. The regime of Clytemnestra and Aegisthus, who had assassinated his brother, had apparently enjoyed a *de facto* recognition by the citizens. Argos is a democracy, ready to try a prince for his life; and, according to Tyndareos (500-3), competent to try even a reigning queen. Menelaus desires not to provoke a quarrel, but to get safe home to Sparta with his wife. Some excusable nervousness is reflected in the formality of his words (356-74), and in one awkward slip when he says (371—2) that he 'had looked forward to embracing Orestes and his mother, thinking all was well with them'. One does not embrace one's brother's murderess. He questions Orestes and listens carefully and without censure to his account; and commits himself to only one expression of opinion — but it is a significant one (416—20):

ORESTES: Phoebus commanded me to take my mother's life.
MENELAUS: A command showing some ignorance of law and right.

ORESTES: What are the gods? We don't know; but we are their slaves.
MENELAUS: Well, after that, doesn't Phoebus now come to your help?

Orestes begs Menelaus to save him; but his own account of the position shows that there is nothing whatever that Menelaus can do. Matters have gone beyond his competence, and it is too late. Before Menelaus has time to reply, Tyndareos approaches, and Orestes' hopelessness is made more poignant by his remorseful memories of boyhood and the kindness he received from his grandparents.

Menelaus, needing time to think things out, is nettled by Tyndareos' tactless attempt to make up his mind for him, and retorts sharply. Tyndareos then analyses the whole moral position (500ff.):

> Orestes' duty was to take
> Lawful proceedings, prosecute for murder, and
> Expel his mother from the palace. In that way
> From his misfortune he would have won a name for wise
> Behaviour, would have preserved both law and piety.
> But now his life bears the same curse his mother bore.

Euripides, like Thucydides, saw the passion for revenge as the great source of evil. Law at least offers some alternative (512ff.):

> Our ancestors established a sound principle:
> The man guilty of murder they forbade to intrude
> On sight or presence of the citizens; his crime
> Must be atoned by exile — not by blood for blood;
> Otherwise always one man's lot is to be involved
> With murder, taking on his hands the last blood-guilt . . .
> The death my daughter suffered was her just desert;
> But it was not for him to execute sentence.

In reply Orestes makes a speech of insane folly, defending his matricide on the ground that, if such reprisal is forbidden, 'husband-murder will become a sport'. He contradicts his earlier judgement by saying that, if he had neglected his duty, his father's Furies would have haunted him. The effect of this speech on Tyndareos is to make him too forget the 'sound principles' he spoke of, and promise instead to urge the Argive Assembly to pass a death-sentence. When he has stormed out, Orestes makes a further appeal to Menelaus to save him, using tortuous arguments and abject entreaties, and including a most offensive allusion to Menelaus' beloved wife (669—72). Menelaus would have been justified in rejecting him as completely as Tyndareos had; instead, his answer is a model of balance, fairness, and candour. He will try, he says, to persuade Tyndareos and the Argives to moderate their fury. Orestes rewards him with an avalanche of abuse; and Menelaus departs. What this long scene has given us is a general diagram showing how the passions aroused by blood-vengeance destroy law, tradition, family bonds, and common sense.

But the scene is not over yet. As Menelaus goes, Pylades arrives from another direction, and a new phase of the story begins. Pylades has an immediate effect on Orestes, as later on Electra and the chorus. His positive qualities are his friendship and loyalty to Orestes; and these are unaffected by any moral consideration (contrast the canon set by *Hippolytus* 997–9). It is the ethic imposed on the soldier, of comradeship in danger, regardless of the enterprise in which the danger is incurred. With each new contribution to the action Pylades makes it clearer that he enters as the human embodiment of Ares, inexhaustible in energy, deterred by nothing, fertile in thoughts of destruction. His venomous allusions to Helen are as habitual to him as expletives are to his modern counterpart. He wastes no time in blaming Menelaus. Orestes, inspired by his friend's positive attitude, suddenly decides to go and speak in his own defence before the Assembly; Pylades undertakes to go with him and support him. They agree to say nothing to Electra (787–9); and Orestes' quoting of the proverb, 'Get you friends, not merely kin', dishonours the debt he owes his sister. The two men set off together for the trial, and the chorus re-group to sing the second stasimon.

The first stasimon was an ode of mourning for the House of Tantalus, wrecked by storms of misfortune. This picture is now focused more clearly (807ff.):

> That splendour of prosperity, that warlike prowess
> Which flaunted its pride over Hellas
> And by the banks of Simois
> Has deserted the descendants of Atreus.

For any who remembered Cassandra's words in *The Women of Troy* 370–83, 'the banks of Simois' must surely recall the harbour of Syracuse. The ode continues (819ff.):

> That noble deed was not noble —
> To pierce a parent's flesh with a fire-born blade . . .
> 'Crime in a just cause' is an impious sophistry,
> An insanity (*paranoia*) breeding in evil hearts.
> What sickness is sharper than the sin that stains
> The hand guilty of a mother's murder?
> Such, such is the act whose accomplishment
> Has destroyed the son of Agamemnon
> With frenzied lunacy (*maniais*),
> With Furies hounding to the death,
> With fugitive eyes rolling in terror.

So much, then, for divine command. There is no doubt that this ode represents in the author's mind the truth of the moral issue behind the whole
story; if this is not so, we must deny him any moral seriousness. Apollo
contradicts it in the epilogue: then it is Apollo who is judged. The chorus
themselves contradict it by subsequent action: then it is the chorus who
are to be judged. In Euripides there is only one final source of moral judgement, and that is humanity, and human perception. This ode is as authoritative a statement as any found in Euripides; and it confirms that the play is
not merely a 'febrile melodrama' but a tragedy in the full sense; and its
tragic quality arises directly from this identification of Orestes and the
House of Tantalus with the citizens forming the audience and with the body
politic which they represent. It is their tragedy that is being enacted; their
belligerent insanity which is leading rapidly to their self-destruction.

The Messenger now arrives to report the trial of Orestes by the Argive
Assembly. His speech was famous in antiquity, especially for its casual
beginning, which Menander imitated in *The Sicyonian*. The man is an old
slave of Agamemnon's; and his report of the trial is strongly coloured by
his devotion to the family. He summarizes five speeches made at the trial.

The first speaker, he says, was Talthybius the herald, who 'twisted eulogy
and censure both together' and was chiefly concerned to please Aegisthus'
friends. Next came Diomedes (898ff.):

> He urged them not to sentence either you or your brother
> To death, but satisfy piety by banishing you.
> Some shouted in approval, others disagreed.

This was the proposal for which Tyndareos spoke convincingly in his
first speech, before he became angry and intemperate. It is the only sensible
speech of the five; the Messenger gives it three lines, as against the dozen
allotted to each of the others; it was not sensational, and clearly was ignored
for that reason. A third speech demanded that the accused be stoned to death;
the Messenger abuses this speaker at some length. The fourth speaker is
described with trite and sentimental enthusiasm as 'a man of blameless
principle and integrity' (917–30):

> He said, Orestes son of Agamemnon should be
> Honoured with crowns for daring to avenge his father
> By taking a depraved and godless woman's life . . .

Tyndareos, the Messenger implies, spoke for the death-sentence; Menelaus
is not mentioned. The narrative ends with an account of Orestes' own
defence, which was as foolish and perverse as his appeal to Tyndareos.
'Yet,' says the Messenger, 'he did not convince the Assembly, though they
thought he had spoken well.' All the features of this narrative — the unsound

arguments used, the irrational responses each argument evoked, the Messenger's prejudiced description of each speaker — form an ironic comment on democratic processes of justice, and well illustrate Euripides' method. But in the end, if the best proposal was ignored, so was the worst; and when sentence was passed (946—9),

> Orestes barely gained this favour for you both,
> To escape stoning; and he promised that his own hand
> Would this day make an end of his life and of yours.

The sentence announces the doom not merely of the brother and sister, but of the House of Tantalus. This is the theme of Electra's monody, in which those listeners or readers — perhaps not many — who had understood the symbolism of Electra's prologue speech and the end of the first stasimon, must have heard a bitter lament for the once glorious city of Pericles (968—81):

> Here is pity, here is indignation
> For the fate of those who will die
> Who once were leaders of the armies of Hellas.
> Lost, lost and vanished,
> Gone is the race of Pelops, root and branch,
> The prosperous home that was the world's envy . . .
> In the length of mortal life there is no permanence.

These last lines echo the Chorus (339—40):

> The greatest happiness is not permanent . . .
> This was the House of Tantalus . . .

Orestes returns, sullenly resigned, impatient of his sister's distress. He relents, they embrace, and are ready to meet death; but one thing that Electra says (1033—4) will be remembered a little later when she is again plotting murder:

> We're going to die. It is impossible not to weep.
> For everyone, life's precious and death pitiful.

The farewell between brother and sister is moving; but it has also a morbid tone. It is a union in both guilt and hatred, and includes the slander of Menelaus (1058—9):

> Succession to the throne was his one thought.

Then comes Pylades' intervention. What has he to gain from it? Apparently nothing, except the enjoyment of violence. It is useless to question the existence of gods; and Pylades, like Ares, is unaccountable. Orestes says to him (1075)

Go back and be your father's son. Don't die with me —

and continues with nine more lines of affectionate farewell. Pylades replies with a fervent protestation of loyalty (1085—99):

I shared the killing with you, and I'll not retract.

This recalls a rather different line from *Iphigenia in Tauris* (709):

I hunted with you; we grew up together.

There, two speeches closely similar to these were made by the same two friends, in a situation where hope of escape, offered to one of them, sweetened and ennobled the emotion expressed. Here the friendship is genuine enough, and Pylades' positive tone suggests that he is going to offer hope of some kind; but this hope is a barren revenge which, instead of sweetening and ennobling, poisons and debases the emotion (1098—9):

So let's put heads together, since we're going to die,
To ensure a share of suffering for Menelaus.

At this point comes an unexpected development not paralleled in any other play of Euripides; one which shows how, after twenty-three years of war, the poet despaired of the very springs of human goodness. The emotion of this scene, intensified by the prospect of death, takes on a false authority which is too much for the moral stability of ordinary people. The women of Argos have listened spellbound; and when Orestes says (1104)

These women are all our friends,

the glow of gratification draws them suddenly into the corrupt ring of loyalty to evil, so that the next line transfixes and transforms them, gripping them by the jealous hatred latent in each:

PYLADES: Let's kill Helen. That will break Menelaus' heart.

In *Medea* and in *Andromache* the chorus protest against proposed murder; in *The Children of Heracles, Hippolytus, Ion, The Phoenician Women*, choruses protest against other forms of wickedness. None of those choruses has pronounced more solemn and authoritative moral judgements than we heard in the second stasimon of *Orestes*. Yet these same women of Argos listen to Pylades' proposal, and to the fifty lines which follow — surely the

most subtly revolting lines in Euripides — and then express and excuse their
full concurrence in words which, because their purport is so habitual, have —
incredibly — hardly ever provoked comment (1153–4):

> The daughter of Tyndareos, who disgraced her sex,
> Deserves the loathing of all women everywhere.

The other daughter of Tyndareos had disgraced her sex and had shed blood
as well; and this same chorus in 831–3 execrated the bloody reprisal
which they now approve. We may surmise that what drives the poet from
his city is not only the degeneracy of the state, the vanishing of public
glory, but the corruption of ordinary people by the miasma of violence.

Orestes and Pylades plan the murder; their object — to cause Menelaus
pain. Neither of them has ever seen Helen (nor has the chorus); but throughout their lives they have heard people revile her and blame her for all the
bloodshed of the Trojan war. As for the crime which this murder is to
avenge, Menelaus' refusal to speak for Orestes has already been shown as
fully justified; Orestes was self-condemned, and the folly of his defence
was unanswerable. There is nothing in the play to support the supposition
(stated as a fact by the writer of the third Hypothesis, on the basis of
Orestes' words 1058–9) that Menelaus hoped to acquire the throne for himself; and it is worth observing that four or five years earlier, in *Iphigenia in
Tauris* 930–1, this slander was suggested and specifically refuted. Another
ancient commentator, the writer of the Hypothesis attributed to Aristophanes
the Grammarian, found 'the catastrophe rather of the nature of comedy'.
In other words, he was ready, like the majority of the first audience, to regard Helen's life as of no importance, and therefore was capable of viewing
the Phrygian's narrative as a merely comic performance. If our assessment
of the whole work favours this kind of approach, then the murder of Helen
(which Euripides invented for this play only) can have no function in the
drama other than its sordid appeal as a piece of sensational violence. This
view seems to me inconsistent with respect for the author; I hold that we
should dismiss it as trivial, and instead build a tragic interpretation on
the strong evidence for a profound moral intention pervading the action
from beginning to end.

The play is about Orestes. The one positive act that Orestes accomplishes
is to kill Helen. Therefore the meaning of the play must lie in the significance
of this act, in the answer to the question, Whom has he killed? What has he
destroyed? The murder represents the very nadir of wickedness; it is
prompted by no traditional duty or divine command; the 'betrayal' which
motivates it is imaginary; Helen is almost as close to Orestes in blood as
Clytemnestra. If the House of Tantalus stands for the city of Athens, then
Orestes' folly and addiction to violence represent the inability of Athens to

extricate herself from a disastrous war; and the killing of Helen symbolizes
that destruction of gentleness, warmth, and beauty which is experienced by
a people who have suffered, and inflicted, a generation of ferocious war.
The gentle virtues hinder and condemn the activities of Ares, whose urgen-
cies cannot afford vision. Aphrodite's husband is Hephaestus the creator;
her seducer is Ares the destroyer. Pericles urged his citizens to be 'lovers'
of Athens, echoing Athena's words to the Eumenides;[14] and what men most
loved Athens for was her creative dedication to beauty. In 408 the Erechtheion
was newly finished; but the spirit which conceived it had endured a long
nightmare of bloodshed and anxiety, and would not survive. So in this scene
the plotting of the two men is written not only for those who will find
pleasure in its vicious slander and unhealthy excitement, but also for those
who will recognize a familiar sickness now grown incurable (1106—16). Part
of it has already been quoted on page 60; and it ends with:

> PYLADES: Well, slaves will have no chance against us.
> ORESTES: True; and if
>   We could bring *this* off, I'd be ready to die twice.

When a plan has been made, the next thing is to sell it to the public.
Pylades comes forward to address to the audience the kind of speech used in
any popular assembly to recommend some doubtful enterprise: 'And my
plan is honourable. Listen ...' The success of its crazed and inhuman
enthusiasm is measured by the response of the chorus (1153—4). In gauging
its effect upon the first audience we should also remember that there could
be few present who had not lost sons or fathers or husbands in the war
(1134—9):

> Helen's death
> Brings satisfaction to all Hellas —to everyone
> Whose son, or father, she destroyed, and every wife
> She made a widow. There'll be cheering in the streets,
> Bonfires will blaze to all the gods, and prayers rise up
> For blessings on us both, because we justly shed
> The blood of a bad woman ...

The rasping irony reaches an apex with the joke in 1145:

> Gods forbid
> That ever Menelaus should thrive, while your father,
> And you, and your sister, all die, and your mother too —
> Well, it's perhaps more suitable to leave her out —
> Only that Menelaus ... should possess your house!

The emotional response of Orestes fascinates by its paranoia. It mirrors the delusion of a city which is, like Orestes, 'now at my last gasp in any case' (1163), and still equating a chimerical 'freedom' with the capacity to take revenge (1167—71):

> I am the son of Agamemnon, whom Hellas
> Chose for command by merit — no despot, but one
> Who had a god's strength in him; whom I will not shame
> By a slave's death, but breathe my last like a free man,
> Getting revenge on Menelaus.

These words are a key point in the play's symbolism. Just as in *The Children of Heracles* Demophon, son of Theseus, represented an age whose ideal had declined since the days of Marathon (see Chapter 7, page 190), so here Orestes speaks for an Athens which looks back to a still more recent 'heroic' age, the age of Pericles. Pericles in 430 told the Athenians plainly (Thucydides II.64) that their empire was a tyranny; and his supporters and opponents disputed whether his own position made him a *tyrannos* — a dispute reflected here in Orestes' words about Agamemnon. (Unless such a reference is intended there can be little point in the phrase 'no despot', since Agamemnon clearly was a *basileus*, a hereditary king, though not strictly a *tyrannos*.) Since then the Athens of Pericles has begotten the Athens of Alcibiades and Cleophon. The trite phrase, 'breathe my last like a free man', may remind some in the audience that in Pericles' day Athens had held a loftier conception of freedom than that which Orestes will claim by murdering Helen to punish Menelaus. Further, the internecine fury of the states of Hellas, all fighting in the name of 'freedom', has destroyed the land which bore and nurtured them; their guilt is that of matricide, and the punishment of insanity falls inevitably on so unnatural an act. Orestes is not merely Athens, but a whole war-crazed generation of Hellenes.

The mounting tension of this scene has still two peaks to come. First, Electra's proposal to use Hermione as a weapon against Menelaus (1199):

> If he attempts to kill you ... cut Hermione's throat.

Pylades' response to this proposal — a grotesque anticipation of wedded bliss (1210) — is a guide to the sense in which we should interpret Apollo's grim blessing in 1659. Line 1130, '*Kill Helen* — that's our watchword', echoes *Electra* 685, 'I give you this password, *Aegisthus dies*', and *Women of Troy* 1030, 'kill Helen ...'. Next, the invocation, 1225—45. Already in *Electra* 671—84 Euripides had parodied the end of the famous invocation in *The Choephori*. There the parallel was close, the difference subtle though distinct. Here the persons involved are the same, otherwise the only parallel is the motive of hatred. The crime to be avenged is imaginary, the victim innocent and unprotected, the danger in execution negligible. The dramatic purpose of the litany is to point the paranoia of the criminals – and symbolically, perhaps, to illustrate the profanation of sanctities as a feature of national demoralization.

The two men enter the palace. The transformed chorus, disowning both the compassion of their first ode and the truth of their second, now eagerly accept Electra's instruction to keep guard on right and left and ensure that the crime is not prevented. The strain of waiting is too much for Electra. She shouts (1284ff.):

> You in the house there! Why do you take so long?
> When will you blood the victim?
> – They aren't listening. O gods, what misery!
> Are their swords blunted at the sight of beauty?

This last marvellous line (see again *Women of Troy* 891–3) keeps Helen in her exact function, still at the centre of the drama. In a world of violence beauty is vulnerable. In the epilogue we shall see the earth deprived of the beauty it could only hate, and Helen mute and remote beside Apollo. Electra, we should observe, is not a unique monster. The desire for Helen's death was fervently voiced by Hecabe in *The Women of Troy*, and by choruses in *Hecabe*, *Electra*, and *Iphigenia in Tauris*; and few commentators have shown surprise at this stream of hate. Now the heroes perform their mission. Twice Helen screams in death, calling on Menelaus. Electra yells,

> Kill, stab, destroy her, both of you!
> Two hungry swords – drive them in!

Hermione arrives. Electra tells her that she and Orestes are condemned, and begs her to go in and kneel before Helen and ask her to secure Menelaus' help (1340–5):

> ELECTRA: Hermione, my own mother brought you up herself:
>   Take pity on us, help us in our misery! . . .
> HERMIONE: Of course I'll go as quickly as I can; and you
>   Shall be saved if it's in my power.

Hermione goes in, and is held prisoner. The chorus, crazy with excitement, rush about shouting, to cover any outcry Hermione or the servants may raise; and they add their blasphemy to that of the murderers (1361–2):

> How justly divine vengeance
> Has fallen upon Helen!

They await the satisfaction of 'seeing with their own eyes the dead body of Helen bleeding on the palace floor'; and then the sardonic, mocking line to introduce the totally unexpected Phrygian (1359):

> Until we hear an account from one of the servants.

But before we study the next scene we must deal with the question, Does Euripides intend us to suppose that Helen was in fact killed by Orestes, or not?

A. P. Burnett says (*Catastrophe Survived* 184) that this drama shows a series of failures beginning with Orestes' appeal for Menelaus' help and culminating in his murderous attack on Helen. The dramatist certainly invites some confusion as to whether the murder is actually accomplished. Burnett and other commentators assume that it was not; they accept Apollo's account of the matter in 1633–4, 'I rescued her and snatched her away from your sword.' On the other hand the Phrygian speaks of 'the bloody, wicked crime which I saw, I saw' (1455–6), and of Helen 'lying bleeding on the ground' (1491). Orestes, being insane, says at 1512 that she is dead, and again at 1534–6 defies Menelaus to avenge 'the blood of Helen'; but at 1580, 1582, being still insane, believes he has not killed her. The Phrygian says (1494–8) that Orestes, interrupted in killing Helen by the entrance of Hermione, turned back 'to the slaughter', but Helen had vanished. When Menelaus enters at 1554 he evidently believes reports he has heard that his wife is dead, and does not believe the contradiction of these reports which apparently the Phrygian had brought him (1558–9). Since Euripides has deliberately left the matter ambiguous there is no point in trying to say exactly 'what happened'; but to applaud Apollo for his 'miracle' in 'saving' Helen seems still more pointless and indeed perverse. If he had saved her she would still be alive. What, then, was the author's purpose in creating this ambiguity?

I think three answers are possible; and they are mutually compatible. First, the wish expressed by the chorus in 1357–8 to 'see Helen lying in blood' demands a response; and the only appropriate response to such a wish is that it be denied; comment is superfluous. Secondly, it is appropriate that the destroyer of beauty should doubt his own success, and surmise that he has opposed a power greater than his own. In the third place, the ambiguity allowed those sentimental listeners who loved a miracle and wished to see Apollo as a saving god to preserve their piety; though why modern scholars should adopt this pious attitude towards Apollo is hard to see. The obvious fact is that, in Euripides' drama, if a god wanted to prevent a kin-murder he could do as Athena did in *Heracles* (1002–6) when the mad hero was about to kill his father Amphitryon; Athena did not wait until Amphitryon was mortally wounded and then translate him to the starry sky, but promptly immobilized his attacker. Or a god could remove the threatened person out of harm's way, as Artemis removed Iphigenia from the altar at Aulis. In both these cases a human life was preserved; but in *Orestes* Apollo does not preserve Helen's life. Therefore the final failed enterprise in this play is not Orestes' murderous attempt, which was blunderingly accomplished, but Apollo's rescue of the daughter of Zeus. We thus find that the one act towards which the drama moves is the destruction of that beautiful, gentle, withdrawn figure who appeared briefly in the prologue, and who appears again, still more withdrawn, and silent, in the tableau of the epilogue.

This too seems clear: it is entirely improbable that the dramatist gave so important a place in this passionately serious play to the worthless and despicable creature he is commonly supposed to have presented as Helen. A character who though invisible after the prologue pervades and focuses the action as Helen does in *Orestes* is certainly one whom the author regards as of some significance. The nature of this significance has been suggested already and will be referred to again at the end of the chapter; but it is now time to examine the Phrygian's scene.

The Phrygian is one of the three persons in the play whom the poet allows us to think of as honest and good. He is an exile and a slave, probably a eunuch. Helen is the accepted cause of the war which destroyed his home and country, she is 'Hell-Helen', *dyselena* (1387); but he does not curse her, he accepts her for her beauty, her divine descent, her human innocence and gentleness. He is a natural, guileless and open-eyed, and his picture of Helen is the loveliest poem in the play (1426ff.):

> I was standing near to Helen
> Stirring the air with a round fan of feathers
> To make a breeze for Helen's hair
> And to cool her cheek — we always do this in the East;
> And she was spinning a linen thread,
> Twisting it in her fingers,
> And the spun thread trailed on the floor.

His horror and revulsion (1455—7) at what was done shame not only the criminals, but still more the ladies of the chorus for their complicity — though to their now corrupted perception he is a comic and nothing else. When Orestes bursts in, sword in hand and recognizably unbalanced (1505), he asks the Phrygian, 'Was Helen justly or unjustly killed?' (1512). With this guilty and menacing question he keeps Helen still at the centre of the drama. The Phrygian answers a madman in his own terms — as the madman recognizes (1514, 1516); and their exchange places the haters and the lovers of Helen clearly in their two camps.

In the short scene where the raving Orestes threatens to kill the Phrygian,

the foolishness of the general creed that Helen was responsible for the war
is once again presented to those who can reason (1515–16). (The line which
saves the Phrygian's life, 'Every man loves living' (1523), echoes Electra's
'For everyone, life's precious' (1034).) Orestes then re-enters the palace; and
a minute later he appears above, holding his sword at Hermione's throat.
Menelaus enters, alone and distracted, having met the Phrygian as he came.
Orestes at one moment (1611) appears to be bargaining with Menelaus,[15] at
another to be about to implement the death-wish which now obsesses all
three criminals (1618–20):

> Electra! Now's the moment! Set this house on fire!
> Pylades, burn these walls and battlements!

The sword is still at Hermione's throat. Flames have been visible in the palace
since 1541, and mentioned three times since, so that they are evidently gaining hold. Purgation by fire proclaims itself as the only salutary end, whether
for the murderers, for the blood-stained palace of Atreus, or for the city of
which the palace is a symbol. Nothing further can be done on the stage.
Apollo appears above, and with him Helen, mute, beyond reach. Apollo
speaks (1625ff.):

> Menelaus, curb the whetted anger of your heart.
> I am Apollo, Leto's son, who speak to you.
> — You too, with your drawn sword on guard at this girl's throat —
> Orestes, calm your fury and listen to my words.
>   First, as to Helen, whom you meant to kill, and move
> Menelaus to rage — your purpose failed; for this is she,
> Whom you see here, enfolded in the sparkling sky;[16]
> Not dead at your hands, but preserved. I snatched her up
> At Zeus her father's bidding, and saved her from your sword . . .
>   So, Menelaus, choose for your home another wife;
> For Helen's beauty was to the gods their instrument
> For setting Greeks and Trojans face to face in war
> And multiplying deaths, to purge the bloated earth
> Of its superfluous welter of mortality.

The question to be decided by the critic at this point is well put by A. P.
Burnett in *Catastrophe Survived*, page 212:

How then does Euripides end his play? Are those critics right who believe that the
poet has purposely found a miraculous solution that is an ugly mockery and left
his play without an end because he meant to announce man's inevitable return to
an abandoned and ferocious savagery?

Put crudely the question is this: How bad has Orestes been shown to be, and how
good has Apollo been proven? Could this god by these means put a permanent stop

to this sequence of violent acts and could he save this group of mortals, according to the play's own evidence?

Burnett answers the first of these questions by saying that Orestes is to be held excusable because of the influence of Pylades and because he is possessed by his mother's Furies (213–17): and answers the second by describing Apollo's gift of Hermione to Orestes as an exercise in *philia*, kindness, which restores Orestes' lost faith in his god, 'and with it his sanity, his *aidōs*, and his normal pious lawfulness'. (*Aidōs* is 'sense of right'.) But the facts of the text are as follows: First, there is no ground for supposing that Pylades influenced Orestes to kill Clytemnestra, since that took place before the play began. Pylades influences him to kill Helen — but not until we have seen Orestes throw away the remnants of reason and goodness which he showed in his first scene with Electra and turn instead to the petulant folly which enraged Tyndareos, insulted Menelaus, and at the trial ensured his condemnation. As for the Furies, their attack (251ff.) comes as an immediate response to lines 247–50 in which Orestes and Electra try to forget their guilt by accusing someone else; and as soon as the attack is over, in the one passage where he appears to be fully sane, Orestes acknowledges his responsibility for the crime, even if he blames Apollo for false guidance (284–93). From the second episode on, Orestes is not only bad, but unpleasantly, stupidly, insanely bad. As for Apollo's 'goodness', it is denied explicitly in the first half of the play, before insanity takes control, by Orestes, by Electra, by the chorus, and by Menelaus — even by Tyndareos. Therefore we must conclude that the end of the play is indeed a mockery; it may be an ugly mockery, but it is none the less serious in its declaration that there is a point beyond which men cannot hope for redemption or recovery; that the reckless pursuit of revenge to the point of kin-murder is wrong, despite all authority of religion. The poet has not 'left his play without an end'; he has declared that the end of bloodthirstiness is insanity and suicide. And his purpose in writing and directing a play to assert this truth is illuminated by the fact that this was the last time he spoke to his fellow-citizens, and that the position of his anti-hero was closely analogous to that of the city which formed his audience. Such an interpretation both conforms and contributes to that view of the poet's character which has begun to take shape as this study proceeds.

Apollo's first, restraining word is addressed — not to Orestes, to bid him take his sword from Hermione's throat, but (1625) to Menelaus who is protesting against the threatened murder. Did a few spectators laugh at this preposterous opening? Apollo's neat indication of *parti pris* is borne out by the whole epilogue. He next tells Orestes to curb his anger; but does not rebuke him for murdering Helen and threatening Hermione (we may note that twenty-six lines later the sword is still held at Hermione's neck). Apollo is evidently concerned only with the ritual aspect of purification, since he promises ultimate absolution by 'most righteous votes' (1651), and exemption from the sentence of the Argive court; and awards him Hermione for his wife. This dispensation, together with the tone of 1658–9,

> Bestow on Pylades the wife you promised him;
> A life of bliss awaits him,

sufficiently confirms an ironic view of Apollo's pronouncements. The assertion that 'I compelled him to shed his mother's blood' (1665) contradicts everything that has been seriously implied throughout the play in regard to Orestes' responsibility for his crime of matricide. As for Apollo's quoting of the epic formula, that Zeus caused the Trojan war in order to reduce the earth's population, at least it exonerates Helen; but the god could not save her innocent life; and such a theory, offered as comfort to Menelaus, is an insult.

At Apollo's side is Helen, and she is mute.[16] Since she spoke with Electra in the prologue she has been an unseen presence at every encounter, her name spoken more often than any other. The world which hated and rejected her has proved itself a world of fools, murderers, and suicidal maniacs — except for the one rather ordinary man who loves her and has lost her, and the simple foreigner who served her. This strangely-matched pair, together with the gentle Hermione, stand for the other, the minority world, where love, beauty, and reason are honoured. In the preceding year *The Phoenician Women* also presented two worlds (see Chapter 6, pages 171–3). There, as here, the one was dominated by Ares; but there the other world of life, warmth, and beauty was presided over by the native divinity of Thebes, Dionysus. Even in *The Bacchae* Dionysus in his creative aspect, when not estranged from reason and gentleness, 'delights in feasting, and loves Peace the giver of wealth and saviour of young men's lives' (*Bacchae* 416–20). In *Orestes* the world to which Athens now belongs is shown as no longer a fit home either for perfect beauty or for the muse of Euripides.

It remains to note Orestes' reply to Apollo (1666–70) — a piece of irony which seems to challenge even the most obtuse to work out its implication:

> Loxias, god of Prophecy! Your oracles
> Were not deceptive after all, but sound and true.
> Yet I confess I felt uneasy, lest the voice
> I heard, and took for your voice, was in truth the voice
> Of some accursed fiend. But all ends well . . .

Thus Orestes joins Apollo in disowning every acknowledgement of truth and humane value which he, Electra, and the chorus expressed in the early part of the play, before Ares assumed leadership in the person of Pylades.

To confirm that the triumph of insanity which we have witnessed is a symbol of the war in which the life of Athens is being engulfed, come the lines of dismissal, 1682—3:

> Go, then, honouring the most noble of goddesses, Peace . . .

There is as little hope here as in Orestes' 'All ends well.'

Readers long accustomed to the attitude which finds Helen a depraved and shallow person rather pointlessly introduced in a single brief scene; which finds Menelaus (in this play) despicable, the Phrygian absurd, Apollo authoritative and benign, Orestes and Electra still royal even if mad, and the whole play an exciting, nondescript entertainment without any particular meaning — these readers will find the interpretation I have offered hard to accept. It has been necessary to anticipate the more complete development of my argument about Helen which is given in Chapter 5, and some ideas from Chapter 6, in the exposition of *Orestes*. When those chapters have been studied, the coherence of my whole view will, I trust, emerge. What the present study sets out to show is that when this principle of interpretation is applied to some seven or eight of the plays often regarded as the most puzzling, the result illuminates a consistent message embodied in them all, and linking them clearly with the more familiar and favourite dramas. It is necessary to insist again — because this is a point easily lost sight of — that the ironic interpretation is not put forward as the only legitimate one. For the nature of irony, as Euripides uses it, implies that some will see it and some will not; and the people for whom *Orestes* was an absorbing piece of escapist melodrama, and *Alcestis* a touching and happily-resolved story of domestic love, comprised a large part of Euripides' audience, and he certainly had them in mind when he wrote. But that section of the audience surely did not include those whose minds were closest to the author's. The unreflective, or the religiously conditioned, response to the play did not need exposition then, needs little now, and is of passing importance; the ironic meaning has an interest and a power which are timeless.

4

WOMAN

There has never been any doubt that Euripides was interested in the nature, behaviour, impact, and social status of woman. Aristophanes presented him as a notorious hater and slanderer of women. In our present century he is more often seen as one who excites pity for the sufferings inflicted on women by gods and men. In this chapter I shall attempt, by looking at the plays and fragments most occupied with this topic, to describe what the author had to say about women and their place in society. The nature of this question, and the incompleteness of the material, both preclude a definitive answer; interpretation will be needed even more than logical deduction. A. W. Gomme's acute and well-balanced essay on this topic[1] several times emphasizes the similarity of situation between fifth-century Athens and our present-day society; and I would add that much of what Euripides has to say about women is directed not to peculiarities of his own society and age but to those features of it which are hardly less familiar to us today – to the almost (though not quite) universal and timeless elements in the relative situation of men and women. I use this last phrase in order to point out, as many writers do nowadays, that while everyone understands what questions are implied by 'the position of women in society', the phrase 'the position of men in society' has no such clear connotation, and could indeed only be discussed if society were as firmly based on the ascendancy of woman as it is in fact now, and was in fifth-century Athens, based on the ascendancy of man.

I believe it was on this radical level that Euripides approached his subject. In our present age, when more social changes of a radical nature are taking place more rapidly than ever before in history, most of us still find it difficult to conceive in realistic terms a state of society so fundamentally different from what we now know. My interpretation of Euripides leads to the belief that he was well aware that the world as he knew it was unalterably committed to male ascendancy and that most people, if they were concerned at all, were concerned only with superficial injustices; that temporary remedies for these might be found, but the real problem was a tension which men and women must endure as long as the race continues. His plays show the effect of this tension on good and sensitive men like Admetus, and on crass and selfish men like Achilles; and on women as different as Phaedra and

Medea, as Andromache and Clytemnestra. In these dramatic mirrors men and women might learn to recognize what was tragic in their own situations.

One of the most useful, and certainly most lively, statements about the position of Athenian women in Euripides' time is the essay by A. W. Gomme mentioned above. There is, he says, 'no literature, no art of any country, in which women are more prominent, more important, more carefully studied, and with more interest, than in the tragedy, sculpture, and painting of fifth-century Athens'. He shows how irrational it is to suppose that, whereas the male characters in Euripides are clearly portraits of the poet's contemporaries, the females are straight out of Homer and the heroic world; and insists, I think rightly, that the mental and moral stature of such women as Sophocles' Antigone and Iocasta, of Aeschylus' Clytemnestra, and a dozen or more women from Euripides, cannot have been a thing unknown and inconceivable to men who sat and watched them in the theatre. Evidence from vase-painting and sculpture all through the fifth and fourth centuries confirms the view that there was available to women a life that gave them dignity, freedom to move about visiting friends or attending festivals, a fairly high level of general estimation, and a possibility of deep affection within the family. Evidence from Aristophanes suggests that some degree of education could be attained by more than a negligible minority of women. If, says Gomme, the common view is correct, that the women of fifth-century Athens were kept in seclusion, oppressed, and generally despised, then 'in that case Attic tragedy and art are in one most important respect remote from Attic life — a phenomenon surely unique in history' (page 115). In other words, he is sure that the charming and relaxed figures we see in vase-paintings or on memorial tablets were recognizable in many ordinary Athenian women; and that the courage, independence, and passion which we see in Antigone, Tecmessa, Phaedra — that such qualities were at least found credible in women by the first audiences of the plays. Most of this seems to me to be soundly argued and probable in itself; but one awkward fact remains.

The phrase 'Attic tragedy and art' is too comprehensive. The vases and memorial tablets harmonize with the general picture of Athenian women enjoying what Medea calls 'an enviable life', zēlōtos aiōn (Medea 243); and the heroines of Aeschylus and Sophocles, whether suffering or avenging, play their parts with a confidence in their role as women, and in the world as it is — its stability reflected in the world of gods — which would, so Gomme argues, be meaningless on the stage if it were not a conscious part of the lives of women in the audience. The same is true of a number of heroines in Euripides — Alcestis, Medea, Phaedra, Iocasta; but in Euripides those of whom it is not true are far more numerous. Macaria's love and anger, unlike Antigone's, must guide her without a faith in any unseen world — 'I hope there is none,' she says (Children of Heracles 593—5); Andromache and

Hermione are alone in the cockpit with their two bewildered and helpless selves; Evadne and Polyxena are isolated, as even Tecmessa is not; the vanishing of Megara is without purpose and leaves no trace, the success of Creusa is hollow and doomed, the defeat of Agaue is (unlike that of Pentheus) hard to relate to any discernible error; Electra in both her plays, and Clytemnestra, and Hecabe, and Alcmene, are women whom life destroys, and without counterparts in the other dramatists. And the lost plays, from the poet's youth to his exile, show a procession of women drawn with contemporary realism, some of them indeed heroic, but all inhabiting a world where enjoyment of the good life, though certainly possible for many, is nevertheless utterly precarious; where rape, imprisonment, destitution, murder, and every form of cruelty, may rob the innocent woman not only of freedom and life, but of innocence and humanity. In presenting this picture Euripides differs radically from the two older poets; therefore to suggest that we can speak comprehensively of 'woman's life as shown in Attic tragedy' is misleading. Yet Euripides was describing the same world in which Sophocles lived; and he was in his middle twenties when he saw the Oresteian Trilogy. How shall we describe, and account for, his different picture?

Aeschylus had already boldly opened the question of the relative rights of man and woman in marriage. In *Agamemnon* the Watchman's description of Clytemnestra as 'a woman with a man's will' introduces a long series of oppositions between male and female which is continued by action and imagery in every scene of the play. The first stasimon of *Choephori* pictures a universal war between the sexes (585–601). In the trial-scene in *Eumenides* Apollo's dubious arguments, and Athena's pronouncement, on her city's behalf, of decisive prejudice in favour of 'male supremacy in all things' (737–8), indicate that the author is aware of an urgent living issue which he places before his audience without offering either judgement or advice. His way of presenting the issue is, especially in Apollo's pleading, ironic. The 'happy ending' of the trilogy stirs and satisfies the emotions rather than the intellect; for it does not erase memories of wounds left unhealed and questions unanswered in the foregoing action. In *The Suppliants* (392–3) Aeschylus states woman's claim to the right of witholding her consent when demanded in marriage:

> Right or no right, I will not be
> Man's chattel won by violence.

However, since Aeschylus appears to have acquired no notoriety for his views on woman's status, it is unlikely that he developed this theme much further in the ninety per cent of his work about which we know nothing.

Sophocles gives us rather more portraits of women than Aeschylus; but in his seven extant plays there are only four heroines (Iocasta, Antigone,

Deianeira, and Electra) and four supporting characters (Ismene, Chryso-themis, Tecmessa, and Eurydice); and again we have but one tenth or less of his work. Whereas in Aeschylus Clytemnestra, Cassandra, and the Danaids all face crises which arise essentially from the fact that they are females confronting the aggressive male, in Sophocles this situation hardly exists; there is a touch of it in Deianeira and possibly in Tecmessa, but it is not the heart of the issue. Sophocles' heroines (the few that we know) face not man but themselves and destiny. They show us, as Gomme says, that most fifth-century Athenians did not hold all women in contempt. They arouse men's admiration; but even Antigone, though it angers Creon that a woman should defy him, is doing no more than a man could have done in upholding humanity against impious tyranny. Also, both she and Creon, though the issue they debate is timeless, belong to the heroic world; a world in which a king may tell a woman that it is not her place to argue with him, but where no man says, 'I can never hate women enough', and no woman says, 'Men hate us.'

Euripides' women are different, and their world is fifth-century Athens; a world where women, though often defenceless against men's cruelty, can on occasion defeat men as Medea defeats Jason, command men as the en-slaved Hecabe commands Agamemnon, and in play after play demonstrate by word and action the weakness, foolishness, dishonesty, and barbarity of men. Not all men are foolish or cruel; if, as Medea says, a woman is fortunate in the man she has to do with, 'her life is enviable; but if not — one must die', *thanein chreōn* (*Medea* 243). Gomme's argument works both ways, and applies as exactly to this line as to Antigone's declaration of moral and religious faith before Creon: Medea's truth would be meaningless on the stage if it were not a conscious part of the experience of women in the audi-ence. The husband whom a young wife found intolerable had been chosen for her by her legal guardian, usually her father. The selfish or stupid or brutal father, whether his name be Nycteus, or Smicrines, or Capulet, or Barrett of Wimpole Street, is one element in woman's situation which, after persisting for tens of centuries, now appears to be vanishing from some few communities; but in Shakespeare's Europe where he still reigned absolute women were still, in spite of him, gracious, lovely, and often happy. For Ophelia, for Juliet, the good life was real but precarious. In any sophisti-cated society widely different attitudes and experiences live side by side and show to the world little sign of their difference. It must have been so in ancient Athens — except that there ill-luck, marital or other, was likely to be (as for Shakespeare's heroines) ruthless in its consequences: 'one must die'. If Gomme's picture of the confident, serene Athenian woman represents the prevailing truth, this line of Medea's will have seemed to the audience who first heard it remote from life; and so will the fate of Antiope, Alope,

Ino, and many others. And if this line was not remote, but voiced the experience of a recognizable minority, then a social problem existed in Athens which naturally did not find expression in vase-paintings or on memorial tablets. It was no one's business to tell the truth about such painful matters except the dramatist's.

And then, half-way through Euripides' career, the war began; and within four years the Athenian male Assembly had voted to condemn every wife in the large city of Mytilene to widowhood and slavery. This decision was revoked the following day; but similar decisions in subsequent years were carried out. Doubtless through years of war the 'enviable life' remained normal for many women; but it grew more precarious than ever; and as enslavement, exile, or death scattered thousands of families, most cities of Greece must have contained their quota of displaced 'free' women whose conditions and prospects were miserable, in addition to the newly enslaved. It is not the adventurous Medea, but her quiet home-loving Corinthian friends, who voice the fear which must often have lain under the graceful surface (643—51):

> O my country, my home!
> May the gods save me from becoming
> A stateless refugee dragging out an intolerable life
> In desperate helplessness!
> That is the most pitiful of all griefs;
> Death is better. Should such a day come to me
> I pray for death first.

And that was written a year before the Peloponnesian war began.

But Euripides is not concerned only with the outward circumstances of women's lives. Intangible realities are no less significant, and he was probably as acute an observer of such realities as any writer of his age. Therefore we ought to be able to gather from his dialogue, which is often clearly contemporary in tone, a valid impression of what the phrase *to gynaikeion genos*, 'the female race', meant to the ordinary, non-analytical ear. We must weigh the admiration which the Pheraean Elders feel for Alcestis with their unquestioning acceptance of her sacrifice; we must set the love of Theseus for Phaedra against Hippolytus' intense hatred of all women, and Phaedra's consciousness that he is not alone in his hatred; we must set Ion's respectful sympathy with Creusa in the first episode beside his readiness to throw her down a cliff in the fourth, and remember Creusa's simple statement that 'Men hate us' (*Ion* 399—400); we must consider passages which show how woman may be woman's worst enemy; and we may speculate on the male audience's reaction to the four ritual murders of girls in religious sacrifice, which we shall discuss in Chapter 7. In describing society's general estimate of women at that period it is usual to quote the famous sentence from the end of the Funeral Speech (Thucydides II.45): 'Your great glory is not to fall short of your nature as women; and greatest is hers who is least spoken of among the men whether for good or for evil.' But Gomme has pointed out (*op. cit.* 101–2) not only how this pronouncement is isolated by its special occasion, but also how much less significant it is than the number of noble and confident women, good and bad, who share the Attic stage with men; not to mention the fact that Pericles was the devoted lover of the most talked-of woman in Athens. The same essay also disposes convincingly of similar arguments for inferiority of female status which have been based on Aristotle's remarks in *Poetics* 54 a 16 about goodness in a woman being 'perhaps inferior' to goodness in a man. In any case this sentence is as isolated a piece of evidence as Pericles' words; what I am concerned with in this chapter is the large body of evidence which comes to us from Euripides' plays, in the form of statements, actions, attitudes, and situations. In studying this evidence we must bear in mind that there was certainly as much variety in opinions about women as there was in the status of women; and that if we find, for example, an oppressive attitude illustrated in a particular male character, there is no need to assume that the dramatist is accusing all men, or even most men, of oppressive behaviour. The proper conclusion will rather be that he is showing such behaviour as a recognizable element in the real life of his day, an element which has its effect on both oppressor and victim.

Earlier in this century some readers of Euripides, under the influence of such movements as the Fabian Society, perceiving that he was aware of the painful social tensions of his own time, were inclined to impute to him the millennial zeal of the reformer. It became easy to dismiss their perceptions by saying that they had recruited Euripides for their feminist or for their pacifist campaigns.[2] Since we are dealing in this chapter with the principal issue of several upon which he may be said to have put forward ethical opinions, I will begin by stating what I take to be the difference between the function and method of the artist and that of the reformer. The reformer observes the social scene with indignation and wants to change it. To gain the power necessary to effect change, he needs to simplify the pattern of what he sees. He concentrates his vision upon the millennial future, and feels uneasy and suspicious about any pleasing features in the present which make the need for the millennium seem less urgent. The business of living in the world as it is interests him, but less than the business of preparing for the world as it shall be. The artist on the other hand is concerned primarily with living in the world as it is. He does not want to simplify the pattern, because the contradictory complexity of it is what most interests him. In so far as he is conscious of millennial visions, he sees them as a feature of the character of certain individuals which sets them at variance with their society and may thus lead to a tragic situation. This is not to say that he approves of things as they are, or accepts them without protest because they provide material for his art. To recall Dodds's phrase quoted earlier (Chapter 1, page 16 — from the introduction to his edition of *The Bacchae*), he feels their tension, and out of it he makes tragedy. This, I believe, was Euripides' attitude in all his work; and it is only on this assumption that we can make sense of his widely varied treatment of women's character and position.

An epitome of the attitude taken by men to women in Euripides' plays is found in the epilogue of *Ion* (1595) in the words of Athena, who on several occasions speaks for the Athenian democratic male:

Apollo has done everything well. He gave you a healthy birth . . . and commanded Hermes to bring the child here, and did not leave him to die.

According to the canons of the heroic age, the act of rape, if committed by a god, was a favour conferred on the woman, and this Athena assumes, as does Ion in 343. (In the same passage Ion twice refers to rape by a man as a 'wrong', 325, 341; while the chorus, 506—8, observe that no woman has ever found happiness in bearing a god's child.) Athena ignores the suffering of the mother as described in 345—69, and the sixteen years of childless marriage spoken of in 425—8 and elsewhere, as not worth mention. The same attitude is shown in *Andromache* when Thetis comforts Andromache for her prolonged sufferings by providing her with a third husband and promising her son a successful life. It is shown in stories such as that of Antiope, whose life of misery in prison is compensated by eventual release, revenge on her persecutor, and reunion with the sons she had not seen since infancy. In such an attitude cruelty to women is not commended, neglect is not censured. It may be men's pleasure to make women happy; but their suffering does not matter much.

This has been a prevalent male attitude to women for thousands of years, as it is today in many kinds of society. Certainly it was prevalent in fifth-century Athens; no less certainly, there were many contemporaries of Euripides whose natural kindness and sensitivity led them in varying degrees to adopt a more humane attitude. *Ion*, like *Medea, Hippolytus,* and other plays, shows a wide variation, from Ion's sympathetic response to Creusa's picture of her maternity (1497) to Xuthus' ruthless plans for deceiving his wife (657—60, 666—7). A dramatist shows the variety of human nature as he sees it around him; but in the epilogue of *Ion* Athena's attitude, which Xuthus and Apollo share, needs no exposition because it is the attitude prevalent in the audience. The opposite attitude, which is rarer, is given full and sensitive expression. Creusa is shown as possessing what we may call either a strong religious faith or an elastic credulity; and thus the end of the play finds her agreeing with Athena that 'Apollo has done well in every respect'; and this no doubt most of her hearers endorsed. But Ion's scepticism in 341, 1521−7, and elsewhere, speaks for a minority; and the scepticism is likely to have been nearer to the poet's own conviction than the credulity, just as sensitivity accords more with his whole work than does the callousness of Athena or of Thetis. This is not to say that he wrote with the purpose either of undermining belief in gods or of campaigning for women's rights; rather, he wrote to mirror the whole spectrum of life and belief. But since so large a portion of his work is dedicated to the characters, conduct, and suffering of women, it is reasonable to conclude that on this question he had instruction to offer to those willing to receive it.[3]

Let us consider a scene which contains a description in fifth-century terms of a privileged woman's life: *Women of Troy* 610−83. It is a passage where irony, so far from being obvious, may not have been intended at all; I do not know that it has ever been suspected. In this scene we are given a picture of Andromache, known from the *Iliad* as a type of the perfect young wife. The *Iliad* showed her foreseeing disaster; *The Women of Troy* shows her enduring it. First the lyric *kommos* wins unreserved sympathy for the misery of the innocent victim, carried away as a slave, with her child in her arms, to be concubine to the son of the man who killed her husband. Then the iambic dialogue begins to deal with facts and reflections; and in this passage Andromache's first couplet is unobtrusively surprising:

Do you see this sight, mother of Hector, the man who killed with his spear the greatest number of Argives?

The Homeric tradition certainly made Hector supreme in valour; but what distinguished him from other Trojans was his generosity and gentleness. If the gentle Andromache had spoken here of his gentleness, her question, 'Do you see this sight?' would have been no less dramatic. Possibly her words recalled to a few listeners a line spoken thirty years earlier in the same theatre, 'Gods do not fail to mark those who have killed many' (*Agamemnon* 461−2); more probably they suggest that Andromache the perfect wife accepts male values in everything. Even this would be a far-fetched conclusion if based on this sentence alone; we must now study Andromache's subsequent speech, 634−83. In doing so we can find a relevant contrast in the ungentle Medea, who rejected male standards and claimed equality with man in moral judgement; we may bear in mind the resolute rebelliousness of Medea's opening manifesto (230−51) as we read Andromache's words describing the chosen pattern of her life (*Women of Troy* 643−56):

I made good reputation my aim; I was fairly successful; but now I have lost what I gained. As Hector's wife I studied and practised the perfection of womanly modesty.

First, if a woman does not stay in her own house, this very fact brings ill fame upon her, whether she is at fault or not; I therefore gave up my longing to go out, and stayed at home; and I refused to admit into my house the amusing gossip of other women. Having by nature a sound mind to school me, I was content. Before my husband I kept a quiet tongue and a modest eye; I knew in what matters I should rule, and where I should yield to his authority.

The picture has a formal charm; and in a gentle and kindly society such a life could represent a degree of real happiness. But the society Andromache speaks of is one where even a virtuous woman dares not visit or invite her neighbours for fear of slander. There is no point in asking whether this was the case in ancient Troy; the fifth-century dramatist had no reason to put it in his play unless he knew that a fair proportion of his audience would recognize it as true of their own society. Euripides' Andromache took for her aim, she says, a good reputation; this aim corresponds to that element in society which endorsed the Periclean dictum quoted above, page 87. As Andromache tells how, in pursuit of this aim, she abandoned the freedom which should have been her royal prerogative, and accepted confinement within the walls of her husband's house, there is no irony in her voice; she has disciplined herself to be content. And it seems certain that most, possible that all, of the original audience remained unaware of irony in her words. But their contact with the poet was mediated by an actor and by all the circumstance of a vast gathering and a moving occasion; to us his words come direct from the page. The poet who also created Medea and Creusa left no rubric to instruct us that one was to be admired or another condemned. Medea's outburst (230–1), 'Surely, of all creatures that have life and will, we women are the most wretched', and Creusa's bitter assertion (*Ion* 398–400), 'Life is harder for women than for men; they judge us, good and bad together, and hate us', both picture the same kind of society as Andromache's quiet acceptance. The two former passages are direct criticism, and delineate two highly individual women. Andromache's speech portrays a less interesting woman; does it in fact contain ironic criticism? It cannot be proved; but Andromache here is describing her former life which, compared with her present plight, seemed blissful to her; and the picture she draws of it is much less than blissful; it is fearful and resigned. If irony is there for those who expect it, it is of the same kind as that which we found earlier in the chorus of *Orestes*: the speaker is sincere, the irony is the author's (see Chapter 3, page 72).

In Homeric legend the position of women shows an ambivalence which has often been noticed by modern writers, and which remained essentially unchanged down to the fifth century and beyond; its safeguards strengthened by law, its disadvantages increased by the increasing complexity of a society organized and administered exclusively by men. In Euripides' day what liberty an Athenian woman had — and it was often considerable — was by

allowance, by custom rather than by constitution, and varied greatly with the
fortune or misfortune, and with the personality, of the individual. The
woman of commanding mental stature, however, can have found little scope
or encouragement for the exercise of her powers outside a purely feminine
circle of friends or the privacy of her home, unless she was prepared to forgo
the shelter of legitimacy and live as a *hetaira*. But the status of Aspasia was as
different as possible from that of Alcmene, and was preferable to that of
Tecmessa, the concubine of Aias, only in its incidental advantages — Pericles
could offer his partner a more interesting life than Aias. The widows of heroes
killed at Troy, whose only hope was a second marriage (see *Andromache*
1039—41) must have found that new husbands were scarce. When a city was
captured, a woman's privilege was to remain alive — as a slave; this convention underwent no change between 1180 and 416 B.C. The ambivalence just
referred to lay in this: that within the framework of a life devoid of any
guaranteed liberty beyond what her family secured for her, Homeric woman
was able to make for herself, if she was at all lucky, an existence in which the
freedom allowed could be enjoyed, and the compulsions accepted, with a
high degree of dignity; so that, in *The Trachiniae*, though the inferiority of
Tecmessa's status is emphasized by Sophocles, she can respond to a tragic
situation no less heroically than the royal Deianeira. In fact, of course, almost
all the mortal women we get to know personally in Homer are either royal
or quasi-royal, or slaves; the ordinary citizens' wives and daughters are
always spoken of anonymously in groups — *Dardanidae bathykolpoi*, 'deep-
girdled Dardanian women'; as in Euripides they appear only in the chorus.[4]
It seems probable, however, that the uncertainty of fortune was still the most
permanent fact about a woman's life in the fifth century. Euripides' women,
then, whether royal, slaves, or bourgeoises, could without difficulty step from
Troy or Mycenae into Pericles' Athens with little need to adapt posture or
behaviour. Their life's task then, as always, was to hold their place in man's
world without man's strength or weapons, but with intangible resources
which, on some occasions only, could win more than force.

Euripides produced his first play, *The Daughters of Pelias*, in 455 B.C. *Alcestis*,
produced in 438, was his seventeenth play, and is the earliest that has survived complete. It comes near the middle of a series of twenty-seven plays
(twenty-three of them now lost) which Webster[5] classifies on stylistic grounds
as constituting his early period. Numerous fragments of the work of this early
period have been preserved, which suggest the lines along which Euripides
pursued the topic of woman's fate for more than twenty years at the beginning of his career. So we will now consider first the plots and themes of some
of these early plays, and secondly four of the plays, known only by fragments,
from the second half of the poet's life; then we shall give more detailed attention to six of the complete plays which contain much of the material for a
study of Euripides' views on the position of women.

Our survey of the early fragments should begin with an acknowledgement to the valuable comprehensive account of Euripidean material presented by T. B. L. Webster in the first two chapters of the book just mentioned. Here it is only necessary to record his conclusion: that between 455 and 428 Euripides produced nine sets of plays, each set consisting of three tragedies and a satyr-play; that it is clear that some, and likely that all, of these sets included one play about a bad woman, one about an unhappy woman, and one about some other topic. Two of these sets can be fully named and dated: *Cretan Women, Alcmaeon in Psophis, Telephus, Alcestis,* 438; *Medea, Dictys, Philoctetes, Theristae,* 431. Even if the tentative table of productions given by Webster (page 32) is viewed as sceptically as it is offered modestly, the evidence he has gathered is enough to establish that during this period of twenty-three years or so — half of his creative life as a dramatist — Euripides was continually concerned with the life of women — so close to, yet so remote from, life as men know it. If the surviving plays are any guide, these earlier works were full of such questions as, Why are women of any force of character likely to be either wicked or miserable? Why do men conceive an indiscriminate hatred of women? If women are of equal importance with men, why is their scope so restricted? If they are naturally slaves, how do they achieve moral heights which shame men into humility?

The fragments we have to consider represent proportions of whole plays varying from two per cent to twelve per cent, and consist of an arbitrary selection of lines. In surveying them it is convenient to use the tentative arrangement by dates given by Webster, page 32. Few inferences can be drawn from our scanty remains of the first twelve of these works. In *Peliades* we find a group of young women easily influenced by the guile of the older Medea and led into a crime which destroyed their whole lives; but we have nothing to reveal how Euripides treated Medea's motivation in this play. Since it is his earliest play, written when he was still under thirty, it is possible that he had not yet developed the conviction which seemed to possess him later, that every legendary crime committed by a woman is seen to be *syngnōston*, understandable, when we take into account the suffering men have inflicted on her. The same may be true of *Aegeus*, which is also among his earliest plays. Here again Medea is presented, this time as a poisoner; which suggests that the stories of her wickedness puzzled and haunted him. His final resolution of her character in *Medea* came only after twenty-four years had passed since he first depicted her. *Alcmene* is the story of a young woman who found herself at once the possession of an irate husband and the instrument of a god; each possessor pursues his purpose or passion, and neither grants the woman a right to her own. *Phoenix* shows a young woman possessed by an old man and hungry for a love suitable to her age. This is also the position of

Phaedra in *Hippolytus*, though the age of Theseus is not emphasized there. The sensitiveness of an Athenian audience, only three generations later, to the pathos of this situation is well reflected in Menander, *The Shield*, Act II, where an old man's resolve to marry a young girl (which he had a legal right to do) is reprobated as an offence against 'decency', *metriotēs*.

With *Stheneboea* (about 440) the theme begins to assume a clearer direction. Three of the fragments (all from the anthology of Stobaeus, an industrious collector of 'talking-points' about women) are evidently among the passages which gave the poet his contemporary image:

Many a man, proud of his wealth and birth, has been disgraced by his wanton wife. (Fragment 663)

O utterly evil − and a woman! What greater reproach could anyone hurl at you? (Fragment 670)

Take her indoors. Any man of good sense should put no trust in a woman. (Fragment 673)

The crime committed by Stheneboea is one common to many stories in many different cultures: that of the wife who, being refused by the man she desires as a lover, accuses him to her husband. This situation occurs in *Hippolytus* and *Peleus*, and similar ones in *Phoenix* and *The Cretan Women*. The judgement passed in all such cases by Euripides' fellow-citizens is not in doubt: the woman was an abominable adulteress, and Aristophanes' word 'whore' (*Frogs* 1043) was generally acceptable. However, since in most of his surviving plays Euripides invited a critical and objective look at accepted judgements, it is at least of academic interest to attempt such a re-statement of Stheneboea's case. We may say, for example, 'She claimed for herself a freedom which, even if reprehended in men, was never denied to them and often excused. Her position when rejected was as shameful as that of Achilles robbed of Briseis, or Aias denied the award of Achilles' armour. Having no power to get revenge herself, and having learnt from men that revenge is the essence of honour, she satisfied the pride which in a man would be an heroic attribute by using male power and duplicity to attack the man who had humbled her.' Yet, even if we assume, as is reasonable, that Euripides' treatment of Stheneboea was not less sympathetic than his treatment of Medea and of Phaedra, it is still more reasonable to assume, on the evidence of the words just quoted from *The Frogs*, and from many other comments on Euripides, that the great majority of Athenians would continue to vilify Stheneboea as a whore and thus illustrate Phaedra's statement that women were 'a target for universal hate', *misēma pasin* (*Hippolytus* 407); and that, in fact, the critical approach and the sympathetic treatment would remain unnoticed and ignored, and the play receive the notoriety of the story in its traditional colours from the unchallenged judgement of male citizens, endorsed by most of their

women-folk. This is speculation; but it is borne out by the history of the understanding and misunderstanding of other plays. In the trial-scene in *The Frogs*
Aristophanes' Aeschylus does not even suggest that Euripides' 'whores' were
presented in a sympathetic light; he simply complains that Phaedra, and others
like her, known by everyone to be whores, were presented on the stage at
all.

A further argument is relevant at this point. We are sometimes reminded
by writers on Greek drama that we must not assume in Euripides any desire
to excuse or mitigate the wickedness of women like Stheneboea, whom the
poet's contemporaries condemned out of hand. But such critics may themselves be making an equally unwarranted assumption, the same that
Aeschylus makes in *The Frogs*, namely, that Euripides chose such topics for
their sensational value, without any deeper human or moral purpose. Those
who allow that this may be the case are open to the same charge as those
who regard *Orestes* as simply a melodrama (see pages 69, 72). It is the
critic's business to seek, by interpretation of the plays as a whole, a clear
and credible character for the author, which can be used with increasing
confidence as a point of reference in the study of difficult questions. Even if
it took Euripides twenty-four years to discover the full depth of Medea's
nature and the significance of her situation, yet the germ of the mature
conception may well have been there in the two earlier plays, as *Stheneboea*
and *Hippolytus I* had their place in the development to *Hippolytus II*. In
fifty years of play-writing Euripides learnt much; but I do not believe that
the author of *The Phoenician Women* and *Iphigenia in Aulis* could have written,
for example, the dull and naïve play which many critics find in the text
of *The Children of Heracles*; nor that the creator of Phaedra had no profound
moral concept underlying his depiction of Stheneboea.

Of the fragmentary plays dated before *Alcestis*, there remain *Protesilaus*,
The Cretan Women, *Alcmaeon* (*Telephus* seems to have been concerned only
with male characters). *Protesilaus* (441?) gives the story of Laodamia,
widowed after one day of married life, and then cruelly persecuted by her
father Acastus for her devotion to her dead husband. The fragments give us
one line of Sophistic theorizing about women (Fragment 655):

Wives ought to be possessed in common —

which may be the father's comment on his daughter's tiresome fidelity; and
four lines containing one of the few sensible and non-ironic general statements about women found in Euripides' work (Fragment 658):

The man who condemns all women together in a single sentence is not wise but a
fool; among a large number of women you will find this one bad, that one endowed
with a noble spirit . . .

The play seems to have offered a poignant and unusually straightforward picture of the undeserved suffering of a good woman whose life was wrecked, first by the common chance of death (Fragment 651, 'He has suffered the fate which awaits you and all of us'), and then by the folly of a bullying father — a theme which occurs also in *Melanippē Desmōtis* and *Aeolus*. *The Cretan Women* tells of Aerope, a woman whose strong sexual nature brings upon her both calamities and cruelties. When as a child she had been seduced by a slave, her father gave instructions for her to be drowned. She escaped, and was married to Pleisthenes, who soon left her a widow. Thereupon, being given as wife to the aging Atreus, she tried to console herself by making love to his younger brother Thyestes. It is possible that in Euripides' version of the story the sons of Thyestes who were killed and served at the famous banquet were Aerope's children. The play seems to have shown Aerope as a woman subjected to successive cruelties which no charge of lasciviousness could excuse; yet the occasional comments of ancient writers do not suggest that they found the cruelties exceptional or unjustified. 'The tears of Aerope' were proverbial; but her fate was the kind of fate accepted without surprise as a woman's fate. *Alcmaeon in Psophis* is mainly concerned with the adventures of Alcmaeon; but a strong 'second subject' appears in the sufferings of his faithful first wife Arsinoe, who was the victim first of her husband's treachery, then of the cruelty of her brothers, who killed her husband and sold her into slavery. Thus in the earliest group of plays four out of the five whose content can be most clearly inferred from evidence present a picture of the life of women as liable, through misfortune, to be subject to injustice, humiliation, calumny, and cruelty; while the plots of four others lend themselves readily to the same theme.

There are three more early plays known only by fragments, from which we can confirm our impression of the poet's preoccupation at this period: *Danae*, *Alope*, and *Ino*. Danae, raped by Zeus, was shut in a golden chest by her father; this fate she accepted rather than the alternative offered, which was that her child should be killed and her own life spared. Alope was raped and deserted by Poseidon, then obliged to expose her child for fear of her father, who eventually discovered that she was a mother. To punish her he shut her up in prison, where she died. *Ino* has a complex plot, the theme of which is the jealousy inevitably bred in women by their dependence on the children whose status as heirs secures for their mother an honourable place in the family.

It is obvious that we must be careful not to build too much upon plays of which we know so little; but several legitimate conclusions can be drawn from those so far mentioned. Euripides certainly did not lack inventiveness; therefore the reiteration of this one theme is likely to have had a serious purpose. The dramatist is making the simple point that the mere fact of her sexual function puts woman at the mercy of man; the risks attendant on beauty, the likelihood of rape, the helplessness of pregnancy and childbirth, all demand from man consideration and mercy; and these are rare, and cruelty common — especially from fathers addicted to punishment. He seems to have recognized that sexual desire in women could be as strong as in men; and since pursuit was less easy than for men, the resulting frustration was likely to have more violent effects. Finally, the love of mother for child is surely used by Euripides not merely for its theatrical appeal, but rather to show that here is yet another chain fettering a woman's liberty, another easy weapon with which she can be threatened and coerced; so Menelaus uses it in *Andromache*. All these desperate disadvantages were always potentially present in the lives even of the most fortunate Athenian women, and liable to be made actual by the first strain on family stability, or by some shift of fortune. The 'enviable life' was real enough, and splendid enough —until something went wrong. Thus the beauty, courage, and helplessness of women provided tragic material in plenty for the first, and largely unknown, half of Euripides' productive life. When we come to the second half, the far fuller material will enable us to see profounder significances and to reach general conclusions which we shall have to fit in with our overall account of the poet's work.

The second half of Euripides' life as a dramatist is represented for us by fifteen out of his seventeen extant plays; therefore out of a dozen or more lost plays from this period of which considerable fragments remain, I propose to mention briefly only four: *Cresphontes, Melanippē Sophē, Melanippē Desmōtis,* and *Antiopē.*

In *Cresphontes* (about 426; perhaps produced at the same time as *Andromache*) the part of Merope seems to be little less important than that of her son Cresphontes. As a young wife Merope suffers first the loss of her husband who is murdered by his brother, then the loss of her child whose life she saves by sending him away; she is taken as wife by her husband's murderer, who offers a reward for the death of the child. A young man arrives to claim the reward; and Merope, unaware that the young man is her son and not her son's murderer, is prevented from killing him only at the last moment. She and her son recognize each other, and together execute revenge on the king. Though some details of the story are romantically heightened, Merope's tragic position and intense suffering are, from beginning to end, the unsurprising consequence of a male attitude to women which had not changed essentially in the seven centuries since the legend took shape, and which has since then been the material of innumerable European dramas, poems, and novels. The powerful effect of this play upon the audience is recorded by Plutarch,[6] whose account confirms the impression that its disappearance is a major loss from the treasury of Attic drama.

Melanippe the Wise is dated by Webster about 422. The story begins with her rape by Poseidon, and the exposure of her twin children. The children, being discovered in a cowshed, are at first thought to be monstrous births of a cow, and Melanippe's father Aeolus therefore proposes to burn them,[7] and commands Melanippe to prepare them for sacrifice. In pleading for their lives she gives an account of the creation of all living species, insisting that monstrous births are an impossibility, that the children must be, and are, normal children, so that to kill them is murder. More than this, Aeolus has been persuaded by his aged father Hellen that these monstrous births are a punishment for some past sin; Melanippe's eloquence shows him how foolish such a belief is (Fragment 508):

Do you imagine that crimes leap up on wings to the presence of the gods, and that then someone in Zeus's palace writes them on tablets, and that Zeus looks at the tablets and passes judgement on mortals? The whole sky would not be big enough to contain Zeus's records of all human misdeeds, nor would Zeus be capable of sending punishment to each sinner. No; justice is here, close to us, if you will take the trouble to look.

Thus a girl in her desperation teaches her royal father both humanity and common sense.

Melanippē Desmōtis belongs rather uncertainly to the period 422–412; Webster suggests (page 117) that it may have been produced with *Electra* as late as 413. Here a different turn is given to the story. Aeolus, finding that his daughter was pregnant, gave her as concubine to the king of Metapontum (a town on the Tarentine Gulf), who happened to be visiting Thessaly. This king took her to Italy, where she bore twin sons, who were exposed, but later adopted by the king. In time the king's wife bore him sons; for their sake she plotted to kill Melanippe's sons, whose identity was still unknown; and in the king's absence she imprisoned Melanippe. The considerable remains of this play should be read in Page's *Greek Literary Papyri*;[8] they include parts of a remarkable speech in defence of women, probably spoken by Melanippe:

Women manage homes, and preserve the goods which are brought from abroad. Houses where there is no wife are neither clean nor prosperous. And in religion – this I take to be important – we women play a large part. In Phoebus' oracle it is women who speak the mind of Loxias ... This shows the right of women in religion. How then can it be just that the female sex should be abused? Shall not men cease their foolish reproaches, cease to blame all women alike if they meet one who is bad? I will make this distinction: there is nothing worse than a bad woman, but nothing much better than a good woman. Their natures are different ...

We also find, among fragments which belong to one or other of the Melanippe plays, a series of attacks on women in general:

The worst plague is the hated race of women. Those who have erred are a disgrace to those who have not. The bad give a share of their ill-repute to those who are not bad. Their attitude to marriage seems to bode no good to men. (Fr. 496)

Punish this woman. The reason why women are troublesome is, that when a man finds he has a bad wife he doesn't kill her. (Fr. 499)

Except for my mother, I hate the whole female sex. (Fr. 500)

These passages, all preserved by Stobaeus, must of course be considered in relation to the whole play, and not regarded as necessarily indicating the heart of the argument.

Antiope is a late play, probably shown in 409 with *Hypsipyle* and *The Phoenician Women*. Antiope's two sons, Amphion and Zethus, were the founders of Thebes. A celebrated scene in the play contained a debate between them, contrasting the life of the musician or poet with that of the 'practical' man — soldier or farmer. This debate seems to present in a less anguished form the opposition between Dionysus and Ares which fills the first two choral odes of *The Phoenician Women* (see Chapter 6, pages 171–3). But the story of Antiope herself is central; and her sufferings are severe and prolonged. She was raped by Zeus; her father Nycteus, finding her pregnant, imprisoned her; but while he was considering what further punishment to inflict, she escaped and was found by Epopeus king of Sicyon, who was visiting Boeotia; and he took her home and married her. Meanwhile Nycteus died, leaving his king-dom to his brother Lycus, with a command to pursue and punish Antiope. Lycus attacked Sicyon and killed Epopeus. Antiope, nearing her time, was conveyed back to Boeotia by Lycus; on the journey, near the slopes of Cithaeron, she apparently escaped, bore her twins by a roadside, and was recaptured; the babies, however, were picked up by a shepherd. Antiope was then kept in prison for some seventeen years, suffering constant cruelty from Lycus' wife Dirce. The play recounts how Antiope was delivered and reunited with her sons, who took a brutal revenge on Dirce, tying her by her hair to the horns of a wild bull which dragged her about until she died — this is the subject of the Messenger's speech. The two sons were about to take a more summary vengeance on Lycus, when Hermes appeared and stopped them. Only two features of this play seem to be clearly established by some two hundred lines which remain. First, the contrast between the lives of poet and soldier; this contrast is changed in the last play of the set into a different key, and becomes a hymn to peace and a condemnation of war. Second, the savage cruelty shown to two women; and here the irony lies in the fact that, while every-one pities the innocent Antiope, when the time comes for execution of 'justice' the guilty man is miraculously saved, while the guilty woman has been put to a horrible death which Hermes did not bother to prevent. As far as we can tell from the fragments no word of censure is spoken against this savage act, for which both poet and soldier were equally responsible.

Hermes tells Lycus to collect the scattered limbs of Dirce, burn them, and cast the ashes into the fountain of Ares; and tells Amphion to build the walls of Thebes by playing his lyre. Neither revenge on Dirce, nor the future glory of Thebes, can alter the half-a-lifetime of misery endured by Antiope; and the two young men are as unconscious of their cruelty as are other young heroes like Hippolytus and Ion.

We now leave the Fragments and turn to the study of six complete plays which together contain material for a fairly detailed account of Euripides' presentation of woman: *Alcestis, Medea, Hippolytus, Andromache, Ion,* and *The Bacchae.*

Because *Alcestis* is for the most part written in fairly simple Greek, it is often the first play read by students and is therefore apt to be regarded as a somewhat elementary piece of work. Nothing could be further from the truth. The astonishing completeness and symmetry of the structure of *Alcestis* has been demonstrated in two fairly recent essays which present opposite, yet in some sense complementary views of this complex play. One is 'The Virtues of Admetus', by A. P. Burnett.[9] The writer calls this essay 'a naïve reading' of the play, and simply describes with acute observation and exact analysis what appears on the surface of the text; an exquisite design is revealed, showing how spiritual values outweigh temporal and *charis*, graciousness, overcomes *dikē*, justice. As an exposition this is both fascinating and true, and is likely to be vindicated by the experience of those who have watched the effect a good production can have on a modern audience. We could accept this as the whole story, if this were the poet's only surviving play. But in fact it followed *Stheneboea* and was followed within a decade by *Medea* and *Hippolytus*; and in itself *Alcestis* shows every sign of its author's full maturity. The subtleties and profound concerns revealed in other plays make it unlikely that this play, a study of the impact of *Anankē*, Necessity, upon an apparently ideal marriage, should avoid the one issue which dominates the author's earlier and subsequent dramas. In *Alcestis* the anguish is gentler, and the only crime is the negative selfishness of Pheres; but the theme is still woman's relation to man, and the question must arise, Is there any meaning here which connects this legend of goodness with those tales of cruelty?

Before attempting my own answer I must refer to a second most valuable essay on this play, 'The Ironic Structure in *Alcestis*', by Wesley D. Smith.[10] This writer sees that the play is permeated by the kind of irony I have described; that Admetus, though loved, admired, and sympathized with by all the other characters except the two slaves, nevertheless at every point fails to say words which would help us to accept a favourable judgement of him, and says instead something inept or self-centred which accuses or degrades him. The writer shows how the play offers 'a critical analysis of the myth's implica-

tions', and how 'the irony is a sour sauce for the happy conclusion', a conclusion which the poet reached only 'by ignoring the tragic view of death to
which he gave the ring of truth a moment before'. This penetrating exposition
demonstrates the technical intensity with which the emotion of the whole
play is presented, and seems to me an indispensable guide to the study of this
masterpiece. But I venture to think that there is still a further dimension to be
perceived, which is hinted at in the last paragraph of the essay:

Euripides' irony is not gentle. Neither is it vicious or bitter. Or if there is bitterness in
the play it is not to be found in the treatment of the person Admetus, who is weak,
who fails his wife . . . What is bitter, if anything, is the failure itself, and the dislocation of values that Euripides describes.

I believe that the purpose of this play is only seen as complete when it is
recognized as a comment on that most fundamental of all assumptions, to
which I referred on page 82, the ascendancy of man; and, in particular, a
comment on the way in which Athenian society, in its attitude to marriage,
applied and developed this assumption, and on the 'dislocation of values'
which resulted from such an attitude.

In beginning this study I must refer back to the former of these two essays,
by A. P. Burnett, who on the first page says:

the story itself makes no evaluation of the husband's acceptance of his wife's sacrifice,
though it plainly condemns the parents. Euripides, then, . . . was not choosing a story
which necessarily dealt with a cad or a coward. . . The audience has nowhere been
instructed to separate its judgement from that of the chorus. Nor has its attention ever
been directed to what must be, in a re-evaluation of the Admetus story, the crucial
moment for revision: the moment when Admetus accepted his wife's offer to trade
her life for his. Euripides, in fact, has gone to considerable trouble to discourage his
audience from thinking of this moment at all.

It is well to state clearly the form of the story as Euripides uses it. Apollo, in
return for Admetus' kindness during his year of servitude, persuaded the
Fates to allow him to 'escape imminent death if he could find another to take
his place'. It is implied that sickness, either then or soon after, confronted
Admetus with *anankē* in the form of 'imminent death'. He tried all his
relatives and friends, and his old father and mother, 'and found no one, except
his wife'. The author leaves us to infer that Alcestis herself offered — or not
to infer it; her dying speech seems to make the matter plain. Whether
Admetus could at any point have declined the bargain is not told us; but
when Alcestis offered, it was too late, and he 'must endure the gift of a god'
(1071). In other words, the course of the play indicates that once he had
accepted Apollo's proposal he was bound to accept any life that was offered.
Burnett also points out that it was Euripides who introduced a new chrono-

logy into the story: 'the death that was offered and accepted was not an immediate death but one set vaguely in the future, allowing a certain amount of continued common life to both the receiver and the giver'. This is a significant detail. By establishing this interval the dramatist presents us with a marriage which has continued over a period of time under this known condition (Heracles knew of it, 523—4), and which can thus serve as a subject for study.

Why did Alcestis offer to die in place of Admetus? Her reason is first given (180) in the speech of her serving-maid who reports her words, spoken with tears to her marriage-bed: 'I am dying because I cannot bear to fail in my duty to you and to my husband.' This view of a wife's duty the chorus recognize as being an ideal which is generally accepted and thought honourable, but very rarely exemplified. It is not an ideal which Alcestis set for herself; she found it already understood by society, but she embraced it with a thoroughness which was her own rare and heroic achievement. This devotion was based not on passionate love for Admetus, but on acceptance of the ideal current in her society of what a 'house' (*oikos*) should be — an institution dedicated to the permanence of the family, to peaceful rule and stable succession. Within this framework Alcestis, being cast in heroic mould, achieves her freedom; but it is not the freedom to live. One strict measure of the freedom to live was given by Apollo to Admetus; and it enslaved him to misery and self-contempt (197—8 *et al.*).

We are now approaching an answer to the question, Why does Euripides carefully avoid mentioning the crucial moment when Admetus accepted his wife's offer? Let us consider a hypothetical answer: Because in every society known to Hellenes or to barbarians it is unquestioningly accepted that, in the broadest terms and in the last resort, woman's life is at the service and disposal of man's. Even if theoretically it was possible for Admetus to decline, yet when his wife made the offer it would actually seem to him to be above all things *right* — right in a degree beyond the achievement of most men's wives; to refuse it would seem to flout an order of nature and to annul a gesture of unique beauty. This is the attitude of the chorus of Pheraean Elders. The play assumes that the audience will not question this attitude, for in the play the only people who question it are the two slaves. It was so obvious that this self-sacrifice was the perfection of wifehood, the consummation of an ideal union. Such is the situation to which Euripides is speaking. He is not saying that this situation is wrong, nor that it is right; rather he asks, What are its effects? Sometimes this principle of the superior value of man leads to evident injustice, as in Jason's treatment of Medea or Agamemnon's of Clytemnestra and Iphigenia; and then it is clear that a principle is being abused. But here, in the earliest extant play, we are shown a good husband and a good wife, marriage at its best, suddenly faced with the *anankē* of death;

and the woman loses her life but gains immortal glory, while the man keeps his life and loses everything that makes it worth keeping. The never-mentioned moment is in fact the focus of the play. This is the 'bitterness' to which W. D. Smith's essay refers; a bitterness rooted in the 'dislocation of values' which must occur when society assumes that in the last resort a woman's life is a reasonable price for a man's life. The story shows the social principle of male ascendancy, established partly by nature and partly by man's power to organize the world for his own purposes, resulting in man's shame and confusion. As a final irony, the poet ensures that this hard lesson shall not be offered to any except the few who will resolutely search for it, by presenting this piece as the fourth of a set, a recognizable substitute for a satyr-play.

The pith of the author's comment on the man—woman relationship in marriage is found in the Female Servant's description of Alcestis saying farewell to her home (170—81):

> Then she went to every altar
> In the whole palace, and before praying decked each one
> With garlands of green myrtle she had picked herself.
> No tear fell, not a sigh was heard. Her lovely face
> Did not change colour, gave no sign of what must come.
> Then, to her room; and now indeed, flinging herself
> Down on the bed, she wept. 'O marriage-bed,' she cried,
> 'Farewell! Here once I gave my maidenhood to him;
> And now my life. I do not hate you; yet you have
> Killed me, for I alone would not be false to you
> And to my husband; and for this I die.

The contrast between the two pictures given here by the Servant is quite different from the contrast Medea spoke of, between the 'enviable life' and 'living death' which a woman might find in marriage. Medea's husband was insensitive and self-loving; Alcestis' husband is sensitive and self-critical. The case of Alcestis is in fact more tragic than Medea's; for the cause of despair is not unkindness but the accepted form of goodness. The status of Alcestis as mistress of a household, as mother of a family, is enviable, a *zēlotos aiōn*, and the recalling of it, as she performs sacrifice at the household altars, induces no tear or sigh. But her situation as a wife, being the most enviable that any woman could hope for, has laid upon her an obligation which calls for unquenchable weeping. Neither in the Servant's narrative nor in the scene which follows does Alcestis speak of love. She 'honours' her husband (*presbeuousa*, 282; the Servant uses *protimōsa*, 155). Only the chorus in 473 use the word *philia*. The tragedy lies in the assumptions of marriage itself, which imposes an obligation without postulating its necessary motive of love. The bed which has taken her life is, in the first place, not one that she chose; Pelias gave her to Admetus, and in that she was lucky — until Admetus fell ill. In the second place the bed stands for the essence of woman's

relationship to man, which is her expendability in his interest.[11] Alcestis'
tears flow not merely on her own account but on behalf of all women. The
chorus agrees that for a wife to fulfil this condition of the marriage-bond is as
admirable as it is rare; but no one, except the Female Slave whose narrative
we are studying, doubts that it is a proper condition and that to fulfil it is
miraculously right. The cost of this condition in a good marriage is spelt out
in lines 183—98. Its cost in a bad marriage is left to the listener's imagination or experience.

The supernatural opening and close of the play provide a frame for its tragic
tableau which, at the cost of a gentle shift from realism to make-believe,
transforms it. Into a hopeless but real situation the wished-for but unreal
intervention of divine power brings hope; the beauty of marital affection
justifies this hope and promises 'a new and better life' (1157); and this scene
sensitively acted on today's stage is always convincing. But in 438 B.C.
Heracles' fight with Death was as much a fairy-tale as King Arthur is to us; the
last phrases of reality which the audience had to remember were Admetus'
question, 'Friends, what have I to live for?' and the chorus's answer, 'There is
no remedy against Necessity' (960, 965).[12] So let us now examine the role of
Admetus and try to define its essential quality.

We shall find this partly in the king's words and actions; but all the other
persons in the play, except Death and Eumelus, express opinions about him,
and these are all part of the account. The first such opinion is the remark of the
chorus, 144.

Poor man! Such a good man, too, to lose such a noble wife!

and the second follows from the Servant in the next line:

Our master does not yet know this, until he learns.

This exchange shows, first, that the chorus are in full sympathy with Admetus.
They are men, and they are free, and these two privileges they share with the
king. As a chorus they represent the society within which the action takes
place (this is the first of the three extant plays which have a male chorus),
and, like both king and queen, have never questioned the relative positions
assigned by that society to men and to women. So while they praise Alcestis
their first sympathy is for Admetus. The Servant on the other hand is a
woman and a slave; she sees there is something that Admetus 'does not
know', because there is a question he has never asked. Since the chorus have
never asked it either, they make no response to a remark they don't understand; they change the subject. At the end of her narrative the servant adds
significantly to her description of Admetus; he not only 'does not know', but
he 'has a memory which will torment him always' (198).

The contrast between this narrative and the choral ode which follows is

remarkable. In the narrative Euripides uses to the full his power to evoke
pity for suffering mortals. The centre of his picture is the wife and mother
about to renounce her life and her rich and deeply enjoyed world. The picture
is so vivid that the audience forget they are listening to a slave. Somewhere
on the edge of the picture, or outside it, is the free man who should have
died. Then the Servant goes in, and the Pheraean Elders begin their chant.
It is as though they had heard nothing, had been blind to the picture which
has moved some of the audience to tears. That picture is not these men's
picture of the situation — they have their own, which remains unaffected by
a slave's words, however true or vivid. They now pray decorously to Apollo
to show mercy — to Admetus; they address Admetus: 'How you have suffered,
bereft of your wife!' What calls for tears is not that Alcestis dies, but that the
king shall see her die (232–3). At last, in 234–6, they speak with sorrow of
the woman; but return at once, 240–3, to the sufferings of the man. What is
implied by this contrast? Surely the words of the chorus are meant to express
the general attitude of men in the audience. (They seldom provoke more than
conventional comment from scholars.) A woman's death may be pitiful, if she
is a good woman; but its importance is limited. The Servant's narrative was
well done — weeping is women's business. But a king is lucky if he possesses a
queen who is at once loyal and pleasant to him, and respected and loved by
his people; to lose such a woman is a serious loss. And we should note that,
when this view is expressed respectably by the chorus, it wins the audience's
assent. Only when it is put in coarse terms by Pheres — 'With a woman like
that, marriage pays; otherwise it's a bad bargain' (627–8) — does it cause
some uneasiness. Few in the audience will have felt the irony in this contrast
between two views of Alcestis' death. If this were the only extant play we
should have no ground for suspecting the simplicity of what is going on; but
the plays we have already looked at begin to furnish an outline of the ironic
method. We are in fact given here a picture, which later in this chapter we
shall recognize in *Medea*, *Hippolytus*, and *Andromache*, of two separate worlds
living side by side: the world of free males, and the world of women and
slaves. The picture of these two worlds offered in *Alcestis* has every appearance
of corresponding closely to the reality of fifth-century Athenian life.

The Servant clearly sees Admetus as guilty (197–8). The Pheraeans, being
free men, do not. But Admetus loves his wife; and with his first utterance
comes the first stirring of guilt below the surface (247):

The Sun sees what we both suffer, and can witness that *we have done the gods no wrong*,
to deserve your death.

Alcestis recalls him to the fact that she is dying, and states clearly the reason:
either Admetus had to die, or, since no one else would, she must take his
place. The children, and the house to which they are heirs, can prosper with-

out Alcestis, but not without Admetus. This is society as men have made it. If Alcestis as a widow had married again, she would have bought her own prosperity at the cost of her children's; this she will not do. This simple argument is Necessity.[13] Its logic has been a torment to Admetus (421) ever since the bargain was made; but guilt is still unconscious. In the next scene, the prevarication which Admetus uses with Heracles is justified on the ground of hospitality; but it is also eloquent of guilt struggling towards the surface.[14]

Then comes Admetus' conscience, large as life in the person of Pheres; and in the presence of the woman who died with a clear conscience guilt abuses guilt. When Admetus returns from the funeral, guilt is at last fully awake. It does not yet know itself; Admetus does not yet identify his moment of sin; but in his last speech of this scene he comes closer to such a perception than had ever been demanded by the simple outline of the popular legend, in which guilt had no place (939—40):

I ought not to be alive now; I have trespassed beyond my fated time, and shall spend a miserable life. At last I realize this.

In the following lines it appears at first that he perceives the truth only because of his present misery; but as he elaborates the picture and includes the condemnation which will come from his citizen-subjects he moves nearer to the truth, and reaches a judgement upon his own action taken at the critical moment when he accepted Apollo's bargain: he is now 'the man who did not dare to die' (955), who 'escaped death through cowardice' and lives the disgraced life of one whose manhood is in question (956—7). Up to this moment the excuse of 'the god's gift' has seemed valid, for many human institutions — marriage, prophecy, war, the theatre — are the gifts of gods and not to be questioned; and Apollo's gift, as voluntarily implemented by Alcestis — by his chance privilege in being married to a heroic woman — simply actualizes the human institution which makes a man's life of greater value than a woman's (the axiom is stated by Iphigenia in *Iphigenia in Tauris* 1005—6). But now Admetus comes to his moment of truth. He comes to it because he is a good man, and therefore capable of learning, and of the sense of guilt for not learning soon enough. Only those few in Euripides' audience who were as honest as Admetus can have known how deep a question was being opened before them. Certainly they could offer no answer; and the miraculous and moving final scene quickly absolved them from the sternness of realism.

Alcestis, then, is a play about Admetus even more than about Alcestis; just as Euripides' whole presentation of woman's life is in fact inseparable from his comprehensive comment on man. This is a play about a good husband and an admirable marriage which, confronted with a crisis of Necessity, suddenly faces not merely the loss and sorrow which are the common human lot, but disgrace and guilt arising from the rare performance of what everyone recognizes as a wife's duty to her husband. The individual character of Alcestis is not important; she is there as the unique embodiment of an ideal of marriage based on the belief that a man's life is of more value than a woman's; and the play submits this ideal to critical and practical scrutiny. We turn next to the first of three plays in which the individual character of women is important: *Medea*. Medea had a secure place among the handful of legendary women execrated for their crimes; the audience would know they were to see a play about a bad woman.

The Nurse's opening monologue provides a balanced portrait. Medea has behaved well in Corinth, but she had contrived murder in Iolcus. She is 'a frightening woman'; but she is also the mother of two little boys; and now the two men on whom her life depends, Jason and Creon, are planning together to get rid of her. Her passionate devotion to Jason had been acceptable while it made her an obedient wife (13–15); when it makes her resent infidelity her husband sees it as a barbarous excess. But though this balanced portrait is important to the drama, there is equal or greater significance in the symbolic function of Medea as an heroic figure championing the whole female world.

She can champion womankind because she is in no sense an average woman. Like her predecessor Clytemnestra, she is the female representative of those miraculous Athenian generations whose men dethroned tyranny, established law and a sovereign people, defeated the Persian Empire, organized the Delian League, sent ships and soldiers adventuring all over the eastern Mediterranean, created the theatre, invented history, founded science, refashioned architecture, design, oratory, argued with Anaxagoras and Socrates — and who in this vast range of achievement gave neither share nor scope to women, apparently never reflecting that the potential energy for these expanded activities must be present to a comparable degree in the other sex. Medea is a foreigner; this provides for the Athenian audience an acceptable explanation of her crime of infanticide, leaving her emancipated intelligence and indignant words free to have their full impact in a statement of women's wrongs. It has been more than once pointed out that all through the play Medea's role as champion of oppressed woman is closely connected with her motherhood (this too links her with Clytemnestra). This is central to what Euripides has to say here about the injustice which fifth-century Hellas inflicted on women. Not only were they excluded from all but the smallest share of the exhilarating freedoms won by men, but they, and they alone, could bring up a new generation of men, to forget their debt to their mothers and keep wives and sisters and daughters in subjection. Jason is interested in his sons in so far as they are necessary to the establishment of his honourable position as head of an *oikos*, a 'house'; yet, in the prospect of begetting new children from Glauce, he has accepted Creon's sentence of banishment for his sons as well as for Medea; and his mild consent (941) to Medea's request that he ask Creon to let the boys stay in Corinth, does nothing to suggest that his indignation in the final scene arose from any real love for his sons. Creon loves his children, he says (329), even more than his country, and so is open to Medea's plea that she needs one day's grace to arrange for her own children's welfare. Aegeus feels his whole life threatened because he cannot beget children. This essential part of a city's life is the function of woman, as necessary and as exacting as that of the hoplite behind his shield (251); this function has love as its beginning, and can be carried out only by the exercise of love. But if a father's love is like Jason's, what is a mother to do? And what would happen to a city if its women, discouraged by men's abuse and waste of love, were to reach the conclusion voiced by the chorus in 1081 – 1115, that the sorrows of motherhood outweigh its joys, and choose to be childless? We shall return to this final stasimon later; for the present, Medea's first scene demands attention.

Before and after the entry of the chorus, Medea's wild laments and terrifying imprecations heard from within prepare us – somewhat uncomfortably – for an extravagant and pitiable person; and the chorus of Corinthian women ask for her to come out so that they can calm her and persuade her to accept what is being done to her. Their position is clear: as fellow-women they sympathize with her deeply and can ignore the fact that she is a foreigner; but they have themselves always submitted to the will of men, and cannot imagine any other attitude being held for long. Then Medea confronts them. She is not shaken with weeping, but cool and self-possessed. She talks like a Greek, not a barbarian. Her first sixteen lines have chorus and audience listening surprised and intent; then she comes to the heart of the matter (230–7):

> Surely, of all creatures that have life and will, we women
> Are the most wretched. When, for an extravagant sum,
> We have bought a husband, we must then accept him as
> Possessor of our body. This is to aggravate
> Wrong with worse wrong. Then the great question: will the man
> We get be bad or good? For women, divorce is not
> Respectable; to repel the man, not possible.

From the Homeric age down to our own century there have been rare periods and scattered places where it was possible for a woman to have some say in the choice of the 'possessor of her body'; for the overwhelming majority of women who have ever lived, this has been a freedom often longed for, always denied. Human dignity has been preserved, heroism achieved, ordinary life lived and endured, within this condition of bodily enslavement; and the rare protests against this condition – of which Medea's must be among the most direct to survive from the ancient world – have been heard as Canute was heard when he ordered the tide back. Medea details the additional difficulties experienced by a foreign wife in a Greek city; but after two lines she is again talking about the position common to all Greek wives – a position where, if you are unlucky in your husband, 'death is better' (238–51):

> Still more, a foreign woman, coming among new laws,
> New customs, needs the skill of magic, to find out
> What her home could not teach her, how to treat the man
> Whose bed she shares. And if in this exacting toil
> We are successful, and our husband does not struggle
> Under the marriage yoke, our life is enviable.
> Otherwise, death is better. If a man grows tired
> Of the company at home, he can go out, and find
> A cure for tediousness. We wives are forced to look
> To one man only. And they tell us, we at home
> Live free from danger, they go out to battle – fools!
> I'd rather stand three times in the front line than bear
> One child.

After this the poet allows those who wish to forget what she has said to forget it, for she adds (252),

> But the same arguments do not apply to you and me –

when in fact everything she has said, except for 238–9, applies as much to every Greek wife as to a foreigner.

Let us look closely at this manifesto. First Medea points out the absurdity that in marriage it is the slave who is forced to buy herself a master; bodily slavery (233) is bad enough, without having to pay money for it. And a woman is not even allowed to choose a man who seems likely to be a good husband; if she is given a bad one, divorce can be got only at the cost of ill repute; if she does not seek divorce, he may rape her every night of her life. Thus to preserve sanity and dignity demands in some marriages the skill of a magician. A man can find other women when he tires of his wife; a woman has no such escape. Finally, an answer to what Orestes says to Clytemnestra in *Choephori* 921, 'It is the man's work that feeds the woman who sits at home.' Medea points out that, though a man by working or fighting preserves the city, the city itself, and the citizen, exist only because a woman bore a son. Every item in this survey of woman's position applies to contemporary Athens; it may be a pessimistic statement, but in fact no girl contemplating

marriage could be sure that her lot would not answer exactly to this description. The statement, moreover, has a peculiar, and significant, dramatic
untruth. Medea, speaking in anger, forgets that she herself, being a woman
in ten thousand, had in fact chosen her own mate; her only dowry was the
help she gave Jason in stealing the Golden Fleece. Her manifesto, then, is
spoken less on her own behalf than on behalf of all the women of Athens.
Further, though what she says is factually untrue about herself, it truly
indicates the character and attitude of Jason. And because it is a stark presentation of current facts to men who are reluctant to consider them, this
is the one place in the play where such a direct statement can have a properly
dramatic function, before the events of the drama have yet begun to move.
Subsequent emotions will safely erase from the audience's memory this subversive challenge.

From here on it is the action that engrosses interest; reflection appears for
occasional moments, as for example when Jason speaks of the force with
which Aphrodite subdues women's hearts as one of the lucky chances which
can help a man in his career (527—9), and wishes that men could beget
children without the aid of women (573—5). A subtle glance at the accepted
status of women comes in the fourth episode, when Jason so readily believes
in Medea's apparent change of heart, and in her words, whose full value is
already revealed to the audience, but not to him (889—93):

> But we women — I won't say that we are bad by nature,
> But we are what we are. You, Jason, should not copy
> Our bad example, or match yourself with us, showing
> Folly for folly. I give in; I was wrong just now,
> I admit. But I have thought more wisely of it since.

In reply to this Jason says,

> You have recognized the right decision. This is the act
> Of a sensible woman.

Jason credits Medea with sincerity here because slavish behaviour is what
he expects from a woman; and his sense of guilt makes him the more vulnerable. The whole drama, in fact, ostensibly reaches the only conclusion which
the majority of the audience would be prepared to accept from such a play:
that sympathy for any ill-treated woman is cancelled by the revenge she is
likely to take unless prevented. But in the first scene the truth was spoken;
and though the audience may forget it, no ensuing wickedness of the woman
who spoke it can make her words untrue.

To read this first speech of Medea, and then to read the chorus's first
stasimon, is to be led to ask, How is it that Euripides' attitude to the status
of women was ever in doubt? And the answer can only be, Because it was so

rare as to be almost unique and therefore, to most minds, inconceivable. It was not a merely emotional attitude but a balanced, rational, and radical one, neither justifying cruelty nor condoning the wickedness it provoked. Euripides' capacity for radical criticism of human values was largely shared by Socrates; but even Socrates had little or none of Euripides' sympathy with women; in this the poet was, as far as we can tell, alone among the thinkers of his day, certainly among writers. It can only have been the solitariness of his protest that made him so consistently provide his audience with an appropriate veil to hide it from their own eyes — in this case the common reasonableness of Jason's arguments, coupled with his candid unawareness of Medea as a human being.

The champion of the female world is confronted, in her husband, with a clearly characterized representative of the male world; a world where most men pursued success in political life, in business or law, in war, in athletics, and a few in intellectual or artistic pursuits. Jason, a political man, has one attitude in common with the athlete we shall meet in the next play: Hippolytus, like Jason, wishes that he could get children without the help of women (*Hippolytus* 618–24). It has already been suggested that a sense of guilt must partly explain Jason's readiness to believe in Medea's change of heart; the sense of failure in ability to deal with women is closely akin to guilt. Hippolytus is without experience either of sex or of marriage; Jason has enjoyed marriage but now wants to change his wife for another. Both despise women as a class and hate them; both therefore have failed a fundamental test of man as a social being — the question of ability to make or find a society in which he can live satisfactorily with the other half of the human race. Hippolytus feels no guilt but is secure in his righteousness; Jason does not feel guilt towards Medea, but towards his sons he certainly does. Lines 914–21,

> As for you, my boys, your father
> Has taken careful thought, and, with the help of the gods,
> Ensured a good life for you. Why, in time, I know,
> You with your brothers will be leading men in Corinth ...

are a hollow utterance for a man who, for the sake of his career, is allowing his only two sons to go into exile — even if he assumed that the money and introductions which Medea refused in 616–18 will now be accepted. The violence of his self-reproach in 1329–50, and the unconvincing anguish of 1395ff., indicate that his bitterness towards Medea gains double sharpness from guilt and remorse. Yet, like those Athenians whom he represents, he is incapable of thought radical enough to renounce the convenience of inherited despotism or to question social tradition. The difference between his world and the world of women is well put by E. Schlesinger:[15]

He cannot comprehend how someone might reproach him . . . and be concerned with such a trifle as the *lechos* ('life in bed'). But it is in this very point, the *lechos* of which Jason speaks repeatedly, that the main difference lies. For him marriage and children – indeed, all human ties, are only a means to an end. The value of life depends on social status and its perpetuation in generations to come. That is why children are important for him.

This depiction of the exclusive male world continues throughout Euripides' work; Hippolytus, Odysseus, Xuthus, Talthybius, Eteocles, all make their contributions.

The female world too is strongly characterized all through *Medea*. It takes shape in the prologue spoken by the Nurse, who accepts women's allotted status and expects kindness in return. When the Tutor enters, the two slaves express their community in bondage (65), and their combined sympathy soon joins with that of the free women of the chorus in support of Medea. Here, as in *Alcestis*, the free woman's world is closer in sympathy to that of slaves than to that of free men. So, before the first free man, Creon, enters at 270, Medea cements her bond of bondage with the women, who promise her their silence (259–66):

> Say nothing. A woman's weak and timid in most matters;
> The noise of war, the look of steel, makes her a coward;
> But touch her right in marriage, and there's no bloodier spirit.

In her interview with Creon she finds that he, like Jason, generalizes about women – which is the last thing a woman of character can stand; and that for him, as for Jason, mutual loyalty between a man and a woman holds none of the sanctity of loyalty between two men. Then with a concession and a threat the male intruder goes, and the female world closes again round the gap, while Medea considers her plans before the listening women, and summons her nerve. She knows what she must do, and that the other world will not suspect and cannot frustrate (407–9):

> We were born women – useless for honest purposes,
> But in all kinds of evil skilled practitioners.

The defiant irony of this couplet – 'we are what you make us, we do what you teach us' – was not observed in the ancient world; and modern readers have sometimes naïvely noted Euripides' sour judgement of the frail sex; but the Corinthian women do not misunderstand Medea. They are not heroic by nature; but after this scene they are roused by her heroic defiance of her oppressors to sing in a rebellious spirit (410–30):

> Streams of the sacred rivers flow uphill;
> Tradition, order, all things are reversed:

Deceit is *men*'s device now,
Men's oaths are gods' dishonour.
Legend will now reverse our reputation;
A time comes when the female sex is honoured;
 That old discordant slander
 Shall no more hold us subject.
Male poets of past ages, with their ballads
Of faithless women, shall go out of fashion;
 For Phoebus, Prince of Music,
Never bestowed the lyric inspiration
 Through female understanding —
 Or we'd find themes for poems,
We'd counter with our epics against man.
Oh, Time is old; and in his store of tales
 Men figure no less famous
 Or infamous than women.[16]

  The interview with Jason follows, with further generalizations about women and the absurdity of their insistence on regarding the sex-relationship as a personal matter (567—73); and after this the chorus sing of Aphrodite and the reality and rich variety of love — a power as essential to the completeness of human life as the sun or the sea. (Jason too, 527—8, knows the name of Aphrodite.) In so far as this ode refers to the dramatic situation, the chorus credit Jason with being deeply in love with Glauce; the audience will be more inclined to believe Jason himself when he says that he is marrying her for expediency (593—7). In more general terms the burden of this ode is the same as that of the other two odes to love, in *Hippolytus* 525—43 and *Iphigenia in Aulis* 543—72: a prayer that Aphrodite may come in gentleness and not in cruelty — coupled with the recognition (voiced also by Phaedra's Nurse) that even when full of pain love is the sweetest of all things. These odes, together with the lyric lines of the desolate Admetus (*Alcestis* 915—21), give us the most direct account available (as opposed to passages tinged with irony such as Andromache's views on wifely devotion, *Andromache* 213—27, or flaming with irony, such as the second encounter in *Iphigenia in Aulis* between Agamemnon and his wife) of Euripides' thought on love and marriage. The odes in *Medea* and *Hippolytus* do not mention marriage at all. The ode in *Iphigenia in Aulis* speaks of the 'twin arrows of Eros — one that bestows life-long content, the other, ruin and confusion'; and prays to the Cyprian to 'avert such ruin from my marriage-bed', and grant 'holy desires'. The love that Admetus recalls is the 'gentle Aphrodite' invoked in the two odes. The natural conclusion is that Euripides saw marriage much as reflective people see it in our society — as an institution accommodating both physical desire and personal affection, but one where the double ideal is rarely attained; that he saw the full beauty and rapture of love as more often bought at the cost of 'ruin and confusion', as when Paris (*Iphigenia in Aulis* 582—6)

Stood before a palace of ivory
And poured his love in Helen's gazing eyes
And was love-shattered in return.

The ode to love in *Medea* ends with a denunciation of false friends; and then the Athenian Aegeus enters, to prove himself a true friend. He shows towards Medea not only sympathy but great respect, which makes acceptable his cautious conditions for helping her — the two meet on equal terms. And after his visit, which gives her plan a clear road ahead, Medea begins to part company with the woman's world which has so far supported her (807–10):

> Let no one think of me
> As humble or weak or passive; let them understand
> I am of a different kind: dangerous to my enemies,
> Loyal to my friends. To such a life glory belongs.

The women of Corinth do not want this glory. Their protest is excused and dismissed; and the Nurse is sent, on her fidelity as a woman, to summon Jason for his overthrow.

A last picture of woman's world is reflected in the ironic opening of the fourth stasimon (1081–93):

> I have often engaged in arguments.
> And become more subtle, and perhaps more heated,
> Than is suitable for women;
> Though in fact women too have intelligence,
> Which forms part of our nature and instructs us —
> Not all of us, I admit; but a certain few
> You might perhaps find, in a large number of women —
> A few not incapable of reflection;
> And this is my opinion: those men or women
> Who never had children of their own at all
> Enjoy the advantage in good fortune
> Over those who are parents . . .

The women who speak, though they are ordinary wives and not heroines, are still 'not incapable of reflection'. They have followed Medea farther than some women would, for they have witnessed her wrongs; the theme of children and the longing for children, and the sight and evident destiny of two little boys, have occupied their eyes and minds ever since the action began; children are their life and their justification for accepting the kind of life allowed them by men. With ironic modesty they offer their opinion on a topic about which their knowledge is as real as Jason's is superficial, and they conclude: that, in the world as it is, the one light and hope of their existence would be better abandoned. They speak not a word of complaint about man's oppression — they have never questioned their role as women; the story of

Medea, now that the irrevocable step has been taken, has transcended such misfortunes and become a comment on the cycle of life and death which includes all human beings — Medea and her sons, Creon and his daughter. Life will go on; but need mortals give thanks to the gods for children?[17] Their last cry (1290—1) is:

> O bed of women, full of passion and pain,
> What wickedness, what sorrow you have caused on the earth!

We come next to *Hippolytus*; and begin our study with one short, telling phrase which, even if it stood alone, should arrest us with its implications. When Phaedra is making her confession to the chorus she says (406—7):

I knew that my craving was a sin; I knew this too, that I was a woman — a thing hated by everyone (*misēma pasin*).

The point to be noted is, that while such a statement is to be interpreted as the utterance of a woman in despair and not as a literal report, nevertheless it tells us something about 'the position of women in fifth-century Athens' which we would not learn from the historians or philosophers of the period, still less from a study of ancient law, or from painting or sculpture; something which it was no one's business to record, except the dramatist's. What reaction was that line intended to arouse in the audience? Indignant denial, or acquiescence in a truth? The world's hatred of women is given fair reason in the two cases shown in this play, where Hippolytus reviles both servant and mistress for offences which are not denied. But the sympathy of the audience is powerfully claimed for both women; for the Nurse because she is a slave with a robust and realistic vitality; and for Phaedra because of her scrupulous self-searching, and because, being attacked by the most powerful of divinities, she chose the heroic defence, to starve herself to death — until her resolution was beguiled and betrayed. Hippolytus illustrates Phaedra's words thus (664—8):

My curse on you all! I shall never have my fill of hating women, even if I am thought to be always saying this. Well, women, it seems, always are evil; so whoever can teach women to be chaste may forbid me to tread their name in the dust.

To this the chorus respond with

How cruel a fate it is to be born a woman! —

a self-evident truth, for the Nurse is now hated by two instead of one, while Phaedra becomes a hater as well as hated, and departs to destroy both Hippolytus and herself. There were surely some in the audience who reflected that hatred is a potent force, and that Hippolytus, in advocating its indiscriminate use by one half of the human race against the other half, can hardly be commended for wisdom. For them, this vicious speech would match the *hybris* shown in Hippolytus' rejection of Aphrodite, and the moral complacency which obtrudes itself in each of his four appearances. Yet it is significant that at no point in the play is there any criticism of his hatred of women. The old Slave gently reproves him for impiety; Theseus mistakenly raves at him for hypocrisy; but the Trozenian women forget his contempt, and love and adore him. In the epilogue his nobility is the leading theme; and it becomes clear that his attitude to women is, for the majority for whom the chorus speaks, a fault easily pardoned.

When Phaedra has gone and the stage is left to the male world we find two passages which invite reflection on the part which that world has played in Phaedra's tragedy. Theseus in his first lament over her says (831–3):

From some distant source I bring back upon myself this disaster sent by gods, because of the sins of someone in the past.

This statement has a curious vagueness. It seems dramatically unlikely that Theseus is referring to the past guilt of the family of Minos, which Phaedra herself has already spoken of (337–41, where she recalls her mother's unnatural love for the bull as the origin of the unhappy love-life of her sister Ariadne and herself); and more likely that the guilt he refers to derives from his own and his family's history, though from which of many incidents is hard to guess. Since the pattern of the drama presents Phaedra and Hippolytus as having in common the memory of an unhappy mother (337, 1082), it is possible that here Theseus is reminded of his cruelty to the Amazons and his rape of Hippolyta. Certainly these lines indicate that a sense of guilt is present as he, an oldish man with a life's record of bloodshed, rape, and violence, looks at the dead Phaedra, still a girl of perhaps twenty or less.

The other passage is from Hippolytus' defence to Theseus, 1002ff.:

There is no man on earth more pure in heart than I ... To this day my body is chaste; I have not known a woman.

It may be that young men as devoted to chastity as Hippolytus were rare in Euripides' Athens, though the sexual freedom of that society and the availability of girl slaves would be likely to arouse some ascetic reaction. One would expect Athenians to regard such puritanical innocence with the same kindly tolerance which the Slave shows in the prologue, knowing that it would soon give place to maturity. But Euripides' picture of Hippolytus reminds us that immaturity does not always pass with the years, and that asceticism is not always innocent. His attitude is not merely one of chastity; it is one of hatred. The savagery of his attack on women, elaborated through more than fifty lines with unrelenting fury (616–68), has in it a touch of the inhuman quality shown in *The Bacchae* by Pentheus; and in both plays this inhumanity is connected with the pursuit, and the vocabulary, of hunting. The point has been convincingly argued in a recent article by Charles Segal.[18] The writer shows that Hippolytus' character as a hunter is exactly analysed by the poet. On the one hand he seeks in Nature serenity and purity; on the other hand his hunting exhibits 'not an ideal harmony, but a harsh opposition between men and Nature'. Phaedra's purity is human, Hippolytus' is inhuman and insensitive. The fact that Hippolytus at the end of the play is accepted as a hero shows that in this character he represents a popular ideal of masculinity; and Segal's article shows that this masculine image, especially in its relation to women, is strongly criticized in this play – though the criticism is so subtly and ironically conveyed that it often passes unnoticed.

The impact of Hippolytus' character on the audience is carefully balanced. The violence of his tirade against women in general, like his sexual abstinence, shows him as immoderate and wins little sympathy; but his harsh treatment of Phaedra would, as we can see from *The Frogs*, be accepted as a just arraignment of a pernicious adulteress. His priggish tone would surely be unacceptable to men, even though they knew him innocent; but the Trozenian women can forget his hatred of their whole sex, and his cruelty to Phaedra; they protest to the gods against the injustice of his death, and mourn for him as one loved and longed for by girls (1140–1). Their acceptance of his arrogant attitude is so much a part of human society that it is embodied in the perennial rituals which Artemis speaks of in her last address to Hippolytus. Yet Hippolytus himself knows nothing of the love suffered by girls who were 'rivals for his bed', nothing of what moves not only the chorus but the Nurse to poetry; he is unaware of love as anything but a matter of unclean lust or necessary procreation. His devotion to athletics (1016) includes a feature sometimes observable in its twentieth-century manifestation – it appears as an escape from the more subtle challenges of living in a two-sex society. Again, everything that is said in this play about the fate of women becomes a comment on the behaviour of man.

It has often been remarked that this play is divided into two halves, the second beginning with the entry of Theseus. What is less often perceived is the nature of the difference between the two halves. From the end of the prologue to Phaedra's exit the stage is occupied by a woman's world: Phaedra, the Nurse, and the chorus together wrestle with a tragic dilemma. Hippolytus intrudes on this woman's world but does not communicate with it; he simply discharges his hatred and departs. The second half of the play has no woman in it except the chorus, who are no longer involved in the action as they were in the first half. Theseus, Hippolytus, and the Messenger constitute a man's world where other assumptions prevail. The first half contains Phaedra's painful and scrupulous search for self-knowledge, and her statement of the pure and noble life as she understands it; as well as the Nurse's robust recognition of physiological fact and her scepticism about the value of a conventional ideal. Each of these courageous women cares about truth in action; but the Nurse fatally misjudges both Phaedra and Hippolytus. Then at the critical moment Phaedra's passionate purity is met and battered by the coarse outrage of Hippolytus' words; and her despair leaps to a wickedness as passionate as her virtue. When we turn to the second half, to the men's world, the picture is different. There is no soul-searching, no serious confronting of any moral issue. For Phaedra's self-knowledge we have Hippolytus' self-righteousness, which deceives not only himself but the women who forget how he hated and insulted them. Here no truth about the nature of gods or the springs of human action is explored. Theseus' sorrow for his lost Phaedra is largely self-pity and is forgotten when hatred for Hippolytus obsesses him. Error is dispelled by divine revelation, but the hatred which was a deeper cause of disaster is never condemned. It is true that Hippolytus pardons his father for causing his death; but this grace extended to another man only makes more noticeable the vindictive fury of his refusal to excuse a woman. Hippolytus pardons his father as a fellow-victim, not as a fellow-sinner; he dies completely convinced of the perfection of his own character. Neither father nor son has learnt to be a member of the human race; their reconciliation is concluded in a half-size world. Phaedra, whose mind and heart are, in contrast with theirs, both human and heroic, is forgotten. In comparison with such a theme − the human race divided into two camps, made for love but dedicated to hate − the war of the two goddesses, the issue of indulgence or abstinence, becomes superficial.

We must now take a further look at *Andromache*. The theme of this play is the position of women in Greek society presented against the background of a war which, years after it ended, is still dominating the life and destiny of men and women, whether they were involved in it or not. Andromache speaks the prologue, and her first sentence unobtrusively echoes what Medea said about a wife having to buy herself a husband:

> I left my home; and with me came a golden hoard
> Of treasures for my dowry.

Hermione, who accepts the economic aspect of marriage without question, in her opening lines taunts the slave Andromache by boasting of the rich dowry Menelaus had provided when she married Neoptolemus. Andromache pictures (347—51) the annoyance Menelaus will suffer when not even a second large dowry will enable him to find a second husband to take Hermione off his hands, should Neoptolemus dismiss her for her present behaviour. The Nurse, in comforting Hermione (871—3), reminds her how much money her father has invested in her. Finally Peleus closes the play with these words (1279—83):

> There, now! Have I not always said how right it is,
> How wise, to look for a wife, or choose a son-in-law,
> From a family of noble blood, what a mistake
> It is to marry beneath you, even if your bride
> Brings with her wealth unlimited? Trust in the gods;
> That is the surest way to safety and success!

The exchange of wealth at a wedding, whether as dowry or bride-price, is a custom which has its congenial and honourable aspect, and in Andromache's opening lines this is not excluded; the other references are less dignified. The humiliation of purchase is, however, only one of a number of wrongs illustrated in this bitter play.

The dialogue between Hermione and Andromache (147—273) has often been discussed as if it were a confrontation of an ill-used heroine by an arrogant and vicious woman. It is true that Andromache, once a princess, is now a slave and apparently in mortal danger, while Hermione is free, royal, and apparently powerful. Andromache is conventionally good, Hermione conventionally bad. Those who like their drama as simple as that may have it — Euripides wrote for them, but not only for them. What this scene, taken as a whole, displays to a more acute perception is a pair of women whose difference of outward circumstance only makes their similarity in unhappiness the more striking. Andromache, though quite defenceless, is mature and confident; Hermione is on the edge of hysteria. Quarrelling is seldom dignified; Hermione is enjoying the quarrel even less than Andromache, and her pathetic and superstitious jealousy drives her to childish sallies and accusations, while her wholesale and irrelevant reviling of Phrygians (173ff.) —

> You orientals are all alike — incest between
> Father and daughter, brother and sister, mother and son;
> And murder too — the closest family ties outraged,
> And no law to forbid any such crime! —

matches the inanities uttered by Peleus about Spartans in the third episode. Andromache is adept at finding the phrase which will hurt her opponent (213):

A wife, even if she has married beneath her, ought to make
The best of it . . .

This duel of shabby insults and vicious threats shows primarily two women
equally robbed of dignity by what war and society — both the creation of the
male — have done to them. Andromache, after years of living as a chattel,
begins to lose some of the grace of royalty. Hermione is as helpless in the
hands of Menelaus, and later of Orestes, as she thinks Andromache is in
hers. Her father gave her to Neoptolemus when it suited him, and will now
transfer her to Orestes because it suits him better.[19] She is almost as much a
chattel as her slave is; but when, half-way through the play, she begins to
discover this, she has not the poise and resolution of the older woman to
help her meet it.

An important passage comes in Hermione's scene with Orestes (929—56);
a vivid description of social life and gossip in the women's apartments of a
prosperous home. These lines have sometimes been referred to as an
irrelevance and a blemish in the play; and so they would be — if the play
were indeed a piece of patriotic propaganda. Since it is a play about the
subjection of woman, this passage is strictly relevant. It shows one of the
strongest fetters by which the subjection of woman could be maintained —
the force of jealousy; it clarifies the implication of Medea's complaint,
'A man can find a cure for boredom; we must look to one man only.' (See also
above, Chapter 2, page 40.) Hermione's words suggest that a wife's best
hope for a quiet mind was to isolate herself entirely (943ff.); and the lines
are therefore complementary to the pathetic account given by Andromache
in *Women of Troy* 647—53 of her resolute effort to be, and to gain the reputation of, a good wife (see above, pages 89—90). The chorus protest that
Hermione has spoken too openly; 'Women's difficulties,' they say, 'should
be decently concealed.'

The women of Phthia, wives of citizens, who form the chorus, are
fortunate to be neither royal nor slaves. As Greeks they patronize the
foreigner (119, 421—2), but they are sympathetic and wish to be helpful.
They believe that what cannot be avoided must be accepted (133—4):

Power will overtake you; you are nothing;
Then why bring trouble on yourself?

They urge Andromache to leave the temple of Thetis; but their advice is
foolish and inconsistent, because they know that her life is threatened
if she quits sanctuary. This foolishness is simply an accurate detail in
Euripides' picture of neighbourly women whose slavish attitude to authority
robs them of common sense. And in the last few lines of the *parodos* these free

ladies demonstrate that 'slavish' is not too harsh a term for their behaviour
(141—6):

> I at least have felt sorry for you
> Since first you came to this house from Troy;
> But for fear of Hermione I have kept quiet,
> Though you have my truest sympathy;
> But I would not wish her to know that I am your friend.

Hermione enters in time to hear this and snubs them suitably (154):

> . . . And that is answer enough for you.

After Andromache's first spirited defiance of Menelaus the chorus rebuke
her for having 'said more than a woman ought to say to a man' (364). Like the
Nurse and Hermione herself, they accept the fiction that the 'plot' to kill
Andromache and her son is Hermione's and that Menelaus merely abets her,
though action and dialogue indicate the reverse. Their view of life, expressed
in the third stasimon, is that the only solution of its problems lies in being
born aristocratic (766ff.) — a belief pathetically belied by the fate of Hermione:

> The kind of life that I would choose,
> The only kind worth living,
> Is to inherit some great and honoured name
> And be brought up in a wealthy house.

Yet even these cosy matrons are elevated by the poetry and truth of their
last stasimon (1009—46), which prepares us to connect fading memories of
the war at Troy with the fresh wickedness of the man who has just departed
taking Hermione away from her home, and with the 'rain of blood' which
the Messenger from Delphi will presently recount. Their mourning with
Peleus is sincere and touching; and they are spared the obligation to offer
any comment on the unbearable irony of Thetis' pronouncements and
Peleus' reply. As for the two royal women, at the end of the play Hermione is
the captive wife of the inhuman Orestes, while Andromache's future is
prescribed for her by Thetis: she is to be freed, and provided with a third
husband, and comforted and compensated for the death of Hector, the
murder of Astyanax, the annihilation of Troy, her years of slavery, and the
murder of her protector Neoptolemus, by the knowledge that her son will
beget a line of kings; for 'even to Troy the gods extend their kindly care'.
But Andromache (on whose noble but unsparkling nature irony would
have been lost) is probably not present[20] to share the gratitude of Peleus for
divine consolation.

We proceed next to *Ion*. The prologue spoken by Hermes gives an outline of Creusa's story up to the time of the action, when she is in her middle thirties. As a nubile girl she was seduced by a lover whom she took to be Apollo, since the incident occurred at the 'Long Rocks' near the Athenian Acropolis, where Apollo had a shrine of some kind (285). She bore her child in secret, then exposed him at the same place where he was begotten. The infant vanished. Later the Athenians gave her in marriage to a foreigner, Xuthus, as a reward for his alliance in war; and Xuthus became king of Athens. Creusa has now been married to him for many years and is still childless; that is why she has now come with her husband to Delphi.

So far Creusa has not found much joy in life. Before she appears, we are given a background against which she will unfold her character to us. Ion comes on stage to get the temple-forecourt ready for the day's visitors. His words poetically evoke the majesty of the Delphic scene and express his own simple piety; at the same time his broom and his bow strike a note of incongruous realism, not to say comedy; for his main concern is in fact to sweep up bird-dung and to prevent birds from fouling statues, altars, and buildings.[21] When the chorus enter (they are female slaves of Creusa) they describe the reliefs and paintings which adorn the temple-court; and each of the scenes mentioned includes some fabulous creature or event from early legend or from the pre-Olympian era — the Lernaean snake, Bellerophon's winged horse, the fire-breathing monster with three bodies, the Giants, the Gorgons, huge Mimas, and the smouldering thunderbolts. When they put their questions to Ion, his matter-of-fact answers repeat the contrast between realism and ancient fable. Then Creusa comes; and the straightforward Ion, who though he has lived for seventeen years in these surroundings has never yet even seen Apollo, at last finds himself talking to someone whose grandfather 'was born from the earth', and asks (269)

Did Athena really take him up out of the earth?

There follow similar questions — he is at once eager to believe and incredulous: Athena's box, a bloody death on the sharp crags: and

Is it true, or merely a tale, that your father Erechtheus killed your sisters in sacrifice? That your father was engulfed in a chasm of the earth?

And Creusa says, Yes, it is all true — and evidently believes it; and adds that her husband is a descendant of Zeus. Ion accepts everything, until she comes to Apollo's rape of a girl at the Long Rocks; then both piety and common sense rebel. The miraculous and fantastic may be allowed as far as the last generation, but into this generation — no! And he answers (341):

Impossible! Some man wronged her, and she is ashamed to own it.

The misery of a bereaved and childless woman arouses some sympathy in Ion; but when it comes to the point (368—9) —

> CREUSA: What of his victim? What does this involve for her?
> ION: There is no one who will ask this question for you.

So Creusa reaches the simple conclusion (398—400):

Life is harder for women than for men; they judge us, good and bad together, and hate us. That is the fate we are born to.

Creusa knows what Phaedra knew — 'men hate us'. She also knows that to make wholesale judgements on all women is none the less common for being stupid.[22] Ion shows in his soliloquy (429—51) that his mind is open as to whether Creusa's lover was Apollo, as she insists, or a man, as he assumed earlier and still believes later, 1521—7; but whichever it was, he judges that the action was an injustice to the woman — though for a brief moment which soon passes (1485, 1488) he shares Creusa's belief and excuses Apollo. In his long reply to Xuthus he pictures his position in relation to Creusa, if he accepts Xuthus' invitation to go to Athens (611—20):

She will hate me, and rightly ... Many a woman, when driven to it, has used the knife or poison against her husband. Besides, father, I pity her. She is your wife; she is growing old without any child.

Xuthus brushes all this aside as not worth considering; and he adds a word to the chorus, his wife's devoted women slaves:

You servants, say nothing about all this. If you speak one word to my wife, I will kill you.

The result is predictable. The gap between slaves and queen closes immediately in resistance to the free male oppressor. The chorus will risk their lives and help Creusa their fellow-victim; and a male slave is there to join the revolt. The old man who had looked after Creusa as a child is an eloquent leader of rebels, and brings to his task a ready-made hatred of Xuthus which surprises no one. He imaginatively expounds his version of Xuthus' iniquitous scheming, and proposes violent action to counter it. But Creusa, encouraged by support, takes her supporters back with her into legend as she recounts her rape by Apollo and tells of the Gorgon's blood which she carries in her bracelet. When the plot to kill Ion has been laid and the chorus are alone, they speak for women's wrongs (1090—1105):

Look now, you who with changeless songs
Slander us women as unchaste,
Breaking man's law and God's to taste
Forbidden joys: to you belongs
This censure! See how the uncounted wrongs
Man's lust commits debase him far beneath
Our innocence. Truth sings
Another tune, and flings
Men's taunts of lustfulness back in their teeth.

When women are wronged, justice sleeps — 'There is no one who will ask this question for you.' But when women rebel justice swiftly awakes (1248–9):

What shall we suffer now? Will not justice punish us?

In comes the admirable young man, Ion, whose eloquence, like that of Hippolytus, finds an inspiring theme in the wickedness of woman, and whose hand turns by instinct to cruelty (1266–8). Fortunately there is yet another woman, the Delphian Priestess, who has authority enough to prevent violence, and for the moment to persuade Ion and Creusa that they are son and mother. But when Creusa still insists that Apollo is father, Ion rebels. He is quite sure now, as he was earlier, that his mother's lover was a mortal man; and her explanation of Apollo's manoeuvres he dismisses as 'mere trifling' (1546). Creusa twice gives Ion her oath, swearing first 'by Athena the Gorgon-slayer', then 'by Athena who fought beside Zeus against the Giants'; and again two worlds face each other — the ancient world of miraculous legend which offers shelter to an ill-used woman, and the realistic world of an honest young man. But the play is over now, and the epilogue returns us to the world of the prologue, where gods are unperturbed by questions of truth or of right. Just as Hermes was mistaken in his factual forecast, so Athena's solution is the same one which Ion has just now rejected as 'mere trifling'. What is the meaning of the play? If this question were put by us to Ion, his answer might well be: 'The trouble with some women is getting them to face facts; but this does not excuse men for exploiting and hating them.'

In the plays we have so far considered Euripides explores the mystery of human nature as it appears in the antagonisms arising between men and women in situations more or less familiar to our experience. In *The Bacchae* (407 B.C.) he looks below the surface of experience for the springs of action and consciousness which generate these antagonisms, for the sense of life itself which in every human being demands freedom as the new-born infant demands air. Dionysus is primarily the god of life and freedom. As soon as human beings begin to live together in a crowded community they find it necessary to restrict their own and each other's freedom with laws, disciplines, contracts, hierarchies, armies; since wine seems to give a temporary release from such tensions (as witness both Teiresias, 280—3, and the Herdsman, 772—4), Dionysus became also the god of wine. In *The Bacchae* we are shown on the one hand a whole city-full of women who, inspired by Dionysus in his primary function of Liberator, cast off the oppressive system which makes them spend their lives spinning and weaving, cooking, cleaning, and looking after children (all these obligations are alluded to in the course of the play), and stream out in a mass to the mountains, where they enjoy the life of Nature in common with wild animals. And on the other side of the picture is Pentheus, master of a palace and commander of an army, with stables for his horses and prisons for all who disobey him; a king who in the past presumably ruled his city in peace, but who now, since Dionysus taught the dances of freedom, is shaken with anger.

Dionysus in the prologue says that he has instituted his worship in 'the walled towns of Bactria and the crowded magnificent cities of the Asian coastline'. It is the administration of large and prosperous communities which most destroys the spontaneity of life. This is an inevitable dilemma; but since it was possible for one section of a community — the free males — to take for themselves the bulk share of freedom and shift the restrictions on to women (the further question of slaves is not included in the pattern of the play), it is women who make an immediate and total response to Dionysus. Women have not had the opportunity, which men have had, of learning how freedom can discipline itself with its own laws and still be freedom. The discipline which rules women's lives is in the main not their own, but imposed upon them. The men of Thebes, alarmed at their loss of authority over the women, will be prepared to obey Pentheus' orders and muster at the Electran Gate; they do not believe that they 'will all be put to flight' (798). Pentheus knows no half-way between being a master of slaves and being 'a slave to his own slaves' (803); so he, the representative of male authority, in order to control his female subjects, goes to spy on them dressed as a woman, until women destroy him.

While Pentheus, baffled, mocked, and mastered, is inside the palace being robed by Dionysus, the chorus sing the third stasimon, an ode expressing the contradiction between the passion for freedom and the passion for self-assertion. The first stanza (quoted in full at the end of Chapter 8, page 224) gives expression to that longing for escape which is so often voiced by women in Euripides' choruses (e.g. *Hippolytus* 732—51). Then comes the anger of the rebel against oppression, resolute

> To stretch a conquering arm
> Over the fallen crest
> Of those who wished us harm.

The antistrophe recognizes that the mysterious operations of Time carry the power of irresistible Law; but rebellion returns in the refrain. The last stanza speaks of the hope — whether of freedom or of revenge — which is all that most men can attain; in hope, we can 'enjoy each passing day'. Of course, all that the chorus say here is as true for men as for women. But ever since Pentheus' first entry these dancing Bacchantes, and their counterparts dancing on Cithaeron, have represented the whole race of women which Pentheus fears, suspects, and hates (215−25, 260−2, 487, 785−6, 796), as Pentheus represents that intractable element in the male world which fosters this antagonism. Legends such as that of the forty-nine Danaids who killed their bridegrooms, or of the 'Lemnian massacre' (see Aeschylus *Choephori* 631−4, Euripides *Hecabe* 886−7) were familiar enough to suggest that the defiance of Pentheus by Theban women might entail a similar peril. 'You will all be put to flight' was not a threat to be ignored.

Because this play treats the whole subject symbolically rather than realistically, and thus uncovers the insoluble depths of the problem of freedom and authority, the dramatist left unanswered all the moral questions of the legend; so that until a generation ago scholars still tended to take sides with Pentheus or with Dionysus. The three male supporters of Dionysiac worship are not impressive: Teiresias, an insincere casuist ready to talk persuasive nonsense; Cadmus, an opportunist ready to 'lie for a good purpose' (334); and the Herdsman, shallow and superstitious (770−4). After the catastrophe Agaue, now in the central role, is first scorned by the women of the chorus, then sentenced by Dionysus. How, then, is the human race to deal with, and how are the two sexes to share between them, this terrible power of life and freedom which both men and women desire and fear? Cadmus, shifty though he may be, has a part of the answer (1344−8): that anger must give place to mercy. In the world of gods this is meaningless; and Dionysus rejects his plea. Once again we see that hope for humanity rests solely in human hands, and then only when perception has been won by suffering. The place of this theme in Euripides' thought will be the subject of Chapter 9.

Euripides, I believe, was first and always a poet and playwright. To call him a feminist is as misleading as to call him a misogynist is untrue. He was a man who felt himself a member of the whole human race rather than of one half of it. He recognized the distinction between royal and common, as he recognized the distinction between good and bad; but he did not equate good or bad with royal or common, nor with slave or free, nor with Hellene or barbarian, nor with male or female. He saw that ordinary women who accepted the position society gave them, whether slaves or 'free', could often achieve, 'on the common level',[23] both goodness and happiness, if they were lucky; but that women of notable character were likely to find in the life allotted to them an intolerable contradiction which led to tragedy.

Further, he saw the mutual hate and anger which this contradiction engendered as something even deeper than the hate and anger which breed
between two men in the pursuit of glory or the defence of pride; for whereas
between men there may sometimes be room for forbearance and relent-
ing, between a man and a woman such a solution is seldom even envisaged –
the nearest approach to such a situation being the remorse of Orestes in
Electra after the matricide, or the reconciliation between Ion and Creusa.[24]
For so deep a problem Euripides has no remedy to offer – any more than
Ibsen had. Perhaps the most encouraging picture he gives us – not a flat-
tering one for male pride, but one strangely free from the poison of hatred –
is found towards the end of *Iphigenia in Aulis*; where the hollow and
egocentric Achilles, suddenly astonished by the vision of courage, is jerked
into reality, into humble admiration, and remembers the terror of death. In
a moment, the sex-barrier which in his first scene made him behave like a
coarse oaf vanishes, and he learns from the child Iphigenia, for the first
time in the play, to become himself.

I said at the beginning of this chapter that its purpose was to describe
what Euripides' plays have to say about women and their part in society.
First, a review of some eighteen fragmentary plays showed that from the
beginning this author devoted far more attention than his predecessors to
the theme of women – the cruelties they suffered and the crimes they were
remembered for. Next, in surveying six complete plays where the material for
this enquiry is most plentiful, we saw that he presents the position of woman
as being, even in the most favoured circumstances, ultimately precarious
and dependent on the will, the good opinion, and the activities of man. We
saw that alongside of characters who regard women with respect – Admetus,
Theseus, Aegeus – there are others, more numerous, such as Hippolytus,
Jason, Xuthus, Pentheus, Orestes, Agamemnon, Achilles, whose attitude
shows at different times contempt, disregard, cruelty, hatred, or guilt;
while women themselves are conscious often of meeting hate where th
should look for love, and in moments of crisis turn by instinct to the
loyalty of slaves for support against man's oppression. I take it as unquestioned that Euripides was among the most penetrating observers of his
age; so that his picture of women's life and status should be placed beside
what we can infer from painting, sculpture, and various kinds of document-
ary material, and given its proper weight as evidence. We shall carry this
enquiry further in the special cases to be examined in Chapters 5 and 7,
where I hope it will appear how closely the theme of woman is related both
to the use of the ironic method and to the second of the poet's principal
themes, the war which began at the mid-point of his creative career.

5

HELEN

The first play for which Euripides chose a plot connected with the Trojan cycle of legends was *Telephus*, which he produced (with *Alcestis* and two other plays) in 438. A fragment surviving from *Telephus* (Fragment 721) gives us this remark, made by Agamemnon to Menelaus when the Trojan expedition was being contemplated:

You go wherever you like; I'm not going to get killed for your wife Helen.

The next was *Philoctetes*, produced in 431; it is not known whether this play contained any reference to Helen. After the Peloponnesian War began in 431 Euripides produced ten 'Trojan' plays, of which eight survive. The two that are lost were *Palamedes* and *Alexandros*; these were the first two plays in a set, produced in 415, of which the third was *The Women of Troy*. The action of *Alexandros* takes place before Paris's visit to Sparta, so it is unlikely that Helen was mentioned. She may well have been referred to in *Palamedes*, but no surviving fragment mentions her. The other nine extant plays, and all the other lost plays known to us, deal with events earlier than the Trojan War. Three of the extant 'Trojan' plays include Helen in the *dramatis personae*; in the other five she is spoken of about forty times, and all these references except two or three are similar in tone to the lines from *Telephus* quoted above − expressions of contempt, hatred, and condemnation.

In the 'Trojan' plays Helen is a figure whose dramatic significance has been seldom discussed, and I believe little understood. The approach to the study of Euripides which I have followed in this book leads to a coherent view of what the author intended by his presentation of Helen. The view here offered is new;[1] and whereas in some other controversial matters, such as the role of Apollo in *Ion*, I regard the ironic interpretation as being the more important of two possible views offered by the poet, in the matter of Helen I find it more difficult to see any way, consistent with respect for Euripides, of accepting the commonly held view as being of any value for even the least enlightened members of the original audiences, and still less for readers of today. The facts given above make it clear that in basing an argument on the eight extant 'Trojan' plays we can be fairly sure that we have before us eighty, perhaps ninety, per cent of the evidence for what Euripides meant in his references to Helen. We are in fact on firmer ground than we would be on almost any other important topic in the study of this author.

Before examining the relevant passages let us look briefly at Euripides' material; and for this, the only source of which we can be sure is Homer. In the *Iliad* more than half of the references to Helen are merely incidental; Paris is called 'the husband of Helen', or the question of 'giving back Helen to the Achaeans' is discussed, or Nestor or Menelaus speaks of her as 'the cause of all our toils and groans'. There are, however, several scenes in which she appears and speaks. The first two come just before, and just after, the duel between Paris and Menelaus in Book III. Then in Book VI we are shown a contrast between two married couples facing the strain of war — Paris and Helen, and Hector and Andromache. In the next fourteen books Helen's name is hardly heard; until at the end of Book XXIV we have her lament for Hector. This is not the place for a detailed consideration of all these passages, but it is possible to summarize them and state a conclusion.

First, it is clear that the picture of Helen, her marriage, and her situation in Troy, is in no way a simple one, but is drawn with much subtlety. Helen is no longer in love with Paris, though he still delights in her. She hates the thought of going to his bed, and her avoidance of him is known and approved by the Trojan women who are her companions. However, her intention to refuse her husband's love is angrily rebuked by Aphrodite, and overcome when Paris takes her by the hand. She thinks tenderly of Menelaus, and is moved to tears when she learns that a duel is arranged between him and Paris. A little later, in Book VI, she sits surrounded by ladies-in-waiting beside Paris in his bedroom. She is not reconciled to him, but tells Hector that Paris 'has no constant mind in him' (*Iliad* VI.352) — he is one day a hero, the next a shirker. The picture is one of marriage overlaid with all the complexity familiar at least to Europeans in every century; but here the painfulness is increased by Helen's peculiar situation in Troy. She is afraid of Trojan women's comments; she is the object of men's admiration; she is certainly chaste. She blames herself for the suffering caused by the war. Priam, however, does not hold her responsible for it; both he and Hector treat Helen with respect and affection, and understand that she has an unsatisfactory husband. To Priam she is always 'my dear daughter'. Finally, her lament for Hector, a most moving passage (XXIV.762–75), shows above all that 'her values are right'. Like so many women in that aggressive, honour-seeking, male world, she was stuck hopelessly in a miserable position; but affection and gratitude speak for the truth of her nature. In the *Odyssey*, Book IV, the picture given of Helen is pleasing but entirely formal, and adds nothing which we need take into account for the present enquiry.

When we turn from Euripides' source-material to look at the picture of Helen which readers from his day to ours have found in his work, the first thing that strikes us is the total lack of subtlety; the second, that her values appear to be all wrong. The Homeric portrait convinces because each feature is questioned or modified by some other, each quality has a living elusiveness; and the general effect suggests that 'temperament' of various tensions which makes a whole and complex character. In Euripides' plays (except *Helen*, which is a special case) the accepted picture is monotonously unpleasant — all alike regard her as a woman undesirable in every respect save one, shallow, vain, false, heartless, vulgar, lecherous. For characters of both sexes, and for choruses, she is a name to curse by. In addition to this, it is never disputed that she was the prime cause of the war and was justly blamed for all the wickedness and suffering which it entailed. What accounts for this difference? It is evident that the unpleasant image was the popular one; there is no record (Gorgias' monograph on Helen is merely an abstract exercise) of any complaint that Euripides was unfair to Helen. Did he, then, accept this view of her? If so, was he incapable of subtlety? Did he compose these refrains of hate and vituperation without any misgiving that they might seem tedious and vulgar to some listeners or readers? When his heroic characters, distracted, maddened, and corrupted by their war against Troy, insist that their crimes and follies are all the outcome of one woman's misdeed, forget the blood on their own hands, and call Helen 'murderess', what message was this meant to convey to his audience, distracted, maddened, and corrupted by their war against Sparta? In play after play this audience was invited by a wide variety of eloquent speakers — Peleus, Andromache, Hecabe, Orestes, Electra, Pylades, and three or four choruses — to join in laying the guilt of war's horrors on the head of one person long since dead, but living as a symbol of the ubiquitous menace of woman. Though there was no rational comfort in this, an invitation to hate and condemn can always arouse in a popular audience a momentary feeling that something has been said worthy of applause. Was Euripides that kind of writer? — for it must be remembered throughout this enquiry that the question is not, What sort of woman was Helen? but, What sort of dramatist was Euripides?

It is clear that between the time when the *Iliad* was written down and the fifth century B.C. popular tradition re-painted Homer's picture of Helen in vicious colours. Is the assumption that Euripides accepted and reproduced this popular tradition supported by his observed attitude in other cases? When we look through the list of well-known heroines who figure in his plays, we find that they fall into two groups, the famous and the infamous. In the first, we have Alcestis, who died for her husband, Alcmene the mother of Heracles, Andromache Hector's widow, Hecabe queen of Troy, the steadfast Electra, the innocent Iphigenia; each renowned for some act of courage or some special degree of virtue. What showing do they

make on Euripides' stage? The impression varies. Alcestis is admirable
enough, if somewhat cold. Andromache in *The Women of Troy* is innocent and
pathetic, but of no great stature; in *Andromache*, though innocent, she is
not weaponless — her cruel tongue can reduce Hermione to tears. Iphigenia
in one play is an understandably self-centred and embittered virgin in her
thirties, in the other a brave child of twelve or thirteen. Alcmene is a
bloodthirsty harridan. Hecabe, heroine of two plays, in each combines
two discordant characters — the tragic, captive queen, and the vicious,
vindictive hater. Electra in both her plays is a mentally disturbed woman
whom we may pity but never excuse. Euripides, in short, regards renowned heroines with a dispassionate and critical eye.

The second group is a shorter list. Many people felt they had reason
enough to hate Euripides because he presented on the stage Phaedra, the
lascivious young wife of Theseus who wanted to go to bed with her stepson,
and Medea, who because she was jealous of her husband's new marriage
killed her own two children to spite him. Phaedra in *Hippolytus* is not white-
washed; she does long for her stepson's love, and when she destroys herself
she does her best to destroy him too. Medea's crimes are not glossed over,
rather they are arrayed in a panoply of horror. Yet each of these women, as
Euripides presents her, wins from an audience a measure of both pity and
admiration, which are the stronger because there can be no thought of
excuse for their wickedness. Two other women in Euripides can be added
to this list; Clytemnestra, who murdered her husband, and Iocasta, who
married her son. Clytemnestra in *Iphigenia in Aulis* is a woman soured, and
perhaps excused, by an unhappy marriage, a lying husband, and a murdered
daughter; in *Electra* she appears, years after her crime, as a guilty, frightened,
lonely woman who has lost her old fire and grown fat and tired, but none the
less has to receive the sword-thrust from her son's hand. Iocasta in *The
Phoenician Women* is given the sole voice of reason and decency in a world
gone mad with war-fever. Yet, none of these four women *heads* the list
of legendary heroines traditionally scorned, condemned, and hated for
their misdeeds. That place unquestionably belongs to Helen, the daughter
of Zeus, whose adultery sent ten thousand Greeks to their death at Troy.
Let us ask, then, Is the poet's attitude to Helen anything like his attitude to
Medea or Phaedra or Iocasta? The question is far from being academic; if our
tradition has been wrong, important features of this poet's meaning and
method have gone unperceived.

We will look first at some of the passages on which the picture of Helen
accepted by both the ancient and the modern world has been based; re-
membering that Euripides mentions Helen's name a number of times in
every play in which it was chronologically possible: in *Andromache* ten
times, in *Hecabe* four, in *Electra* six, in *Iphigenia in Tauris* six, in *Iphigenia in*

Aulis a dozen times. Nearly all these references (a notable exception is *Iphigenia in Aulis* 582—6) name her in the most hostile terms as the prime cause of the Trojan War, guilty of all its sufferings because of her immoral behaviour.

In *Andromache* two not very subtle gibes are aimed at Helen (who has no part in this play) by Andromache when she defends herself against Hermione (229—31):

> Your mother Helen, my girl, was much too fond of men;
> Don't you try to outdo her. Look at your mother's bad
> Example, and avoid it, if you have any sense.

And later (247—8):

> HERMIONE: It is Troy Thetis hates. You Trojans killed her son.
> ANDROMACHE: Your mother killed him, not I. Helen killed Achilles.

These are scoring-points excusable in a woman at bay, threatened with death; Helen was the mother of Andromache's enemy. Later a full-scale attack on Helen is delivered by Peleus in a series of lurid passages — 'A wickeder woman never lived' (602—12, 619—23, 627—31); and in this scene Peleus firmly establishes himself as a buffoon, a brave, blustering old fool incapable of reason. In *Hecabe*, the chorus in the second stasimon call Helen 'the loveliest woman that ever lived', and in the third stasimon pray 'that she may never reach her father's house, but be drowned in the salt sea'; while Hecabe (265ff.) names her as the cause of Achilles' death and therefore a suitable victim to be slaughtered at his tomb. In the early part of *Electra* Helen is twice mentioned in condemnation by the chorus (213—4, 479—86), who in both passages bring in the topic quite irrelevantly; and in the latter passage, where these neighbourly housewives express a vivid desire to see Helen's throat cut, and 'her life pour forth in blood', it should be noted that these are the same women who later (1226), commenting on the murder of the other daughter of Tyndareos — the one who killed her husband — will say of Orestes' act of vengeance, 'Could any act be more dreadful?'[2] In the final episode Electra's hatred and Clytemnestra's guilt fairly balance each other, but the two murderesses are at one in their condemnation of Helen in three successive passages (1026—9, 1062—5, 1083—4). In *Iphigenia in Tauris* Iphigenia complains (354—8),

Yet Zeus never sent wind or ship to convey Helen, my destroyer, to this shore, that I might take due vengeance and make a second Aulis for atonement here;

and the chorus echo her soon after (438—46), wishing that Helen's throat might be cut by Iphigenia's hand, and the blood flow down over her hair;

while sister and brother, at last reunited, agree — twice — in their execration of Helen. Iphigenia forgets how fervently, at the beginning of the play (380—91), she condemned Artemis for demanding human blood. *Iphigenia in Aulis* shows a variety of approaches to this theme whose sordid monotony (which distressed few among the masses in the Dionysiac theatre) generations of scholars, in their reverence for the perfection of Greek tragedy, appear either not to have noticed or not to have found incredible. When Agamemnon is quarrelling with his brother, Helen is the handiest missile for barbed abuse (382—4); and Menelaus too, in his mock-repentance, endorses the popular view of his wife (488). There are six phrases uttered by various speakers referring responsibility for the war and its cruelties to Helen (467, 683, 1168—9, 1253—4, 1334—5, 1417—8); yet the action of the play clearly shows the death of Iphigenia as due to the moral delinquency of at least three of the adult characters, backed by two corrupt schemers and by the blood-lust of the mutinous rabble they call their army; while even the Aeschylean excuse of a north-east gale is specifically erased from the story (10—11, 813). The chorus, however, refer to the love of Paris and Helen in touching and romantic terms free of any censure, making the viciousness of others the more noticeable. We may observe, too, that this is a chorus which in all three stasima shows itself morally serious and perceptive, and undergoes no change of character like that of the chorus in *Orestes*.

Again we must remember that the important question is, What sort of writer was Euripides? These passages, at the least, show a special kind of interest in Helen which needs to be explained; and when we add to them the expressions of murderous venom which we have already found in *Orestes*, and which we shall find again in *The Women of Troy*, it should be evident that we are confronted here with a fact of some significance in the later half of Euripides' life's work. Why did he write these passages in play after play? Was he concerned to remind his hearers of the disastrous consequences of adultery? Did he commend these censorious attitudes and bloodthirsty aspirations? Can we close the question by remarking that it was a very different world from our own? Or should we seek an answer in the opposite direction, and see these vicious speakers as condemning themselves by their words? The part of Peleus in *Andromache* could perhaps never be tedious; but the Athenian audience must surely have been divided between the many who enjoyed Peleus because they agreed with every fatuous word he spoke, and the few who enjoyed him as a caricature of their less intelligent fellow-citizens. Many whose image of Electra had been settled by Aeschylus and Sophocles would listen to her reviling of Helen in *Orestes* carelessly unaware that this Electra was a different person; a few would examine the significance of her change of character. When anonymous innocents like the chorus in *Iphigenia in Tauris* echo the vindictive hatred voiced by their superiors, an

average audience will follow them uncritically. The whole of Euripides' work
tells us that he regarded vindictive hatred as the most pernicious of common
faults. It is also clear both from his plays and from the history of the period
that this fault must have appeared to him almost universal, perhaps
invincible, certainly ineradicable; then, as now, a fault defiantly clung to
and justified in the name of morality by most of his fellow-citizens, and
therefore one which could not be openly attacked without inviting contradiction. To invite contradiction is not the best way to persuade; so the poet
holds up his ironic mirror, and offers no judgement other than what we can
infer from the moral or dramatic status of the person who speaks the ironic
lines.

For those who find it hard to believe that so vital a point in Euripides'
meaning was missed during his lifetime by most of his admirers, and after
his death by readers and critics, it may be instructive to look at Aeschylus'
treatment, forty years earlier, of the theme of *hybris*. Here it is generally
accepted that we now perceive what was missed then. In *Agamemnon*, after
the prologue, the chorus enter and describe their memory of the day when the
Argive army set out for Aulis. They speak of the two kings as being sent on
their vengeful mission by Zeus himself — doubtless the view held by
Agamemnon and his brother. They recount the long days of waiting for the
north-east wind to abate, the dwindling stores, the rotting hulks, the dis-
contented army. The question which the kings asked Calchas is not given,
but it can be inferred from the answer (198ff.): they asked, How can we
induce the gods to change the wind? It did not occur to them to reason that,
if gods could change the wind, the north-east gale indicated divine disapproval of the expedition, and therefore the question was impious. The
answer given was a suitable answer to impiety. The monstrous *hybris* of
annihilating Troy is prefigured in the ritual murder of Iphigenia, just as it
is echoed later by the *hybris* of walking on purple from the chariot to the
palace door. The connexion in thought is made clear by Calchas' reading of
the portent of the pregnant hare torn by two eagles. It is no less clear that
this straightforward interpretation of Aeschylus was missed by most ancient
critics. Even in recent years it has sometimes been assumed that in Aeschylus'
view Agamemnon was right at least to consider seriously the command of
Calchas to sacrifice Iphigenia, instead of recognizing it as a diabolical reply
ad hominem — a menacing challenge to a stubborn king who had asked the
wrong question. Euripides' thought is a close successor to the thought of
Aeschylus; and his handling of the Helen-myth suggests that he may have
been aware of both these points — the nature of Agamemnon's question and
the nature of Calchas' reply.

This is not to suppose that either Aeschylus or Euripides thought of Helen
as innocent. Helen was guilty — of infidelity to Menelaus. Menelaus was

guilty — of the war and all its cruelty and bloodshed. Greeks over the next six centuries smoothly omitted the middle term and found it economical and satisfying to say simply, Helen was guilty of the war. Why did this sleight-of-tongue become so universal and so popular? It is not indignation that demands a scapegoat, but guilt. Euripides knew that you cannot argue people into recognizing their own guilt. He tried to help them to make the discovery for themselves, in two ways: first, by showing on the stage this habit of condemnation and hatred in all its absurdity, tediousness, and malice, as we see it in Peleus, in Electra, in some of the choruses; secondly, by placing Helen's misdeed side by side with the misdeeds of others, both men and women, who made her their excuse. Menelaus massacred a nation to appease his injured pride; Agamemnon, Clytemnestra, Electra, all murdered members of their own family; in *The Women of Troy* we have Hecabe, who has on this occasion no power to commit murder herself, begging Menelaus to commit a murder in no way different from those committed by Clytemnestra and Electra, except that the fault it was supposed to avenge was not murder, but adultery.

There, of course, was the rub. Every myth, every tradition, made adultery a less polluting crime than murder; but who dared proclaim this openly before a national audience? A dramatist could ask for a measure of sympathy for Medea or even for Phaedra, whose desire was never fulfilled; and though he would of course provoke an outcry, he would still be able to put on another play next year. But to claim sympathy for a successful adulteress is less in the region of bold theorizing; it may belong to comedy, but it is too near the bone for tragedy. The line of defence which Euripides gives to Helen in *The Women of Troy* is stated by her twice (946–50, 1042–3): 'I was in love, and went willingly with Paris. Aphrodite is irresistible. Forgive me.' Her case is stronger than either Medea's or Phaedra's; they both found passion irresistible, but allowed it to lead them towards murder. Love did not lead Helen that way; it led her to fidelity till death — for the abuse heaped on her never included any hint that she was unfaithful to Paris. Agamemnon and Menelaus could have justified themselves by saying that it was Ares who made them bloodthirsty, revengeful, and unscrupulous; but they do not name him, for he is the god whom other gods abhor. Helen names Aphrodite. Gods and men alike fear laughter-loving Aphrodite, but they do not abhor her. They reverence and prize her as the central, indispensable power of — to use Shakespeare's phrase — 'great creating Nature'. Aeschylus had celebrated her invincible divinity in the famous fragment from *Danaides*; Sophocles in the third stasimon of *Antigone*; this was no new theme, but an acknowledged truth. Helen, who obeyed this divinity, makes only one plea, for pardon; a plea rejected in the modern as in the ancient world.

It should now become clear that, if we are to impute to Euripides the

ironic intention which I believe underlies all his references to Helen, we
must ask the question, What did he himself think of the act which was
the ostensible reason for such general condemnation, namely her adultery?
The question is neither irrelevant to the present study, nor unscholarly to
ask, nor impossible to answer. The only reason why it is seldom posed is that
one particular answer is usually assumed. Euripides' plays have nearly
always been interpreted on the assumption that about this matter he shared
the view of his contemporaries. This is in itself unlikely, since he disagreed
with them in so much else. It is important for the modern critic to remember
that the reason why Euripides' contemporaries disapproved of adultery was
not the same as the reason why modern citizens, or Christians, or sociologists,
diaspprove. It was neither religion nor — except superficially — sentiment, but
self-interest. Athenians recognized, as we do, the beauty of womanly fidelity;
but the argument of Chapter 4 has made it clear that it was admired less as a
moral quality of the woman than as a fortunate asset of the husband (see
Pheres' remark, *Alcestis* 627–8, and Chapter 4, page 104). We may feel
touched on hearing young women pray, like the girls from Chalcis (*Iphigenia
in Aulis* 555) that their desires may be lawful, *pothoi hosioi*; but we should
remember the male ferocity earned by any other course — a ferocity shown
unchanged in a modern story such as Kazantzakis' *Zorba the Greek*. But the
poet who composed Medea's protest against the 'double standard' (*Medea*
244–7; see also 410–30), and put into lyric verse the indignation of Creusa's
slaves (*Ion* 1090–1105), was not a man for whom the mere word 'adultery'
was a sufficient condemnation of any woman. His lifelong insistence that
men and women should be judged by equal standards is expressed, with an
exquisite irony derived from the play's context, in the same chorus from
Iphigenia in Aulis:

> The quest of virtue is a wonderful thing;
> Whether in women, to avoid unchastity,
> Or in men, whose manifold devotion to discipline
> Exalts a city to greatness.

To conclude: we have little chance of understanding what Euripides meant
by his treatment of Helen unless we reject the notion that he himself regarded
her leaving of Menelaus as the act of a whore, and recognize that his presentation of the story is everywhere impartial. The simple fact about Helen,
as he shows her, is that it did not occur to her to accept as final the rules men
had laid down for marriage. Her sister Clytemnestra was a conscious rebel;
she chose violence and reaped punishment. Helen was not a rebel, but a
natural woman; she loved Paris, left Menelaus, and reaped years of suffering.
Generations of Hellenes recognized that Clytemnestra's rebellion had failed;

they condemned her as a murderess. They knew that Helen's gentle non-acceptance had defeated them, and feeling powerless against beauty and spontaneous confidence they decided that Helen, no less than her mannish sister, must be labelled murderess; and knowing that this was illogical nonsense they repeated it loudly and frequently. This is the posture which Euripides holds up for ironic comment by those capable of looking in his mirror. There is no record that anyone in the fifth or fourth century perceived the poet's mockery; it was too gentle. Had it been less gentle, how long would the male board of selectors have continued to accept the plays he submitted each year for the Dionysiac Festival?

We have now looked at the most important references to Helen in the five plays in which she is not a *dramatis persona*; we must look next at the plays where Helen herself is presented. The treatment of her in *Orestes* has been fully described in Chapter 3; and there it was necessary to anticipate part of the present argument. We proceed now to *The Women of Troy*. To describe the part assigned here to Helen will entail an exegesis of the whole play, since in successive scenes Hecabe, the chorus, Cassandra, and Andromache all take her for their theme, until Menelaus arrives to present her in person to the audience. It is, moreover, probably true to say that the concept of Helen prevalent in today's world of literature, and in current classical scholarship, is derived more from this play, and from its central scene, than from any other source.

Helen is first named by Poseidon in the prologue (34–5). The Greeks, he says, justly reckoned her as a war-captive; and she is now with the Trojan women who are awaiting allocation to the various chiefs. When Hecabe rises from the dust and speaks, she names 'hated Helen' as the cause of the war (132), and says that Helen 'cut the throat of' (*sphazei*) Priam. When the chorus enter a few lines later, we know that they have left Helen inside the building from which they appear; and before long they too speak of 'hated Helen' (211). Then Cassandra enters; and when her frenzied dance has given place to reasoned speech, we again hear Helen's name spoken, but not with hate or condemnation. Cassandra states – what no one denied – that Paris's marriage with the daughter of Zeus was for him at once a glory (398–9) and a disaster (357); and further, that Helen eloped with Paris willingly –which Helen herself will freely admit (946). Cassandra does not speak one word in censure of Helen. The war, she says, was caused by the folly of the Hellenes and of Agamemnon (368ff.):

They, for the sake of one woman and one love-affair, went in pursuit of Helen and destroyed ten thousand lives; their sage commander, to win what he most hated, lost what most he cherished – sacrificed his daughter, the joy of his home – for the sake of a woman who was not abducted by force, but went willingly.

In her last line before leaving the stage Cassandra repeats that the war was caused, and the House of Priam destroyed, not by Helen but by the sons of Atreus. The one person in this play who neither hates nor condemns Helen is the prophetess whose word was never believed, and always true.

The second episode belongs to Andromache. She comes 'drawn in a Greek chariot, beating her breast; and Hector's son Astyanax is with her . . . and beside her Hector's sword and armour of bronze, and other spoils of Troy . . .' (569—74). When her lament, shared with Hecabe, calms itself from cries of despair to coherent speech, her first sentence finds the cause of her suffering in the fact that Paris was not killed in infancy, but lived to destroy his country 'for the sake of his hateful marriage'. This is a double irony. First, the real cause of disaster, correctly identified by Cassandra, is illogically rejected by Andromache as by everyone else, in favour of a remote cause. Secondly, later in the scene her own infant will be taken away to be killed, ostensibly to prevent future wars. (Exactly the same irony is found in *Andromache*, where the chorus, who in 293ff. wish that Paris had been killed at birth, in 491 exclaim in horror at Menelaus' proposal to kill the child Molossus.)

Then Talthybius announces that Astyanax is to be thrown from the battlements; the sentence had been proposed and urged by Odysseus, and agreed to by all the other chiefs. Andromache curses Odysseus in one line (724):

> By a like sentence may his own son be condemned!

She accuses the other chiefs in two lines (764—5):

> Hellenes! Inventors of barbaric cruelty!
> What has he done? Why will you kill this child?

Then the distracted mother devotes eight lines, the heart and weight of her curse, to Helen:

> Tyndareos' daughter! You were never got by Zeus!
> You had many fathers; the Avenging Curse was one,
> Hate was the next, then Murder, Death, and every plague
> That this earth breeds! I'll swear Zeus never fathered you
> To fasten death on tens of thousands east and west.
> My curse on you! The beauty of your glance has brought
> This rich and noble country to a shameful end.

When she is silent, the chorus yet again ascribe all this wickedness and suffering to 'one woman and her accursed love'.

Then Menelaus comes, saying that the Greeks have handed over Helen to him, to kill or not to kill (874ff.):

> And I've decided not to carry out sentence here
> But take her back to Hellas, and there see that she
> Pays with her blood for all my friends who died at Troy.
> (*To the soldiers*) What are you waiting for? Get in and fetch her here,
> Drag her out by the hair — bloodthirsty murderess!

In the scene that is to follow, Menelaus and Hecabe will find themselves
allies, with a common enemy; Menalaus has already stated his purpose —
to kill Helen; and Hecabe will do all she can to ensure that he carries it out
(890ff.):

> I applaud you, Menelaus, if you will kill your wife;
> But avoid seeing her, or she will take prisoner
> Your tender heart. She captures men's eyes, destroys cities,
> Burns houses to the ground, so potent are her spells.

A few lines later she will add that Helen is to be punished not only for leaving
Menelaus and causing the war but for 'the mischief that she made in Troy' —
the irrelevance of which no one comments on:

> The whole indictment, once complete,
> Will ensure her death; there can be no chance of escape.

Menelaus is not impressive, but Hecabe is. The poetic solemnity of her prayer
(884—8; this will be studied below, page 144) wins attention and respect both
from Menelaus and from the audience. When she explains her meaning —
that she wants Helen killed, this is consonant with Menelaus' already
expressed wish. If there are some in the audience to whom this seems a crude
debasement of the solemn prayer, they are given no chance to pursue so
uncomfortable a thought; for Helen herself enters immediately, to face this
grotesque alliance of destroyer with victim, and to learn that sentence of
death is already passed. Before we study the ensuing speeches, we should
look at this scene as a whole and at its part and place in the drama, and
ask whether it is artistically satisfying, dramatically effective, and consistent
with what we know of the author.

The usual interpretation holds that Helen, by her appearance, manner,
and words, shows herself a shallow and worthless person; that the audience
is left to reflect on the infinite agony of a war whose achieved purpose is to
restore an immoral wife to a brutal and stupid husband. The atmosphere of
cruelty and anguish pervading the stage has steadily intensified and reached
its peak with the exit of Talthybius and his prisoners. When Menelaus
enters after the second stasimon, cheerfully saluting the splendour of the sun,
the change in tone is startling; the audience realizes that it has witnessed
as much sordid misery as it can bear for the present, and feels that some

dramatic surprise is due, that some new aspect on the tragedy will now be revealed. If the traditional view of this scene is upheld, such expectation is disappointed. Helen is the dull and nasty creature everyone has spoken of; no deeper insight into guilt and responsibility, into the significance of Aphrodite or the myth of the Judgement, is offered us; the set speeches are what we thought they would be, so is the result of the 'trial'. There is no real choice or decision; nothing whatever happens. When Menelaus and Helen have gone, and the chorus has pictured the daughter of Zeus gazing in her golden mirror, and prayed that she may never reach home, and Talthybius returns to lay before Hecabe Hector's son dead on Hector's shield — then actors and audience together re-enter the gloom with jaded senses and unrefreshed. The imaginative experience of the whole drama had after all no rise and decline, no contrast, no architecture, no illumination; its focus was a dead fire. The emotions have been racked, but remain unpurged for want of a vision. The condemnation of cruelty wins the spectator's tired assent but leaves him with no new thought to ponder. For those who demanded from a tragic poet something more than a passion torn to tatters, the satyr-play *Sisyphus* which followed this tragedy must have been unusually welcome.

Is the accepted view of this scene consistent with our knowledge of the author? We have already noted (page 130) that Euripides' habit is to look at a familiar and condemned figure from a new angle, and to take an intimately personal view of a human situation. In *The Women of Troy* tradition insists that his picture of Helen is exactly what everyone expected it to be, a formal and superficial image of a standard bad woman. If there is one ethical opinion which can be ascribed to Euripides without dispute, it is that he regarded vengefulness with abhorrence and reprisal as a crime, pardon as an act of virtue. In this scene two women kneel before the vengeful Menelaus, one begging for blood, the other for pardon. The argument could be extended, but enough has been said to show that the usual view of this scene is far from satisfying, that time spent in seeking a better interpretation will not be wasted.

Menelaus in his opening speech three times refers to his intention to kill Helen; she has reason to know that she is hated (898), but she keeps her nerve. She is rational enough to know she is dealing with the irrational, both in Menelaus' anger and in her own experience. She must say much in a short time; but she must say it for her own, and her author's, satisfaction, since no one on the stage, and few in the audience, will understand or listen. As soon as she begins it would be clear to many Athenians that this 'trial' which Menelaus conducts is (like a Black Mass) a reversal of a sanctioned and familiar ritual: sentence is already pronounced, the accused speaks without hearing the charge, the prosecutor accuses without fear of reply. In such a travesty of *dikē*, who is on trial? No one is there to ask that question; Helen stands alone not only against characters and chorus on stage but against Athens and the world. She must speak, then, to the few, if any, either in that audience or in the audience of the future which Hecabe imagines in 1244–5 – 'to give songs to poets of a later age' – the few who judge justly though Zeus has vanished (1060ff.), who know that truth is more subtle than simple, and have not learnt to be afraid of beauty.

The man standing before her as judge holds her guilty of the war. Helen has for ten years listened to this accusation and knows that logic cannot defeat hatred. She speaks *ad hominem*, using contemptuously an exaggeration of the argument he holds as valid against her (919–22):

> Hecabe here produced the first cause of our troubles
> When she bore Paris. Secondly, this city, and I,
> Were doomed by Priam,[3] when he ignored the warning given
> By a dream of firebrands, and refused to kill his child.

This evidently carries an allusion to the prologue of *Alexandros*, which told the story of Hecabe's dream; but it is hard to see how anything in that play could mitigate the foolishness of such an argument, unless it is intended as a mockery of the inveterate Greek habit of finding remote and still remoter causes to ease the guilt of those responsible for a crime. Of course Helen's action made her in part a cause of the war, and in the *Iliad* she is bitterly conscious of this; but popular opinion in fifth-century Greece – as is clear from the passages we have noted in this chapter – complacently made her the author of every crime that accompanied the war, from the murder of Iphigenia to the murder of Astyanax, and the others that followed. Confusion of *post quod* with *propter quod* can be an illogical comfort to conscience.

That Euripides' interest in this fallacy was recognized in the ancient world is shown by two later writers, Cicero (about 46 B.C.) and Clement of Alexandria (about A.D. 200), in passages discussing the theory of cause.[4] Cicero says that we should take the 'cause' of an action to mean not simply that which precedes it but that which makes it happen. We should not say that Hecabe 'caused' the destruction of Troy because she bore Paris (a reference to Helen's words in this scene), nor that Tyndareos 'caused' Agamemnon's death because he begot Clytemnestra (a reference to *Orestes* 585–7). It is equally foolish, he continues, to say (here he quotes from Ennius' adaptation of *Medea*), 'Would that pine-trees had never been felled on Mount Pelion' (see *Medea* 3–5), since it was not this that caused Medea to fall in love with Jason. Clement too refers in detail to these lines from the opening of *Medea*, with similar comments. Passages such as these from Euripides illustrate the way many people respond to catastrophe by going back in imagination to an earlier moment and searching for some other possible turn of events which

could have led to a different result. This searching is natural at a time of
anguish; but it may also be foolish and pernicious. It may be foolish because,
as Cicero says, you might just as well wish there were no such mountain as
Pelion; and it may be pernicious because in fact it will often happen that one
of the supposed causes is a person still living, against whom all our anger will
be directed. Medea's Nurse does not curse the woodman who felled the pine;
but in Euripides' plays Helen is repeatedly cursed by both men and women
(e.g. *Hecabe* 943–9, *Orestes,* 1116). So, when Helen blames Hecabe and Priam,
her words are an ironic *reductio ad absurdum* of the same argument applied
to herself. A similar instance appears in *Andromache* 293–300, though there
the irony is the author's, not the speaker's. In such passages Euripides shows
how the precise interest of an intellectual theory, and the helpless anguish
of a human being, both contribute to that Greek propensity for fixing the
blame on some convenient scapegoat, which demonstrated itself in innumerable cruelties throughout Greek history and, as Thucydides observed, reached
a new level of atrocity in the Peloponnesian War.

Helen's first argument, then, is either the kind of silliness which ceases to
be interesting, or it is irony of a kind which will elude Menelaus and Hecabe,
but presents itself for our interpretation. Her second argument offers the
Judgement of Paris as a factual account of events leading to her elopement
from Sparta (923–34):

What happened after that? Listen – this is how the story goes. This Paris was judge
of the three goddesses. Pallas's bribe to him was that he should destroy Hellas at the
head of a Phrygian army; Hera promised that he should rule over all Europe and
Asia. Aphrodite spoke extravagantly of my beauty and promised to give me to him
if she won the prize. After that – see how the story goes: Aphrodite defeated the
other goddesses; and my marriage with Paris brought Hellas this benefit, that you
are not now ruled by barbarians, not conquered in battle, not oppressed by tyranny.

To exhibit this naïve acceptance (if that is what it is) of such a myth in the
presence of the coarse and earthy Menelaus and the realistic physical and
mental suffering that has been presented on stage, carries ineptitude several
tedious steps further – unless here too we should look for a second meaning
below the surface. *Alexandros* may well have supplied a clue; but even without that play we can ask a question too seldom asked: What was the meaning
of this most famous of all myths? What was the story of the Judgement of
Paris about? I suggest that it was about that elusive quality, greatness; that
the man who rejected the gifts of Hera and Athena was a man born with
potential qualities to make Priam and Agamemnon look small, but without
the desire to use them. Choosing instead the pursuit of beauty, he lived liked
and patronized but not greatly honoured and still less understood in a world
darkened by the shadows of Hector and Achilles, men who had embraced the

gifts of Hera and Athena; mocking both himself and his warlike brothers, taking nothing seriously, and dying before his time; a man 'of inconstant mind' (*Iliad* VI.352). The fragments of *Alexandros* are consonant with such an interpretation; they show the adolescent Paris presented as an unknown shepherd-slave who proved invincible as an athlete, defeating Hector and Deiphobus. The overtones of such a story include many thoughts: that greatness is unpredictable; that great men and great passions kindle wars, change dynasties; that no one can ever tell what different results would have followed different decisions, or learn from one error how to avoid the next, or how to apportion gratitude and blame; that history cannot be changed, and justice is relevant only to future action, never to the past.

The extreme compression of this early part of the speech, 919—37, conveys a reserved refusal to explain anything. Helen cannot have expected her judge or her accuser either to accept this story as a factual account or to light on any understanding of its symbolism. She is speaking to an angry and mediocre man about a man far superior to him. Her lines 936—7, 'I am reviled for my beauty, for which I should have been crowned', unite her with her one-time lover, who in *Alexandros* (Fragment 59), finding his life threatened, says, 'I shall be killed for my sense of honour, which for other men is their salvation.' Helen's repeated phrase, *hōs echei*, 'how it is', or 'how the story goes' (923,931), used in preference to 'how it happened', also suggests that what she is talking about is not so much past fact as current fable, which to her hearers means something different from its meaning for her.

The next part of her speech, 938—50, recalls another experience which eludes explanation in banal statements: her helplessness under the spell of a passion which a few years later had evaporated — a memory which still seems to her more real than anything that has happened since, and which can only be spoken of in supernatural terms. Since her accusers look for causes, she will do the same: if Menelaus had not chosen the moment of Paris's visit to sail off to Crete leaving the pair of them alone, all the agony would have been avoided. She has as much right to call him 'most wicked', *Ō kakiste* (943), as he has to blame her.

It is often said that in this scene Helen evades responsibility for her own action by shifting it on to the goddess (948, 1042). Hecabe certainly regards Helen's reference to Aphrodite as mere self-excuse. (Modern editors usually put the same interpretation on Helen's statement in *Orestes* 79 that she eloped from Sparta *theomanei potmōi*, 'by a destiny of god-sent madness'.) All through Homer we find actions or decisions of mortals ascribed to an impulse imparted by a god. Doubtless belief in this degree of divine agency was often used as an excuse for misdoing, and it is not surprising that the indignant Hecabe uses this weapon against Helen. But it was not a valid weapon. In the *Iliad* Agamemnon was blinded by Zeus and Moira and Erinys so that he robbed Achilles of his prize (*Iliad* XIX.87—8); but when he saw the results of his folly he accepted responsibility and offered extravagant recompense (*ibid.* 137—8). Aeschylus in *Agamemnon* 218—25 crowds into two sentences words emphasizing both sides of the timeless dilemma: there was 'Necessity'; but Agamemnon himself 'put on its bridle'. In *Hippolytus* Phaedra analyses with painful scrupulousness her own situation: Aphrodite is irresistible, yet Phaedra knows herself responsible for her actions. So in this scene of *The Women of Troy* it is clear that Hecabe's view is crude, and will seem convincing to the large proportion of the audience whose stereotyped reaction to Helen is equally crude; but Helen herself, like Phaedra, has reflected scrupulously. She says her elopement was prompted by a powerful goddess, Aphrodite; but the words she uses in 945—50 show that she no more denies responsibility than Agamemnon did when he offered compensation to Achilles. Her act was a decision of her own mind, her *phrenes*:

My next question I put not to you but to myself. What happened in my heart to make me (*ti dē phronousa*) leave my home . . .? Punish the goddess . . . but me you should forgive.

Since there is no compensation she can offer, Helen asks Menelaus to pardon her, both here and in 1043; and it is clear from Menelaus' line to which she is replying ('so that you may learn not to put me to shame', 1041) that she asks pardon for leaving him, not for causing the war. However, unlike Agamemnon, though she asks for pardon, she does not say that her act was either foolish or wrong. Why not? In the *Iliad*, as Euripides certainly knew, Helen expresses bitter regret for having eloped with Paris. But now, in this play, Paris has been dead for a year, and Troy is dead too; Helen sees all the past ecstasy and misery in perspective; and she knows that on the day when she obeyed Aphrodite there was nothing else to do. Besides, she keeps her pride before Menelaus. She neither evades responsibility nor pretends that she had any alternative.

Then why is her speech so veiled, so elusive, so easily misconstrued? Because this is the central scene, the apex of the play, and what she says will be remembered. Let us look back again at what Medea, sixteen years earlier, said in her first speech, before the action had begun (see above, pages 108—9): 'Men choose their wives, and when they are tired of them find other women. A woman can neither choose nor reject the possessor of her body. We are the most wretched of all creatures; if marriage is unhappy, death is better.' Helen had claimed what men regarded as solely theirs, the freedom to choose and to reject. To be explicit, she would have said, 'I had the right to leave the husband I accepted under duress, for the man I loved; and if you chose to make my action your excuse for a ten years' war, that was your doing, not mine.' If the Helen whom Euripides conceived — a character developed from the Homeric model — found such explicitness beneath her dignity and inconsistent with her view of herself, if she knew that profound truth never wins conviction by argument but either is perceived or is not perceived: are we prepared to disagree with her? Her claim is consonant with the whole tenor of Euripides' view of woman as one equal half of the human race; but since in Euripides' day this claim was entirely unacceptable, we should not be surprised that a dramatist preferred to leave it implicit in a play performed at a national festival.

After Helen's speech the chorus in three lines urge Hecabe to 'come to the help of her children and her country, and demolish Helen's persuasiveness'. It is usual for commentators to tell their readers (e.g. Kitto, *Greek Tragedy* 213) that Hecabe in her reply does exactly this. It is not to be disputed that Hecabe has suffered immeasurably and that her resentment is natural. But the standard interpretation of her speech goes further than this and insists on seeing the whole situation exclusively through Hecabe's eyes. Let us scrutinize the portrait of her which the author has given us up to this point, and try to see it in perspective.

She is commonly described as a figure of sublime tragic dignity. In fact a perusal of all her words discovers hardly a single sentence to lift the hearer's thoughts above the immediate agony, the obvious pathos, to show the fact of cruelty or pain in a cosmic setting, or to identify the solemn essence of tragedy. Hecabe compares the misery of Troy with past glories, her own fate with her once royal fortune. When told of her assignment to Odysseus she utters a lament longer and more passionate than for others whose fate is similar. To Andromache's total despair she replies that 'while there's life there's hope', and urges her to forget Hector and reconcile herself to Neoptolemus. Hecabe speaks of the gods only to say that they are 'treacherous allies' (469) and that to call upon them is a mere convention (*echei ti schēma*), or to accuse them vaguely as authors of her sufferings. Not until Menelaus arrives, announcing his intention to kill Helen as an act of revenge, is Hecabe at last inspired to a serious and poetic utterance addressed to Zeus, and equating bloody reprisal with justice (884—8):

> O thou, this earth's upholder, throned above the earth,
> Great Zeus, whoever thou art, mysterious and unknown,
> Be thou human intelligence, or natural law,
> I praise thee! For thou movest on a noiseless path
> And guidest all the affairs of men to their just end.

There is in her whole behaviour an entirely excusable, but undeniable, self-absorption (we may contrast the pure selflessness of Polyxena in *Hecabe* 197ff.), which does not belong to sublime tragic dignity.

A further point of curious significance must be noted. This play was produced as the third of a set of three, of which the first was *Alexandros*. A papyrus first published in 1922[5] gives part of a scene from that play in which it is clear, despite the incomplete state of the text, that Hecabe and her son Deiphobus plot together to kill the unknown youth who has defeated the royal princes at athletics. The three plays may not be strictly a trilogy; but the first play shows Hecabe as a queen at the zenith of her prosperity, driven by jealousy to murder; and when in the third play we see the same Hecabe pleading that Helen be killed, it is reasonable to enquire whether our text suggests the same motive.

Hecabe's accusing speech begins with ridicule of the naïve story of the Judgement of Paris. I have already argued that, if we are to suppose Helen intended her reference to the story to be taken literally and factually, then the author is presenting us with a degree of silliness which, in this context, ceases to be interesting. Hecabe devotes twelve lines to knocking down this Aunt Sally; she dismisses the idea that Hera would 'bargain away Argos to barbarians, or Athena see her Athens subjected to Troy'. But in fact Athena herself in the prologue has planned with Poseidon to destroy the Greeks by thousands, out of personal pique. Thus Hecabe's first argument is shown to be based on error. She then turns her ridicule to Helen's statement that Aphrodite came in invincible power with Paris to Sparta; this too Hecabe affects to treat as a factual description of events. It is unlikely that many in the audience would take it in this sense; but anything is good enough to score a point against Helen. Hecabe answers Helen's question, What happened in my heart . . .? (946) with a timeless popular cynicism (989—90): 'Men call every foolish lust Aphrodite.'[6] Let us grant to Hecabe, for the sake of argument, that in every country in every age most unions are based partly on vanity and lust; but must a tragic poet be a cynic? Between the Phrygian prince who declined government and conquest, and the world-renowned daughter of Zeus, was love not to be admitted? It has been resolved almost universally, and without critical reason, that (however we interpret Homer) Euripides identified his judgement in this matter with the bitter and jealous Hecabe, the desperate Andromache (in both her plays), the buffoon Peleus, the resentful Iphigenia (in *Iphigenia in Tauris*), the morbid Electra, the insane Orestes, and the captive choruses in *Hecabe*, *The Women of Troy*, and *Iphigenia in Tauris*. For readers to assume, as these characters do, that according to the mind of the dramatist Helen in leaving Menelaus was moved by mere vanity and lust, is to prejudge the whole nature and value of a major writer's work. When Phaedra loves Hippolytus rather than her husband, both the chorus and the Nurse speak of love as something beautiful, mysterious, dangerous. It was not they who called Phaedra a whore, but the cultured Aristophanes, to please his groundlings; even Theseus in the last scene speaks no word to condemn her. Euripides' lyrical descriptions of love (e.g. *Hippolytus* 525ff.,

Medea 627ff.) include fear of its results with reverence for its sweetness and truth. The possibility that Aphrodite in her most profound, tender, and glorious aspect may have been absent from the marriage of Helen with Menelaus, and present in her encounter with Paris, is not one that we would expect Helen to talk about in this scene; but it is as firmly ruled out by commentators on Euripides' plays as it would be if they were appearing for Menelaus in a divorce-court. It has yet to be shown that the poet ruled out such a possibility. In his last play he allowed his chorus (*Iphigenia in Aulis* 582—6) to picture Paris arriving in Sparta

> To stand before a palace of ivory
> And pour your love in Helen's gazing eyes
> And be love-shattered in return.

Like Menelaus, Hecabe ignores Helen's confession, implied by her question in 946 and confirmed by her plea for pardon, that she went with Paris willingly; she asserts (998):

> Well now, you say my son abducted you by force,

and sarcastically refutes what Helen did not say. Hecabe makes this false statement either deliberately or because she did not listen to Helen's defence. It was Deiphobus, not Paris, who took Helen by force, as Helen tells us in 959—60 (from *Alexandros* we already know Deiphobus as an unsavoury character). Wilamowitz, being sure that Hecabe could speak only the truth, deleted these two lines as spurious; and other scholars have followed him. There is no reason whatever to suspect their genuineness; what they show us is that yet another of Hecabe's rhetorical arguments is false. Hecabe follows her statement with an irrelevance equally inadmissible: 'When you heard of a Greek victory, you would praise Menelaus, to gall Paris's heart; when Troy gained ground, Menelaus was nowhere.' This, following on 996—7 ('Menelaus' palace was too confined a sphere for your luxurious insolence'), is designed to sharpen Menelaus' anger against Helen. To compass the death of the woman she hates, Hecabe will resort to any flattery of the man who has destroyed her home, family, and city (1023): 'You have the impudence to lift your eyes to the same sky as your husband!' The final exchanges between this preposterous pair of allies in inhumanity present a bitter edge of irony which has — inexplicably — been seldom noticed. The fact that the chorus here range themselves entirely on one side of the *agon* indicates that the author did not expect more than a very few of his audience to see the perverseness of his tableau.

All this, it will be said, is imaginative interpretation. I hope it is; irony by its nature can appeal only to the imagination. And what is the alternative?

It is banality, the death of imagination; a view which makes this central scene of *The Women of Troy* a moral vacuum occurring at the apex of a deeply moral play, and robs the focal figure, Helen, of all interest. The accepted view of this scene, moreover, carries with it a view of all Euripides' references to Helen, in the five plays where she is not a character, which ought to make us question whether Euripides has, after all, any subtlety in dealing with a human situation, any conception of a moral issue as part of a dramatic pattern, any universal or timeless message at all. Yet further, unless we perceive the horrifying change which comes over Hecabe when the presence of Helen gives a tongue to her jealousy, we miss not only the truth of this scene, but the power of the scene which follows. When Hecabe kneels beside the murdered child, the sublimity of mourning rises at last above the self-centredness of the earlier scenes; it not only restores Hecabe to her former dramatic authority, but transcends both her anguish and her wickedness. This is the true essence of tragedy. I would say that the right way to study this play is, on the evidence of all the other plays, to reject out of hand the usual view together with all the dubious assumptions on which it is based; and to look again, with minds as unbiased as we can make them, at the text itself, on the more rational assumption that the author was a great artist and a wise man; and that when he made his meaning obscure he knew what he was doing, and knew why he chose to challenge our imagination rather than encourage our prejudice.

In the end, then, we have to accept that the poet refuses to tell his audience plainly what sort of woman his Helen is, apart from the fact, attested by Hecabe, that she has in full measure the beauty tradition gave her. She is brought to judgement; and those who listen either agree with the sentence, or see the prosecutor, witnesses, and judge alike self-judged before their prisoner. The words Euripides wrote for Helen offer little satisfaction to someone who feels indignant against the source of so much evil. She is not obviously even a bitch; a translation or a performance which so presents her is in danger of falsifying the text. The end of the scene shows the chorus as implacably, if excusably, vindictive, Menelaus as cruel, coarse, and stupid, Hecabe as hating to the point of perversity, since she pleads in the name of Greek widows for Helen's execution. Helen kneels, with the sentence of stoning in her ears, to speak these two lines (1042–3):

I beg you, by your knees, do not hold me guilty of the *nosos* –

the word means not merely 'disease' but the helplessness of love, and its whole train of disastrous consequences –

which the goddess sent upon me; do not kill me, but pardon me.

This tableau has been almost universally received as symbolic of justice meted out by the righteous against the wicked. A more objective view will see here a tableau which we have observed already in *Orestes*: beauty surrounded by hatred. When in Chapter 9 we review all that Euripides has to say about anger and its cure, we shall find that if he has one central message for moral despair it lies in this word *syngignōske*, 'pardon'; and there we shall study its exact meaning — for it differs somewhat from the Christian idea of 'forgiveness'. Here we need only notice that in this scene-ending which includes the chorus-leader and all three actors the two lines voicing the thought most characteristic of the poet are given to Helen.

Our survey so far has established that Euripides gave much thought to the person of Helen; that he saw her as a figure somewhat reserved and mysterious, a symbol of that world of experience which ignores the lure of adventure, violence, and power — the gifts of Hera and Athena — and offers the indefinable essence of beauty itself. What seems chiefly to have haunted the poet was the treatment accorded to this unique person by later generations: the embodiment of beauty had been, almost everywhere, re-painted as a whore. She whom in the *Iliad* Priam habitually called 'my dear daughter' was now a byword for vain and vulgar selfishness. How, then, would it be possible to present, for once in a lifetime, this irresistible character in her proper person, full of charm, honesty, warmth, and wit, without rousing the fury of traditionalists? Aphrodite is laughter-loving; and Euripides wrote what we today can only call a comedy, though its form is that of the tragedies[7].

The play called *Helen* is unique. It can be, if directed with care, imagination, and taste, a highly entertaining piece on today's stage. On the surface it appears as a sophisticated and light-hearted patchwork, mainly of scenes, phrases, and situations from *Iphigenia in Tauris*, *Hippolytus*, and *Andromache*, with hints and echoes from other plays. A first reading may suggest that Euripides is here making simple fun of his fellow-citizens by saying, as it were, 'All they object to in Helen is her adultery; then I will remove the adultery.' He takes the story used by the sixth-century poet Stesichorus, that Helen herself, being tempted by Paris, was at Hera's command conveyed by Hermes to Egypt, to the palace of Proteus, there to be kept safe for Menelaus; and that Paris sailed off to Troy with a phantom Helen which Hera made from 'ether', whom Menelaus captured when Troy fell, and took on board with him, thinking she was his real wife. The shipwreck of Menelaus on the coast of Egypt seven years after the fall of Troy, his meeting with Helen and their escape together, are the material of the play. The comedic nature of the dialogue, one may assume, secured the poet from suspicion that he really thought Helen an adorable creature; and in any case his Helen, though nowhere condemning the conduct of her phantom, credibly claims for herself the most demure chastity.

A single passage, however, is enough to suggest at the outset the possibility that those who knew Euripides' mind and method would recognize them here too. The blind hatred of Helen which already in five tragedies had been voiced by men and women alike, drawing from audiences that severe endorsement which is the common response today – that furious posture is presented yet again in the prologue of *Helen*; but here the inanity of it approaches caricature (71ff.). Teucros, son of Telamon, turns up, meets Helen; knows her by face immediately, and – of course – hardly restrains himself from killing her on the spot. 'The daughter of Zeus is hated all over Hellas,' he says (81). The promptitude of his response is in itself enough to indicate irony; the dialogue which follows confirms it. Why does he so hate Helen? He has been exiled, he replies, by his own father. Why? Because he did not prevent the suicide of his brother Aias. Why did Aias kill himself? Because Achilles' armour was awarded to Odysseus. Why did Achilles die? He was fighting at Troy to recover Helen. This is rather like the old nursery rhyme, 'There's a hole in my bucket, dear Liza . . .' The principle of the scapegoat – the fallacy of the remote cause – could not be better instanced. What is more, two further examples of this obsessive habit of mind occur within the next few pages, at 229ff. and 386–92.

Besides this, there are repeated allusions to the fact that Helen 'is hated all over Hellas', that it is her lot to 'bear the guilt of countless agonies and countless deaths' (198–9). Why should she suffer for crimes which she did not commit (249–51)? The very seriousness with which this story of the 'phantom Helen' is treated in, for example, the splendid 'Nightingale Ode' (1107–64) leaves ample room for the thought – indeed invites the thought – that the Helen of popular tradition, whose 'name is shouted with execration through the cities of Hellas' (1147–8), the she-devil guilty of the blood of thousands – that this Helen is indeed a phantom, a figment of men's guilt for their own bloodthirsty wars. The one play where the poet is free to present his true image of the woman Homer created as the embodiment of all beauty, is the comedy where it will be assumed that he writes with his tongue in his cheek; while the solemn, preposterous, or criminal haters and revilers of Helen who fill the Trojan tragedies are applauded as champions of morality and justice. And finally, the exquisite poetry of the lyrics and choral odes in *Helen* proclaims the whole piece as a celebration of beauty; that current disease, the war-begotten hatred of beauty, whose pain is a theme in *The Phoenician Women* and in *Orestes*, has no place in *Helen*.

What I have so far described, however, appears only on the ironic surface. Below this surface lies a philosophical structure, a verbal design of fascinating complexity. A recent article by Charles Segal, 'The Two Worlds of Euripides' *Helen*,[8] has revealed the whole play as a detailed and intense exploration of the antithesis of illusion and reality. The *eidōlon* story (the 'phantom') provides a basis upon which the play builds a pattern of related antitheses — supposition and knowledge, name and body, death and life, the cruelty of Hera and the counsels of Zeus, the horrors vainly suffered at Troy and the hope revealed in Egypt, the curse and the blessing inherent in beauty. And this pattern, as Segal traces it, moves nearer to the antinomies operating in the social and political world before which the play was presented; it becomes a vehicle for yet another statement of the poet's lifelong concern with the two major blunders of human society as organized by men. Though it might seem at first that Troy should represent reality and Egypt illusion, it soon becomes clear that the opposite is true. The violence of war raged around a non-existence and a lie; the truth existed and was revealed in a place so remote that no news from outside ever reached it. 'In this strange world,' Segal writes, 'the male, heroic values of mainland Greece, perpetually kept before us in the theme of the Trojan War, prove ineffectual and even encumbering. Hence Menelaus' discomfiture by the Portress is not just a bit of humorous stage-play, but dramatizes the alienness and inappropriateness of those martial, Trojan values which Menelaus embodies.' In the Egypt of this play 'the men may bluster and threaten, but the real power lies with the women'. Menelaus is as much a child before Helen's mature sensibility as Theoclymenus is before Theonoe; so that 'masculine aggressiveness has to yield place to the life-fostering, private, mysterious ways of women'.

The scope of Segal's penetrating study is far broader than the question which the present chapter seeks to answer; the reader who pursues it in detail will find, whether or not he agrees with every argument, that *Helen* is not only a moving romance and an entertaining comedy but also a profoundly intellectual statement of relative values. This quality in the play gives significance to the fact that here Helen is offered to us as the embodiment not merely of physical beauty but of feminine warmth, grace, power, sensitivity, and wit; in short, as the woman *par excellence*. Thus the theme of this chapter is linked with that of Chapter 4. The hatred and slander which Helen endures are the same which Phaedra and Creusa recognized as the usual lot of women; and in her case they are intensified by the fear which beauty arouses in the destructive male. The devotion and respect which Menelaus receives from her are the same which many men in the first audience accepted as a due tribute from the wives they ruled. In fact, once we recognize that *Helen* is a serious and philosophical play, it is no longer possible to reconcile its picture of Helen with the picture traditionally found in the seven other 'Trojan' plays; and the only solution is to accept that the abusive passages in those plays are ironic in intention and condemn not

Helen but her condemners. The inference offered by this play is that all pretensions of male aggressiveness, whether directed against a neighbour state or against a wife or daughter, belong to the world of illusion; while woman, both symbolically (as Segal explains, it is Helen 'who administers to Menelaus the bath and the change of garment') and practically (in the devising of escape), organizes a successful response to a real situation.

But above all the 'two worlds' to which the title of Segal's article refers are the worlds of life and of death: Menelaus is everywhere the dealer in death, Helen the dispenser of life. It would be superfluous to begin here to detail the complexities which Segal unravels in his close study of key-words and images. But it is worth noting, first, that *Helen* presents once more the picture of the separate worlds of man and of woman which we have found in *Medea, Hippolytus, Ion*; and secondly, that in *Helen* these two worlds correspond with the two worlds imaged in *The Phoenician Women* as the domains of Ares and of Dionysus (see Chapter 6, pages 171–3). A year after the Sicilian disaster, with the origins and the objectives of the war long ago out of sight, this play calls both reflectively and romantically (as *The Phoenician Women* calls desperately) for a sane choice between life and death. The theme of home-coming from war to peace fills the final stasimon. The longed-for home is indeed Sparta, not Athens; but it is a place of 'the season of dances' by the banks of Eurotas, of 'the enchanted night when the Spartans revel for Hyacinthus'; and this festival, as Segal points out (page 597), was dedicated to the theme of 'renewal after sterility'.

In the earliest of his extant tragedies Euripides challenged Athenian society of his day as a system unjust and oppressive to women, a community where one half enslaves the other half. Aeschylus had opened this topic with his Clytemnestra and the suppliant Danaids; Euripides made it more articulate not only in *Medea* and *Andromache* but earlier in *Alcestis*, and alluded to it in many other plays. It is true, as Gomme, Kitto, and other writers maintain, that the spirit of Greek women in the fifth century claimed and won for them a kind of life which in many cases offered some dignity, some variety, even a degree of freedom; but it was also true, as Medea implies, that this was something allowed to them by the expedience of men or yielded by the weakness of men, but never recognized as a right. It seems at least possible that the universal hatred of Helen which was apparently accepted among Euripides' contemporaries developed as one symptom of the bad conscience of Greek society over its oppression of woman; though it must be remembered that in the plays she is as often victimized by women as by men. For the average woman the most profitable course was to ally herself wholly with the Greek male as he instinctively unloaded his guilt from both its sources — injustice to women and bloodthirstiness in war — at once upon a single victim. For the persecuted figure of Helen is there, also, to reduce to absurdity, to reveal in its true colours, that vindictiveness which knew an easy answer to the daily agonizing question asked by Athenians in 415 B.C. and for a generation following: Who is responsible for this disastrous war? The principle of the public scapegoat had been familar in Athens from early times.[9] Public manifestations of this instinct are no less familiar in the modern world; and the reader of Thucydides can see how it coloured the conscience of the fifth century B.C. Who was to be blamed for the war with Sparta? The Athenian citizen knew — it was Pericles; it was Alcibiades, or Cleon; it was, above all, Socrates, the corrupter of young men's thoughts. In the plays we have been studying, the 'woman hated throughout Hellas' casts an ironic light on that same vindictiveness which, in an Athenian law-court five years after the war ended, condemned to death the most noble scapegoat in Greek history on a charge which might with no less justice have been brought against Euripides if he had remained in Athens.

What, then, was the poet's message — that particular part of his message which he embodied in this reserved, gentle, ironic figure that hovers around his plays? In taking the central person of the myth of the House of Atreus, and showing her again and again as the target for unquestioning contempt and hate, being herself neither guilty of all nor innocent of all, but human, dignified, unfathomable, and a symbol of eternal beauty surviving in a world controlled by unwise and angry men — in presenting this vulnerable figure upon his stage Euripides was surely not inviting the unwise and angry men in his audience to align themselves with Electra, Peleus, Orestes; was not encouraging them to applaud and reinforce the least creditable of their innate prejudices. He was offering, to those few of them capable of thinking unfamiliar thoughts, an invitation to overcome their uneasy antagonism towards woman, to renounce the fear and hatred of beauty; to shoulder their own guilt; and learn to find a place in their harsh and censorious world for that intangible and unpredictable mystery whose gentleness and ruthless power are combined in the divinity of Aphrodite.

6

COMMENT ON WAR

Euripides was a little over fifty when the war against Sparta began in 431 B.C. At that time he had written only two of the plays now extant, *Alcestis* and *Medea*; the other fifteen complete plays, and about twenty known to us by their fragmentary remains, were composed against the background of that savage struggle which ended in 404 with the defeat and humiliation of Athens. The extant plays of Sophocles, of which several were written during the same period, contain little identifiable reference to the strains and anxieties which occupied the lives of author and audience outside the theatre; but, of Euripides' fifteen war-time plays, nine either deal directly and primarily with the subject of war, or contain clear comments on such topics as the difference between a just and an unjustified war, the treatment of refugees, the concept of sacrifice, the principle of reprisal, the fate of the defeated. And alongside such comments we can follow in these plays a developing series of pictures of the behaviour of Athenian citizens and of the Athenian state in the conduct of the war. The nine plays to be considered are: *The Children of Heracles, Andromache, Hecabe, The Suppliant Women, The Women of Troy, Helen, The Phoenician Women, Orestes, Iphigenia in Aulis.* Six of these have already been studied in certain aspects. We shall now look at them all in turn, noting passages which seem to be significant for their criticism of war in its nature and in its effects.

The difference just mentioned between the work of the two poets is of course well known. A play of Sophocles called its audience away from the practical decisions, the hates and desires, of yesterday and tomorrow, inviting them to weep and tremble in a world of heroically clarified issues. A play of Euripides, for those who listened reflectively, spoke in a different voice. It confronted the war-weary citizen with yesterday's failure and tomorrow's terror. It held up mirrors in which he could contemplate himself and what he was doing with his world, in an embarrassing, a shocking, new light; yet the mirror-image was often so veiled in irony as to be visible only to those who demanded truth, while those who sought the comfort of self-delusion could still find it. Among the later works of Euripides there is only one, *The Bacchae*, which departs from this function and assumes instead a function nearer to that which we associate with Sophocles. Both kinds of function have remained ever since as legitimate activities of the theatre. In the modern study of Greek drama critics have, in general, concentrated their interest understandably on the universals of Sophoclean drama, and have been critical of those who were lured by the realism of Euripides' stage into interpreting his views on moral or social topics. Especially in reading the plays about war, they have been reluctant to assume that any real community of experience can exist between an ancient Athenian writer and ourselves; or that we today can in any significant measure see what these plays meant, or were intended to mean, to their original audiences — apart from such general statements as Cassandra's in *Women of Troy* 400, that 'a wise man will avoid war if he can'. This attitude is in some degree justified. The difference in scale of twentieth-century events, the global impact of any disturbance, the force of technology, the growth of international ethical feeling, have given modern war a very different aspect from that of the struggle between Athens and Sparta. But Euripides in his plays does not, in general, look at war like a historian, or a sociologist, or even a philosopher, still less as an economist or technician. From the complex pattern of a war situation he picks out one point where two or three human beings are acting or suffering, each a factor in the whole nexus but aware of it only from the place where he stands. This is the aspect of war which remains unchanged in our day. It is an aspect sometimes little regarded, then as now, by the controllers of strategy; yet they too are a personal and human part of it, and because they see both the broad and the narrow reference of what they do or suffer, their words can be pregnant. It is here that we meet a community of experience joining the ancient world to our own.

It is always hazardous to find in an ancient writer a message relevant to the modern world. I am aware of the temptation to see analogies on right and left, and to claim classical support for moral attitudes foreign to the ancient world. On the other hand we have already observed, in studying Euripides' criticism of the behaviour of his fellow-men towards women, that his attitude in that fundamental department of social life was indeed foreign to the climate of his time; and it seems probable that this alienation, among other things, aroused the hostility which made him leave Athens. The modern tradition has sometimes, in interpreting Euripides, clamped its own timid limitations on his daring and unpredictable mind. The result has been to present us with an author whose moral judgements contradict each other, who affronts now our intelligence, now our sense of humour; and whose dramatic methods call for apology or despair — as, for example, when Kitto tells us, in his often excellent book on Greek drama,[1] that *Iphigenia in Aulis* is 'a thoroughly second-rate play', and proceeds to explain that a second-rate play is what Euripides intended to write — and how brilliantly he succeeded.

A. W. Gomme in an essay on Thucydides[2] says that he 'regarded war not as an occasion for glory ... but as an evil. The Peloponnesian War did more material and moral harm than any other had done; it threatened to destroy Greek civilisation altogether'. He continues a little later (page 121):

[Thucydides] knew that a war fought on that scale, with such intensity, and over so long a period, at once became more serious than any problem it was called upon to solve. That is why he lays so much stress on certain incidents which had very little influence on the military result of the war — on the victory of Athens or of her enemies — but were symptomatic of the evils generated by it: the struggle for Plataea, the Corcyrean sedition, the conquest of Melos; Plataea particularly.

What Gomme has pointed out in this acute comment is in fact the strong dramatic and tragic element which can be felt all through the History, and which at many points shows how closely his thought coincided with that of Euripides. Later in this chapter we shall examine the connexion between *The Women of Troy* and the conquest of Melos; and we shall see in Chapter 7 how the drama of Plataea illuminates the fabric of *The Children of Heracles*. In studying *Orestes* we have seen that Orestes, Electra, and Pylades exemplify with painful detail the mental self-corruption, the destruction of the truth of words, which Thucydides memorably describes in III.82.[3] In that passage, moreover, the historian lays a similar emphasis on the obsession with revenge, as a chief cause of disaster, to that which we find in the tragic poet. Later in the same essay Gomme insists that dislike of war was normal to Greeks. Another way of putting it is to say that the concern of any government, then as now, was to assure its own citizens that their dislike of war was commendable, but unique and therefore to be overcome. Belligerence and love of peace are both equally normal, in different circumstances, to most human beings. Segal, in the essay quoted in Chapter 5 (page 150), shows how Menelaus (in *Helen*) and the warlike world which he represents belong to the realm of illusion; and adds that 'the opposition to war which this rejection of heroic values implies is part of a larger issue important in late fifth-century thought, an increasing movement away from the public toward the private realm' (page 575). But the 'movement' which he speaks of was itself, of course, confined within the private realm; that is to say, thoughtful individuals became emotionally less identified with the state, while public policies remained unaffected.

  The purpose of this chapter is not so much to argue that Euripides disliked war — that needs no proof; but rather to describe the particular elements which we find illustrated in his comment on war: the self-deception, the corruption of truth, the avoidance of responsibility; the yielding to mass excitement, the disregard of helpless suffering, the unreason of revenge, the suicidal insanity of obsessive bloodshed. All these he exposes in personal terms as his male heroes manoeuvre and dispute, fettered by their bronze armour as slaves by their chains; and at every point these nine plays remind us that war is a destructive ritual indulged in by one half of the human race, who in their manic devotion to warlike causes treat the other half as expendable.

It is convenient to begin with two plays which are sometimes called Euripides' 'political' plays – though there are others I would include under that title: *The Children of Heracles* and *The Suppliant Women*. *The Children of Heracles* (427) deals with one common reason for armed attack, namely the indignation that one city feels against another city which gives shelter or comfort to its enemies. *The Suppliant Women* (421) deals with the opposite side of a similar situation. The help requested in each case is of a kind prescribed by religious sanction: protection for refugees, and burial for the dead. In both cases the cause of war is presented as a just one – the obligation to help, at risk to oneself, a suppliant who is unjustly treated; and in both cases the justified battle issues in victory for the just cause. That is to say, in these plays warfare is considered as a necessary instrument of political action, and interest centres on the purposes which should employ it and the limits which should control it.

The Children of Heracles will be studied in detail at the beginning of Chapter 7. It is far from being a simple play. Its plot is complicated by a painful analogy with current events, by some phoney oracles, by disgraceful equivocation on the part of the king, and by several daring shocks in theatre technique. However, what the play has to say about war is simple and confident. The chorus, being Elders of Marathon, stand for the best military tradition of Athens, which the victory of Marathon had illustrated and glorified; a tradition based on trust in the supreme power of Zeus, guardian of suppliants, of oaths, and of the ties of kinship (766–9). The victory over Argos reported in the Messenger's speech vindicates faith in Zeus and justice. It is still only the fourth year of the war; the Athenians, in spite of mixed fortunes in battle, the suffering caused by the plague, and guilt at their failure to help Plataea, still maintain the buoyant courage with which they entered the struggle; and their spirit is reflected in this play. Yet, though the play records an Athenian victory, it adds three riders to question its value and sour its rejoicing. Eurystheus at the point of death prophesies to Athens that 'these are faithless guests whose cause you saved'; the gratitude of a neighbouring city will not be assured as the result of just warfare, Argos is not another Plataea. Worse than this, even the integrity of the victors is endangered by their obligations to allies. The Elders of Marathon firmly assert an Athenian principle, 'We do not kill those taken alive in battle' (966), which Eurystheus affirms (1010–11) is upheld by 'the laws of Hellas'. Yet Alcmene is absolute for the prisoner's death; and even if Demophon should reappear (which the defective text makes uncertain) we cannot see that opportunist ruler winning a battle of wills against Alcmene. As far as we can tell the play ended with the civilized Athenian principle overruled by the vindictive refugee Athens had protected — and this in spite of the chorus's prayer (926—7),

> A relentless nature, obsessive hatred —
> God keep me guiltless of these!

The words refer ostensibly to Eurystheus' persecution of Heracles' children; but since they are spoken just before the scene in which Alcmene turns the tables on her enemy, their reference is evidently two-edged. The third rider is the most disturbing of all, and expresses a truth which the poet referred to again in *The Phoenician Women*. The sacrifice with which the victory was bought is forgotten at once; nobody even troubles to ask whether in fact Macaria's heroism had any effect on the result of the battle. This matter will be discussed more fully in the next chapter.

We come to the tenth year of the war, and *The Suppliant Women*. The message is less simple here; three separate wars are presented for our reflection. First we are told in some detail of the war Adrastus made against Thebes. It was a war in which the prince of Thebes, Polyneices, marched to attack his native city — a blasphemy in itself — and, still worse, to meet his own brother in battle to the death; his allies, Adrastus king of Argos and five others, had involved themselves with little reason in a cause whose justice was far outweighed by its impiety. The assault on Thebes ended in defeat; of the seven leaders only Adrastus came home alive. The second war is the expedition of Theseus against Thebes to recover the bodies of the dead leaders. Theseus' behaviour is correct in every point. He tries persuasion first; when Creon refuses to allow burial of the dead, Theseus immediately attacks and defeats him; and having recovered the bodies, instead of pressing home his victory and sacking Thebes (which is what every other Homeric hero would have done, thereby perpetuating the cycle of revenge), Theseus leads his army straight home to Athens. There is no question but that this is presented as the action of a rational and just man, to whom war is a weapon which he draws and sheathes at will, not a fiend enslaving the man who unleashes him. Yet the play ends on a note of despair. What can a single rational and just ruler accomplish against a thoughtless and inexperienced younger generation resolute to be so enslaved? In the last scene a second chorus enters, a group of little boys, the sons of the dead leaders. They were not present when the Messenger told how Theseus had refused to destroy Thebes, leaving a door open for peace. The chorus of suppliant women, these boys' grandmothers, were there from the beginning, and they had received the lesson of Theseus' action; but boys do not listen to their grandmothers. Instead they speak to the urns which hold their fathers' ashes, and promise a third war (1143—52):

> Father, your son mourns for you!
> Do you hear? Shall I one day,
> Shield in hand, avenge your death? God grant it!
> Justice for my father's blood —
> It will yet come, with the favour of heaven.

The mothers of the dead know that they will not be listened to. They reply:

> This evil sleeps not yet. Why must we always weep?
> I have had enough of disasters and of misery.

The sons ignore them and continue:

> The day will come when I march bronze-clad
> To avenge my father's death.

When Theseus addresses the boys, he bids them remember what Athens has done for Argos, but himself appears to forget his own equally significant act in sparing Thebes from massacre and pillage. Why is this? The picture given of Theseus so far has been strangely contradictory — a mixture of courage and pomposity, firmness and instability, idealist action and unrealistic theorizing. At this moment he has before him two choruses: the desolate mothers who plead for an end to weeping and slaughter, and the warlike children who talk of bronze shields and vengeance; and Theseus keeps a cowardly silence, and neither reassures the mothers nor rebukes the children. This, unhappily, is a true picture of Athens — and perhaps of any state in a similar position. She had the moral and the physical power to lead Hellas to peace, but instead conformed to the popular posture; so that 'this evil sleeps not yet' (1147). Theseus had missed his moment for speaking the truth — a truth which he acted, but acted out of sight; and now it is too late. Athena appears, and she speaks with the unmistakable voice of the Athenian democratic Assembly. She sees on one side Theseus and the bereaved women of the chorus; on the other, the little boys impatient for revenge and blood. The chorus she ignores; Theseus she instructs and rebukes; the boys she encourages and incites to armed reprisal. 'Nothing else is possible,' she says (1224). The poet does not denounce his fellow-citizens; he silently holds up a mirror. In reply to Athena Theseus says — like the accused in a certain kind of political trial —

I will obey you, Athena; by your voice alone I am saved from error, led in the right path. Only guide my decisions; while your favour rests on us, Athens will live henceforward in security.

With these words Theseus revokes the civilized principle of reason and

peace which comprised one half of his central action in the play.[4] The bitterness of this final irony is equalled, I think, only in *Iphigenia in Aulis*. The war
is now ten years old; it will continue for seventeen years more.

This closing tableau has been prepared for in earlier passages. The eloquence
of the Herald who comes from Thebes to warn Theseus against interfering
shows two characteristics familiar to us from many speeches in Thucydides:
first the argument from expediency — it will not pay you to go to war; second,
the irrelevant argument — that the men who attacked Thebes were wicked.
But the main part of his speech is in fact a lucid exposition of the suicidal
nature of war, the blessings of peace, and the folly of democratic governments which make reason yield to emotion (484—5):

> If Death stood there in person while men cast their votes,
> Hellas would not be dying of war-mania.

This is the first appearance of the image of war as insanity, which becomes
more insistent in the later plays. The Herald continues:

> We know what good, what evil is;
> How far peace outweighs war in benefits to man —
> Peace, the chief friend and cherisher of the Muses; Peace,
> The enemy of revenge, lover of families
> And children, patroness of wealth. Yet these blessings
> We viciously neglect, and embrace wars.

It is Euripides' ironic way to put the truth where the careless listener will
least expect it —as here in the mouth of the Theban Herald, who is obviously
on the wrong side. So, later, he gives to the foolish and wretched Adrastus two
separate passages which would speak home even to the less intelligent bulk
of the audience, who all knew that a few years earlier, after the affair at Pylos,
Sparta had offered peace on moderate terms, and Athens had refused it. First,
Adrastus speaks after the news of Theseus' victory (737—49). Once, he says,

> We thought ourselves irresistible, superior
> In numbers and in youth; so, when the king of Thebes
> Offered us peace on fair conditions, we refused;
> And then we were defeated. Next, the tables turned,
> Victorious Thebes acts like a poor man newly rich;
> Grows insolent; and in turn insolence leads the whole
> City of Cadmus through stupidity to ruin . . .
> O foolish states, who have the power to avert defeat
> By conference, yet choose instead the ordeal of blood!

And presently, as the funeral procession forms, these lines (949—52):

> O wretched race of mortals! Why must men get spears
> And spill each other's blood? Stop! Lay this rage to rest;
> Live quiet with quiet neighbours, and preserve your towns.

It is surely fair to observe further the difference between those two passages. The first is a reasoned comment on the behaviour of two warlike states, each lacking the judgement to make peace at the right moment. The second is unreasoned and emotional, and thus suited to its occasion, the mourning of the mothers for their sons. The plea for conference (749) is unanswerable; but Theseus' justified military action has already given a sound answer to 'Why must men get spears . . .?' However desirable it may be to value peace more than war, not all the arguments used in this case are cogent. In 421 Euripides is still careful to state both sides of the argument; by 409 (*The Phoenician Women*) he will have a case which cannot be over-stated. Here he is content to place before his audience a choice of judge-ments. The twentieth-century playwright, in some countries at least, can make heresy or rebellion explicit with little risk; if he gets a theatre at all, boldness increases his chance of a run, and a 'success' can be floated on a fairly small group of sympathizers, so that irony is not necessary. Euripides had one performance in which to address the whole nation. His offering was twofold: first for those who would hear, not what was said, but what they assumed was going to be said; secondly, for those who looked for his support and guidance in considering the gamut of possible judgements and soberly choosing their own.

Between these two plays came *Andromache*, first acted about 426.[5] It is a densely-packed play combining the two themes of woman and war, though the former is paramount. The thematic design up to the end of the second episode is worth noting. First Andromache's elegiac monody pictures the impact of war upon one life formerly prosperous; then the *parodos* urges, from the safe position of those who have not suffered, acceptance of such miseries as inevitable. Then enters Hermione the daughter of the man who made and won the war, to demonstrate that her father's victory has brought no more security, happiness, or freedom to her than to Andromache. Then comes the irony of the first stasimon: the war could have been avoided — how? — by Hecabe if she had obeyed Cassandra and killed Paris at birth. Here is yet another pointer to the folly of 'reference to the remote cause'; for Andromache has already told us how the Greeks murdered her infant son, and in the next scene our chorus will exclaim in horror when Menelaus proposes to kill Molossus. The ode ends with this thought (304–8) for the Athenian citizens after five years of their modern war:

> Hellas too would have been spared the agony
> Of those ten years when her young men

> Fought to and fro before the walls of Troy;
> Spared the widow's lonely bed,
> And old men's tears for their dead sons.

In the next episode we see Menelaus as the embodiment of successful war, bland, heartless, and false; and the pattern of the first half of the play reaches its climax in Andromache's denunciation of Sparta (445—53):

> Spartans! The whole world hates you above all other men!
> Lies are your policy, treachery your accomplishment,
> Your craft is crime and cruelty; your hearts warped and sly,
> Your minds diseased, you lord it over the Hellene world;
> Justice lies dead. What wickedness is not in you?
> You add murder to murder, you make gold your god;
> The whole world knows your speech is one thing, your intent
> Another. My curse on you!

Thus in a little over one-third of a play devoted primarily to exhibiting the predicament of woman, the nature of war and its effect on human lives has also been illuminated from many different angles; which shows how closely related, in the poet's view, were the two chief aspects of male ascendancy.

After the episode with Orestes (already discussed in Chapter 2, pages 38ff.) three comments on war conclude the action. The fourth stasimon elaborates the theme of lines 304—8 quoted above, that the disaster the war inflicted on Hellas was only a degree less lamentable than the death of Troy (a theme recurring in *Helen*); that war extends its curse from continent to continent and (here the chorus anticipates the news later brought by the Messenger) from decade to decade (1044—7):

> This plague — Hellas too has endured the plague.
> The thunder that shattered Troy
> Has passed to our pleasant fields,
> And death is with us in a rain of blood.

It was three years since the plague in Athens had abated; and barely two generations since the invading army of Mardonius had vanished from the Greek mainland. The second comment is the tableau of mourning for Neoptolemus: the hero who survived the battle to die by treachery; the old man's tears for his desolate house, for the glory of his youth now mocked and debased. The third comment is the most bitter. Why do men and women, generation after generation, accept as inevitable the monstrous follies of warfare? Because they have learnt to blind and comfort themselves with trivial make-believe. The hollowness of Thetis's message to Pelcus is underlined by a subtly cruel touch: Neoptolemus' body has just been carried all the way from Delphi, but Thetis tells Peleus he is now to carry it all the way back. After that he is to 'sit down . . . and wait until I come out of the sea . . . to escort you home'. Peleus neither questions her command nor wonders if it will be a long wait. He is rapturously comforted, and confirmed in his two main articles of faith: noble blood, and the favour of the gods. When consolation is so easy, how can indignation hope to combat evil?

Hecabe was produced in 425 or 424. It is an unsparing detailed statement of the corruption which attacks human life as the result of war. The action bears no reference to fighting, but shows what results follow when political causes have been allowed to take their conventional course in violence. The chorus's account of the council of Hellene chiefs (116ff.), and Agamemnon's diplomatic musing (852–6), are two of many passages glancing at the nature of war-time politics.

The first and all-pervasive evil, which forms the background of the drama, is the sheer physical chaos and horror which the victors have accomplished, the mass of charred ruins which a few days ago was a city full of life. The instructions Hecabe gives to Polymestor (1008–10) for locating the supposed hidden treasure provide an imaginative glimpse of the devastated city. What remains of Troy is represented by the women of the chorus, a handful of captives. The second corruption displayed is the treachery of a friend: Polymestor, king of Thrace, a friend of Priam and Hecabe, has murdered the young son they sent to him for safe keeping, for the sake of his gold. Next comes the morbid superstition which demands human sacrifice; a barbarity excusable in brutalized masses, but not in their leaders. Agamemnon, whose weakness betrayed his own daughter ten years ago, is not likely to behave any better now; while Odysseus insults Hecabe with a smooth-sounding, question-begging speech typical of the official explanations which tend to be used by any authority from that day to this. Odysseus neither believes that his reasons answer the case nor expects Hecabe to accept them as valid; but for such a decision (107–8, 116–40) there has to be an official reason. After four corruptions, suddenly there is a blaze of purity: Polyxena's spirit is one thing that war cannot change or destroy. When she has gone, corruption returns. Talthybius' report of the sacrifice is sympathetic and sensitive; but he describes with approval the guilty sentimentality which made the Greek soldiers pay fulsome honour to Polyxena's body. Next, when the dead Polydorus is discovered and Hecabe appeals to Agamemnon for acquiescence in her revenge, the victorious commander-in-chief displays his abject dependence on the good opinion of his subordinates, and accepts without protest Hecabe's words (864, 869–70):

You are, like all men, a slave . . . I will set you free from this fear; know what I do, but take no hand in it;

whereupon Agamemnon agrees to betray his ally Polymestor. Meanwhile Hecabe has spoken eloquently to Agamemnon (798–805) of the majesty of Law as the only upholder of right. But when the king has declined to act in the name of Law, and leaves justice to his slaves, the distinction between Law and primitive revenge has vanished. Finally the tragic and noble Hecabe (like Theseus in *The Suppliant Women* and the chorus in *Orestes*) is herself corrupted and becomes a maniacal murderess, under whose eye the pitiful king ratifies her travesty of Law. The tale of corruption is completed by the prophecy of the blinded Polymestor, that Hecabe will be changed to a dog and will die there in Chersonese, while Agamemnon will be murdered by his wife.

This procession of evils born from war was composed when the war was entering its fifth year — the year of the Corcyrean revolution whose devastating effects on Hellenic moral values Thucydides describes in Book III.82–4. The condemnatory tone of this play is so much more outspoken than that of *The Suppliant Women* that one would expect it to be the later work. Murray, while giving 421 as the probable date of *The Suppliant Women*, says[6] that its style suggests it had been written some years earlier. Webster assigns both plays to one set, dated before 423. After these two plays six years passed before Euripides again took war as his theme; *Heracles* and *Ion* contain no reference to it. Then came the annihilation of Melos in 416, and Euripides wrote *The Women of Troy*. Much has already been said about this play in Chapter 5; and its meaning in regard to the suffering endured by war's victims needs no exposition. The prologue, however, contains a contribution to the poet's total statement about war. The dialogue between Athena and Poseidon makes two points. First, that in war the outcome is always unpredictable. The Greeks have defeated their enemies, captured Helen, sacrificed Polyxena to ensure a safe homeword voyage, and are eager to set sail. But Athena — in spite of Hecabe's assurance (974) — is scheming with Poseidon to destroy the fleet on its way home; and in the first episode we learn from Cassandra that Agamemnon will survive the storm only to meet death by treachery. (The end of *Erechtheus* illustrates the same truth; see Chapter 7, page 197.) Secondly, even if it were possible to influence future events by appealing to gods, divine operations are in fact only another way of describing haphazard chance. The casual pettiness which guides the conversation of Athena and Poseidon tells us that no moral principle underlies the pattern of history; that justice is something which on occasion man may achieve by his own efforts, but it will never be guaranteed by any god. It is not, as Aeschylus hopefully asserted (*Agamemnon* 750–81, 1001–16), a cosmic principle of balance which works automatically. As Thucydides points out, the Melians put their trust in the gods, and the Athenians destroyed them. There is more meaning in this than a mere rejection of outmoded myth. The play is about war; and the character given to gods in this prologue states that the making of war and the ending of war are like other decisions, solely man's responsibility. Divine powers indeed exist, as part of the mystery of the universe; but the only one of them that man can claim to know is Chance, who can be relied on to be unreliable. The conclusion reached is one which the poet points to in many plays: trust no god, blame no god; look only to yourself.

When *The Women of Troy* was produced the Athenians were on the point of despatching to Sicily the most powerful force sent overseas by any Greek state since the Trojan War. The first episode in this play is dedicated to Cassandra — known as the prophetess whose words were always true, and never heeded. Here Euripides follows a practice we have noted in *Medea* and elsewhere: he places his unacceptable message where its effect on the audience will be dimmed by the emotional scenes which follow it, while those who later remember and reflect will understand what had been said (366—83):

This at least is no mad raving: the Greeks led ten thousand men to death; their sage commander, to win what he most hated [the reluctance of Nicias to take command was well known] lost what he most loved . . . When the Greeks came to our shores, what did they die for day after day? To repel invasion from their borders or siege from their city's walls? No! When a man was killed, his limbs were not laid to rest by his wife's hands; he had forgotten what his children looked like; and now his bones lie in alien earth. In their homes things were no better; their women died in widowhood; fathers sank into childless old age longing for the sons they had brought up, and were buried with none to honour their graves. Certainly Hellas has much to thank her army for!

To utter such ill-omened words on such an occasion was perhaps less extreme than to mutilate the Hermae (see Thucydides VI.27), but it could be seen as showing a similar spirit. Euripides seems almost to challenge accusation in these words of Talthybius (408—10):

If Apollo had not driven you crazy, my general would have had you punished for inviting ill-luck by such words just as he is setting sail.

The chief purpose of the play, however, is not to denounce a foolish policy, but to place before the eyes of citizens the invariable cost of war paid both by defeated and by victors — the anguish of the individual, of children, women, and the aged; to combine in one cry the causes and claims of Macaria, Polydorus, Polyxena, Hermione, Andromache, Molossus, the mothers of the Seven, Iphis, Evadne — of all whom the makers of wars disregard as expendable. The poet's despair of ever making his point clear even to the victims is shown in 610—11. Cassandra has already given us the picture of Greek women dying in widowhood (380); now the gentle Andromache points to Hector's armour on its way to Neoptolemus' ship, and the first thing she says about her dead husband is that he killed more Greek men than any other

Trojan. If this line had originated from anyone but Euripides, it would call for no comment. In the same way even Andromache, when told of the sentence on Astyanax, illustrates again most women's acceptance of male judgements in everything, by directing the flood of her imprecation (766–73) not against the callous Odysseus but against her fellow-victim Helen.

It was suggested in Chapter 1 that Euripides' two main themes could be seen as presenting the guilt of man for *hybris* in two spheres. In most of his work this guilt is alluded to indirectly, and every concession is made to the reader who prefers to ignore it; for example, in *Alcestis*, where guilt is clearly depicted, the comedic element acts as an analgesic. In *The Women of Troy* we are given a figure to carry guilt written in his face. Talthybius is only obeying orders, reporting and executing the will of his superiors. Heralds as a class are vilified in several other plays; but here, where we recognize a decent, sympathetic man, Cassandra gives him even harsher treatment than heralds receive elsewhere (424–6):

This ignorant servant! He is a herald: a fine name, 'herald', for creatures universally loathed, lackeys and menials of courts and governments!

It is clear at once to the audience that Cassandra is unfair to Talthybius – who is in fact exactly like themselves. (No one ever heeds what Cassandra says.) He is not brutal like Menelaus or Odysseus; he treats the captured women with respect and consideration, knowing that until a few days ago they were free, rich, and noble (299–303) – though duty to his superiors comes first (305). He has a touch of plain humour, and sees Agamemnon as a man like himself but with an erratic taste in choosing a woman (413–20). He tries to spare Hecabe the news of Polyxena's death (260–70). He is reluctant and sensitive in telling Andromache of the sentence on Astyanax (709–25); and knows that what he is doing is work 'fit for a man without pity or decency' (786–9). When he comes back with the dead child he is again considerate, and sees that by being helpful to the captives he can get through a busy day with no waste of time (1147–55). In his final appearance he prevents Hecabe's suicide and gets her safely off to Odysseus' ship according to orders (1285–6). Only at one point has he felt it necessary to be unpleasant, when he told Andromache that if she caused him trouble over Astyanax she would be overpowered and her child refused burial; and he took care to show that this threat was not his own, but made by authority of 'the Achaeans' (726–39). An autocratic decision by a single chief can perhaps be appealed against, can certainly be dismissed by an audience as un-Hellenic; but a majority decision is faceless and democratic. Talthybius refers twice to the sentence on Astyanax, in terms regularly used for decisions of the Athenian *ecclēsia*, *edoxe* (713), 'it was decided', and *psēphos ekranthē* (785), 'a vote was taken and ratified'.

Whether there is a keener moral sense in modern Europe than existed in fifth-century Hellas is a question whose vagueness leaves it open to debate. Both then and now, the writer who can see a moral issue and place it clearly before his fellows is a rare phenomenon; some can understand what he is saying, a few can act upon it — but the great majority who heard will be unaware that anything has been said; and for them, if you will, it has not been said. But if there was one man in the theatre at the Great Dionysia in 415 B.C. who had used his sword, under orders, in the mass killing in Melos some nine months earlier, Talthybius spoke for him; for it is unlikely that he had forgotten the occasion. Athenians were not, like Spartans, systematically brutalized by their training, and practised in the periodic massacre of Helots. And for those who did not carry out the killing but voted for it, Hecabe speaks (1158—66):

O you Achaeans, you are fine fighters; but where is your pride? Did you so dread this child that you must invent an unheard-of death for him? Did you fear that he would raise Troy from the dust? ... With the city taken and every Trojan dead, still you shook with fear before this babe — are you not proved cowards? There is one thing worse than fear — that is, fear without reason.

Recent comment on Euripides,[7] in its anxiety not to impute what is called 'the modern conscience' to an ancient Greek, has been apt to neglect the indications in this play of an intended reference to the destruction of Melos. In my view, not only is there a general analogy, but the killing of Astyanax is used to give particular point to the indictment of Athens. The inner significance of these opening lines of Hecabe's speech is further suggested by the fact that they, like other bold statements (e.g. *Medea* 230—51; see page 109), come at the beginning of a passage whose subsequent concerns will for most listeners erase the memory of them. During the next few years after this play Euripides soft-pedalled the theme of guilt for war, for the disaster in Sicily had made words unnecessary. It reappeared in *The Phoenician Women*, and filled *Orestes* and *Iphigenia in Aulis* from beginning to end.

We have already, in Chapter 5, looked at the comedy and the irony of *Helen*, produced in 412. This play was written soon after news was brought that the hundreds of ships and the tens of thousands of men Athens had sent to Sicily would not come back. Though much of the dialogue is light-hearted, and some of the lyric may be felt as poetically escapist, we hear a serious note in 362—74, where again the community in suffering of victors and defeated is described:

But listen! Loud and full
Through Hellas too the same river of weeping runs,
And hands are clasped over the stricken head,
And nerveless fingers clutch and pull
The unfeeling flesh till the nails are red.

And a second familiar theme, that the warlike spirit is a disease, an insanity, recurs in 1151ff.:

You are out of your minds, all you who acquire reputations for courage by war and the point of the spear, ignorantly trying to check the undertakings of men; if bloody conflict is to decide these matters, war will never leave our cities.

And the corollary a few lines later:

It would have been possible to settle the quarrel for Helen by negotiation.

But in the three plays we have still to consider, these quiet comments and grievous lamentations give place to a steady stream of eloquent denunciation of the continuing war as a pageant of hypocritical stupidity and an obsession of madmen.

First, *The Phoenician Women*, 409 B.C. Kitto's full and imaginative account of this play in his *Greek Tragedy*[8] pictures Euripides as carefully designing something like a new *genre*, in which chief importance is given to interesting incident, exciting narrative, unexpected characterization; while the loose structure of the piece is explained by calling it 'a dramatic pageant' presenting 'the whole lively history of the line of Cadmus'. This may well be part of the truth; viewed in this light the play is, as Kitto says, 'very good cinema'. Another view is that of Webster,[9] who calls it 'a play about a whole family affected by the utter selfishness of a single member'. But these are surely less important aspects. The real significance of this play lies first in the truth it presented to a population which was beginning to feel itself besieged; and secondly in the lucid diagram it offers, to readers of subsequent ages, of the springs of war in the emotional attitudes of men. The play is addressed directly to the citizens of Athens on the one topic which in 409 confronted them afresh every day, especially at the time of the Dionysia, when one more — the twenty-third — summer's military activities were about to begin. The theme is war — the war of the Seven against Thebes; but from the outset Thebes is clearly and deliberately identified with Athens in the minds of the spectators. Iocasta as Prologue tells the listeners that the scene is Thebes, a besieged city, and that the issue of the drama is to be the quarrel between Eteocles king of Thebes and his brother Polyneices who has come with a foreign army to attack and destroy the city of his birth. This all too real situation is made almost visible in the prologue to an audience who for several years past have watched from the walls of Athens the movements of Spartan troops, now permanently based at Decelea, an hour's ride to the north. The city is so closely besieged that Antigone on the battlements can recognize enemy leaders by face. It was of course known that in the legend Thebes had repelled the besiegers; but an ominous note is struck when her Tutor says to Antigone (154–5)

Yet our enemies come with a just cause.
My fear is that the gods may see this all too well.

When the chorus enter they describe the situation thus (250—60):

Now raging war stands at the city's ramparts
With a blaze of blood threatening death to Thebes . . .
All around this city
Gleaming shields mass like a dense cloud . . .
O Pelasgian Argos,
I tremble before your fierce strength
And before the hand of heaven;
For he arms himself in a just cause
Who fights to recover his home.

The issue of the whole action is the implacable enmity between the two brothers Eteocles and Polyneices. In the first scene Polyneices tells how he came to be allied with Adrastus king of Argos. Adrastus had been advised by an oracle to marry his daughters to a lion and a boar. He himself told us this story in *The Suppliant Women* twelve years earlier; and there Theseus had roundly called him a fool for paying heed to an oracle of that nature. Now Polyneices tells us again how he and Tydeus had been acclaimed as two fighting beasts because of their ferocity. As the play proceeds Tydeus is forgotten, and the image of two fighting beasts is transferred to Eteocles and his brother in a number of passages where they are compared with boars and lions (1296, 1380, 1573). When Eteocles enters, his speech in reply to Polyneices reproduces exactly the tone of the Athenian democracy as we know it in Thucydides, first in a moderate form from the speeches of Pericles, then with full explicitness in the speeches of Cleon, of the Athenian spokesman in the exchanges with Corinth and Corcyra, and later in the dialogue with Melos. There is no such thing, says Eteocles, as 'equal right' or 'justice'. These are mere words; in fact they do not exist (504—6):

I would go,
If it were possible, to the regions of the stars,
Explore the sunrise, probe the depth of the earth, to win
That greatest of all goddesses, Absolute Power.

And he ends his speech thus (521—5):

So now, let fire and sword be let loose; yoke your teams,
Fill the whole plain with chariots. I will not give up
My throne to Polyneices. In all other matters
Piety is well; but since there must be wickedness,
There is no nobler pretext for it than a throne.

The four or five points of Eteocles' argument are remarkable for their correspondence to a pattern recognizable today in most public disputes, industrial or political. The mirror here is not merely undistorted, it is timeless. Further, since from the beginning Thebes is identified with Athens, the recurring image of two fighting beasts attaches itself to what becomes, as the action proceeds, a picture of the struggle, now twenty-two years old, between Athens and Sparta. After this speech it is no longer the collective city of Thebes that symbolizes Athens, but Eteocles himself; he is the very spirit of the Athenian war-party. He and Polyneices, who openly pray to the gods, each that he may kill his brother, cannot but present to a fifth-century audience the two contestants for supremacy in Hellas. As everyone knew before the play began, in the legend the gods answered both their prayers.[10]

Iocasta's reply to her two sons is a lucid and powerful plea for the only secure basis of lasting peace: equity, fair measure. Her prime argument is not the evils of war, though they are alluded to later, but the positive and civilized rationality of peace between cities, presented as the human aspect of the eternal law of Nature. In *The Suppliant Women* the blessings of peace were described by the Herald, and the benevolence of Nature by Theseus; but both those passages were set in a strongly ironic frame. Here there is no irony; Iocasta's speech is sincere in every word. If we read it as a direct address to the citizens of Athens, begging them to regard reason, justice, and their own welfare before it is too late, it is hard to imagine a more cogent appeal. Here is the first half of it (528—57):

> My dear son Eteocles, not all the qualities
> Of age merit contempt; experience has words
> Wiser sometimes than youth. Oh, son, why set your heart
> Towards the most evil of divinities, ambition?
> She is a corrupt power; shun her. Many prosperous
> Cities and homes have entertained her, and thereafter
> In degradation and despair watched her depart.
> She has possessed you. There is a nobler course: to honour
> Equity, which binds for ever friend to friend, city
> To city, ally to ally. Nature gave to men
> The law of equal rights. Want is the inevitable
> Enemy of wealth, and works towards war. Equality
> Settled for men fair measure and just weight, and fixed
> The laws of number. Night's dark face shares equally
> With the bright sun the travelling of each yearly round;
> Each yields in turn, and neither burns with jealousy.
> Shall day and night give equal service to mankind,
> And shall you scorn your lawful share of your own home,
> Deny your brother equal right? And is this just?
>   Why set so high, so extravagant a value on

> Sovereignty — that injustice crowned by good fortune?
> Is admiration precious? It is an empty gain.
> This wealth you long for — what advantage comes with it?
> For a mere name, it costs you endless toil. Enough
> To supply need contents the man who knows himself.
> A man's possessions are not his in private right;
> We hold in trust, as stewards, what belongs to the gods,
> Who, when they will, in turn take from us what is theirs.

Eteocles shows by his answer that he has closed his ears to everything Iocasta said, that his mind was closed before he came. The two brothers next give a verbal demonstration of the image of fighting beasts; and Eteocles concludes (624):

> To hell with our whole house!

Three statements about the nature of war are offered in the course of the action — offered, that is to say, by implication from the dialogue and the events presented.

First, war is excused by self-deception and carried on by self-contradiction. Polyneices demonstrates the former when he says to Iocasta (433—4),

> I call heaven to witness that I come in arms
> Against my kin and country most unwillingly.
> I have no choice —

which was no more true for him than it was for Agamemnon or for Orestes. A little later he adds (438—41):

> The thing
> That gets most honour in this world, and wields more power
> Than anything else, is money. That's what I've come here
> To get, with twenty thousand spears to press my point.

This was true enough, but somewhat unrelated to the 'just cause' spoken of by the chorus in 258—60, which Polyneices will himself urge in 484—96. Eteocles, after asserting that 'equal right' and 'justice' are meaningless terms, goes out to battle with these words (781):

> As I set forth,
> Justice, my ally, promises me victory.

And then, forgetting that in his discussion of strategy with Creon he has made four rash and thoughtless proposals in a row, he prays, for success and safety, to 'Precaution, that most helpful deity'.

The second statement: war inspires nobility, then wastes and ignores it.

Teiresias prescribes the sacrifice of Menoeceus if Thebes is to win the battle. This proposal, properly described in its Euripidean context (see Chapter 7) as a hoary imbecility already discredited in at least five earlier plays, none the less rouses a response from the heroic patriotism of the young and innocent Menoeceus, who thereupon goes off to kill himself, saying as he departs (1014):

> I will purge our country from her sickness.

Not only was this a false hope, since in spite of his sacrifice the sickness raged as before till it had obliterated the royal house; but the prince's self-sacrifice is mentioned again only perfunctorily, and when his distracted father re-appears he cannot, even to comfort himself, regard any supposed connexion between his son's death and the Theban victory as worth speaking of.

Thirdly, the pretentious arrangements of war never work. The carefully arranged interview with Polyneices was never meant to work. No one knew whether the sacrifice of Menoeceus worked, and apparently no one cared. In the first battle, when masses of dead bodies already covered the field, to save further bloodshed Eteocles challenged his brother to single combat. Not only did this decide nothing, since at the end of the duel the two armies at once fell to fighting again, but this final battle was thereupon won by a mere accident (1466—9); and over the corpses of the brothers their mother killed herself. In this last tableau, since Thebans, like Athenians, claimed to be sprung from the earth they inhabited, we see a symbolic picture of two cities which, having ferociously destroyed each other, have at the same time destroyed their common mother, the land that bore them. This imagery appears again in the next play, *Orestes*; but there is still one further point here which we should notice, voiced by the Phoenician girls who form the chorus.

Here is the first strophe of their second choral ode (784—800):

> O Ares, bringer of agonized exhaustion,
> Why are you dedicated to blood and death?
> Why does your trumpets' blare
> Untune the songs of Bacchic festivals?
> When the ripeness of youth is crowned with flowers,
> And girls dance together,
> You are not with them, tossing your hair to the wind;
> When breath fills the flute
> You sing no song to make the Graces dance;
> You assemble warriors and weapons, you inflame
> The fighters of Argos with thirst for Theban blood;
> No music of pipes sweetens your merrymaking;
> Your running is not graced

With the wild whirl of thyrsus and fawnskin;
You rush with a rattle of chariots, ringing of bridles,
Thunder of hooves beside the quiet Ismenus;
You inflame the earth-sown race of Thebes
With hatred for the men of Argos;
You marshal your joyful dancers
Whose food is the fury of war
To match their massed bronze against walls of stone.
Hatred, that god of terrible power,
Has devised this misery for the royal house,
To exhaust with anguish the descendants of Labdacus.

In this superb poem Euripides draws a contrast between the destructive excitement of the war-god Ares and the creative excitement of the life-god Dionysus, a native of Thebes. Throughout the play these two gods are presented as governing two opposed worlds, of death and of life; human communities may choose, or be fated, to live in one world or in the other. The first choral ode (638—75) introduced this theme, telling first the story of the joyful birth of Dionysus, then the story of Ares' dragon and the cruelty and slaughter which it caused. Allied with Ares and the dragon (from whose teeth the Theban race was born) is the dreaded Sphinx, who devoured Theban citizens (906—11, 1019—42) until Oedipus overcame her. The power of these two monstrous enemies to life, together with the image of the two beasts locked in combat, forms a recurring *motif* of the play; and interwoven with this theme is its opposite — the joy of Dionysus, 'the ripeness of youth crowned with flowers'.[11] But Ares prevails, and Dionysus fades, till at the end Antigone, returning with the bodies of her brothers and her mother, speaks of herself as 'a Bacchant of the dead'. The urgency of the choice between Ares and Dionysus, death and life, is pointed to by Teiresias when, speaking of the two brothers, he says (880),

Creon, death for each by the other's hand is very near.

But Teiresias is himself already committed to the wrong choice. His answer to the predicament of Thebes takes account of Ares (who in Sophocles, *Oedipus Tyrannus* 190—202, was recognized as the enemy of Thebes) and urges Creon to 'gain Ares for his ally' (936); but ignores Dionysus, who is a son of the Theban royal house. There is no other play in which the malevolent influence of Ares is so specifically and exclusively invoked; yet in the first two stasima the chorus makes it clear that Dionysus, bringer of joy, is no less a god than Ares, if Thebes would but claim his protection. Instead, the heroic Menoeceus dedicates his life to Ares (1006). Creon has been generally called ignoble because he rejected Teiresias' words outright; but a study of the play as a whole, and of Euripides' writing as a whole, points to an opposite conclusion — that irony is at work here in the poet's characteristic manner. If Agamemnon and Orestes,

faced with their menacing oracles, had trusted their natural instinct as
Creon trusts his, Hellas would have been spared the agonies of the house of
Atreus. Such, then, is the central purport of *The Phoenician Women* — a message
to bid Athens choose, before it is too late, between these two worlds, between
death and life; and make peace with Sparta. It is hard to imagine a play
filled with a more urgent prophetic tone for the moment of its production.

The message of *Orestes* has already been studied in Chapter 3, and it is only
necessary to give a brief recapitulation. There is here no fighting, no Messenger from a battlefield; instead we are shown in symbolic form the roots of
the disease from which arise such disasters as we witnessed in *The Phoenician
Women*. *Orestes* asserts that the result of prolonged war is mental and moral
deterioration in those who yield themselves to its influence. The fighting
youth of Hellas have, in the name of an imaginary 'freedom', destroyed the
land that gave them birth; and this deterioration is now indistinguishable
from insanity and is incurable. The sudden corruption of the chorus in the
middle of the play after the arrival of Pylades is a reminder that the destructive potency of war works not only on leaders, not only on fighting men, but
on the whole civil population, including women. The propaganda of war
deludes its victims with false comfort, rouses contempt for gentleness, and
destroys beauty. Athens has thus destroyed herself; and the poet, about to
leave her, bids farewell to her lost greatness.

Finally, *Iphigenia in Aulis*, written in 407 in Macedon, and posthumously
produced by Euripides' son in Athens, probably in 405. There is no need here,
as in *Orestes*, to interpret symbolism. The play is about war, its distinguished
leaders, its anonymous soldiers, and its innocent victims. The fleet of a
thousand ships is at anchor in the Bay of Aulis; the great army is waiting for a
fair wind to Troy. The chorus are girls who have come over the narrow water
from Chalcis to gaze at the famous heroes, at the tents, weapons, chariots, and
ships. At first they are lost in admiration. Later they ask themselves, What
are these men going to Troy to do? They know (776—9):

> There will be heads forced back, throats cut,
> Streets stripped, every building gutted and crashed;
> Screams and sobs from young women . . .
> God grant that neither I nor my children's children
> Ever face such a prospect.

And they picture the women and girls of Troy (784—92)

> Sitting before their looms, asking each other,
> Who will be the man
> Who twists his hard hand in my silken hair
> And like a plucked flower drags me away
> While my tears flow hot and my home burns?

Athens had inflicted this upon other cities; now it was every Athenian woman's recurring nightmare.

The story of the sacrifice of Iphigenia was very well known to the audience. But in this play, even more than is usual in Euripides, assumptions about what we are going to be given are misleading. That, in fact, is the play's chief comment on war: that in a war nothing is what it seems to be. For example, ever since Aeschylus' *Agamemnon* everyone had known that the expedition to Troy was held up at Aulis by a stormy wind from the north-east, which could only be stopped by sacrificing Iphigenia to Artemis. Many modern readers have tried to interpret this play — have tried to enjoy it — on that assumption. But we are in fact told, first in the prologue and later by Achilles (9–11, 813), that there is hardly any wind at all. Yet the sacrifice is still demanded. Why? No explanation. Agamemnon tells us he is reversing his decision to send for Iphigenia. But Agamemnon knows exactly how many days it takes a horseman to ride from Aulis to Argos, and how long it takes a carriage to come back; and he has delayed sending his second message until it is probable that Iphigenia is on the point of arriving, when the decision will be taken out of his hands. Menelaus, again, is ruthless at first, and leads Agamemnon into a fine posture of righteousness, a protestation that he will not sacrifice his daughter, that the whole war is a piece of lunacy. Then Iphigenia arrives, and Agamemnon sheds tears. Menelaus softens: 'Compassion moves me for the unhappy girl,' he says; 'why don't we kill Calchas?' — and his brother, like a puppet on strings, now insists that the sacrifice is inevitable. What is shown here is a phenomenon only too familiar in our modern world: the fact that in a corrupt society a destructive pattern of events, once set in motion, advances automatically, fuelled by the self-interest of numerous individuals, towards its prepared conclusion, regardless of the presence or absence of any rational motive. So in this painfully realistic scene between Menelaus and Agamemnon (471–542), we cannot be sure that any word or gesture is what it seems to be. There is indeed a driving force behind what happens, but it only becomes evident later in the play: the mutinous army. It was the superstitious rabble of soldiers who, once the idea was leaked to them by Odysseus or Calchas (518, 524, 1361–2), insisted on the sacrifice (1346–52). This aspect of the familiar pious story was specifically put forward by the Elders of Argos in Aeschylus' *Agamemnon*;[12] and here in *Iphigenia in Aulis* the talk between Agamemnon and his brother (471–515) is not the emotional and touching picture it has sometimes been taken for; rather it suggests a plain instance of the ritual dance of diplomacy, in which forms of words follow a pattern felt to be necessary. There is really no problem; Agamemnon yielded a long time ago; now the two progress by formal steps towards an accepted outcome.

When Achilles enters, he plays a different tune in the same key. He learns that Agamemnon had induced his wife to send his daughter to Aulis with the tale that she was to be married to him, Achilles, when in fact he was intending to cut her throat at the altar of Artemis. Achilles is outraged; cold-blooded ritual murder, we assume, stirs his horror. Not at all. 'Agamemnon ought to have asked my permission before using my name as a decoy. Of course I wouldn't have refused.' Two other figures of authority in the army are named, Odysseus and Calchas; the commander-in-chief knows that he can trust neither. All these characters were familiar to the audience from Homer, where, if they are not to be unreservedly admired, they can be moderately respected. What Euripides is showing in this play is what twenty-five years of war have taught him: the power that falsity has over truth; the commanders who cannot command, the reasons which are covers for real reasons, the loyalty which is expedient, the resolves which are provisional; the banner of freedom held aloft by men who know their own slavery and find 'freedom' a useful excuse for doing what they intend to do.

The Epode in the third stasimon will summarize what the poet has to say about his warriors and their war. The chorus have just heard Achilles giving emphatic assurances that 'no one shall lay a finger on Iphigenia'; but the words of their ode do not countenance one shred of hope that he can or will carry out his boastful promises. Nor do they suggest that there is anything either religious, or beautiful, or noble, in the notion that a victim should be sacrificed, nor that military necessity provides any excuse. The girls from Chalcis waste no sympathy on the distressing dilemma of Agamemnon; they condemn outright the murder demanded in the goddess's name (1089—97):

> Where now can the clear face of goodness,
> Where can virtue itself live by its own strength? —
> When ruthless disregard holds power,
> When men, forgetting they are mortal,
> Tread down goodness and ignore it,
> When lawlessness overrules law,
> When the terror of God no longer draws men together
> Trembling at the reward of wickedness?

Which does in truth matter more — the achievement of a political end, or the right of an individual to life and security? This is a perennial question, and a practical one. In Euripides' time, as in ours, the answer must either be that the individual's right matters more, or it must demonstrate that this cannot be secured unless the political end is first achieved. Agamemnon's answer to this question, the speech with which he walks out of the play, not staying for an answer, but leaving his final words to echo in Iphigenia's ears, is a masterpiece of Euripides' characteristic 'mirror-irony'. Here it is in full (1255—75):

I am well aware what's pitiable and what is not.
I love my children; and I'm not an insane brute.
I shrink in dread from carrying out this act, my wife;
Yet if I do not, dread remains. I must do this.
Look at this fleet of war-ships marshalled here, this huge
Army of bronze-mailed warriors from the Hellene states,
Who cannot sail against the walls of Troy, or raze
That famous city to its foundations, unless I
First sacrifice you, as the prophet Calchas commands.
A strange lust rages with demonic power throughout
The Hellene army, to set sail immediately
And stop barbarians from raping Hellene wives.
If I refuse to obey the oracle, they'll come
To Argos, and kill me, you, our whole family.
Menelaus has not made a slave of me, my child;
I came to Aulis not to serve his purposes;
I am slave to Hellas. For her, whether I will or not,
I am bound to kill you. Against this I have no power.
So far as lies in you, child, and in me, to ensure,
Hellas must be free, and her citizens must not
Have their wives stolen forcibly by Phrygians.[13]

          Exit Agamemnon

We shall look again in Chapter 8 at the several layers of significance which wrap Agamemnon's thought about his own freedom; for the moment we will consider only their impact upon Iphigenia. In the next scene Achilles bursts in to say that his own soldiers, the famous Myrmidons, threaten to stone him if he opposes the sacrifice; that the whole army is in an uproar, and is coming, led by Odysseus, to take Iphigenia to the altar. Iphigenia knows now that there is no escape. She is a brave child; at least she can preserve dignity; she makes a virtue of necessity – Achilles uses that very phrase (1409); and offers herself for sacrifice. But, to support her courage in the face of such brutal superstition, such baffling nonsense, she snatches at the one poor threadbare reason which has been offered for this irrational cruelty: she echoes her father's parting words. Their falseness has been glaringly shown, she is hardly aware of what they mean; but they are better than nothing, and men have died for such phrases, and will again (1378–81, 1400–1):

          The power of all Hellas now looks to me . . .
     No more forcible abductions from our happy homes, when once
     Paris has been made to pay the price of death for Helen's rape . . .
     Greeks were born to rule barbarians, mother, not barbarians
     To rule Greeks. They are slaves by nature; we have freedom in our blood.[14]

And that final utterance, which, I regret to say, has most often been interpreted by readers and by scholars as straight patriotic sentiment, is one of the most powerful instances in Euripides' work of the method he used for the expression of his most deeply-felt beliefs. For he shared with Socrates two gifts — the knowledge that no mind can receive new truth unless it is looking for it, and the ironic self-restraint to put that knowledge into effect.

This rapid survey of nine plays has set forth in summary what seems to me to constitute the most fully developed criticism of war as an established human activity that has come to us from the ancient world. To appreciate the originality and force of Euripides' message one should read what remains of his writings in close and constant comparison with the History composed by his contemporary and — in some sense — his fellow-dramatist, Thucydides. Neither was what we mean by the term 'pacifist'. Both regarded war as a necessary part of political life, however painful; they criticized the particular war from which Athens proved incapable of extricating herself. The historian saw the foolish decisions, the perverse judgements, the loss of control, the reckless gamble, the surrender to superstition. The poet saw all these no less; and most of them are shockingly evident in *Iphigenia in Aulis*; but he saw always and insistently one further thing, which Thucydides was not concerned with: the individual victim. In a war there is always sacrifice; sometimes exacted, sometimes offered; sometimes effective, sometimes wasted; but always to be pitied and valued, never to be ignored. When at last Athens fell, those who died of famine in the final months, innocent or guilty, were the victims whose suffering, according to Euripides' code, merited more serious consideration than the fortunes of demagogues or diplomats. That is a truth which in our day — and we may be thankful — is more often and more forcibly stated than ever before in world history; but the fact that it seldom influences a major political decision is one reason why the plays of Euripides, if understood in the full force of their bitter irony, bear a needed message for the modern world.

7

SACRIFICE FOR VICTORY

Sacrifice was the central act of most religious observances in ancient Greece; and many of the essential activities of secular life, whether routine or occasional, were adorned, protected, and validated by sacrifice. Sometimes the offering was of corn, cakes, flowers, or wine poured on the ground; but ritual often demanded a living victim, and the sight of a bull, goat, sheep, boar, or cock ceremonially slaughtered was familiar to every Greek. In course of time, and in private company, this familiarity bred contempt. There are scenes surviving from two different plays of Menander where a scrawny old sheep is dragged on to the stage and heartless jokes are made about the risk of its dying of old age before the guests arrive for the party. But as late as the time of Euripides, and especially on public occasions, the prestige of sacrificial ceremony preserved its vitality.

One aspect of this prestige was the emphasis which custom laid upon the individuality of the victim selected. It had to be the most perfect animal available, and thus had often been designated for this purpose from birth, kept under special conditions, watched and tended with religious care. If it was tame under the hand it was the less likely to invalidate the ritual by resistance; but a beast that had been used for labour was generally regarded as unsuitable for sacrifice. Therefore the victim was more likely than other beasts to be one which had been reared with personal affection like a domestic pet. It walked to the altar decked with wreaths and ribbons. These details combined with the solemnity of the occasion, the total silence prescribed for the moment of death, and the beauty and innocent helplessness of the animal, to strengthen the worshipper's sense of identification with the life thus visibly spent on his behalf. Such a significance would be clear enough if the sacrifice was a thanksgiving for success or an expiation of guilt; it was still more vivid when a commander on the eve of an expedition or a battle was — to quote again Aeschylus' phrase — 'implanting willing boldness in dying men' (*Agamemnon* 803—4) by inflicting on a bull the death each man was ready to risk but hoped to avoid.

These emotions were familiar to everyone in fifth-century Athens, and they have their analogies in our society today. In Homeric times the numinous impact even of a simple routine sacrifice, where an animal was killed, must often have made the unseen world very real to some of those who participated. But when, as in Agamemnon's case, the victim whose throat would provide the reassuring blood was

> Not an animal grazing to the farm-boy's pipe
> Or the herdsman's whistle,
> But a girl reared at her mother's side
> To be bride to an Argive prince (*Iphigenia in Aulis* 1083—8)

—then the intensity of the spectators' feeling, the depth of their identification with the victim, was something entirely beyond our modern experience, and perhaps only remotely real to most of those who in the fifth century B.C. sat in a theatre to watch these strange but compelling enactments of tales from a yet earlier age.

The sacrifice of Iphigenia is the whole theme of *Iphigenia in Aulis*, and is treated retrospectively in *Iphigenia in Tauris*. The sacrifice of Polyxena is the theme of the first half of *Hecabe*, and is reported and lamented in *The Women of Troy*. The sacrifice of Macaria, though neither seen nor reported, completes the first half of *The Children of Heracles*. The sacrifice of Menoeceus occupies about two hundred lines in *The Phoenician Women*; the sacrifice of Otionia, a daughter of the Athenian royal house, is a central theme in *Erechtheus*. Each of these sacrifices was made to ensure the victory or safe passage of an army. Aeschylus dealt retrospectively with the sacrifice of Iphigenia in *Agamemnon*; no such sacrifice occurs in his other extant plays, none in Sophocles. To include in the category of 'sacrifice' such deaths as those of Heracles in *The Trachiniae*, or of Alcestis, or of Helen in *Orestes*, is to confuse the issue. (Pentheus in *The Bacchae* is a true sacrifice, but of a different significance from the cases we are now dealing with.) The five instances in Euripides of 'sacrifice for victory' plainly constitute a theme which he wanted the Athenians of his day to consider; and all seven of the plays which present these instances were written during the Peloponnesian War. What, then, was Euripides' purpose in returning so often to this theme?

The usual approach to such a subject as 'the concept of sacrifice in Euripides' would be, I suppose, to collate allusions to sacrifice in Homer and Hesiod and other early writers with the findings of anthropologists, examine the legends involving human sacrifice which are treated by Euripides, and assume that the form in which these legends appear in his work arose from his awareness of the place which religious sacrifice held in the practice, and in the conscious or unconscious beliefs, of his contemporaries and of recent generations. Such a study is obviously of interest and value. An enquiry of that kind, however, would involve much material that is outside the scope of this book; I shall therefore confine myself to asking, in regard to each of the relevant plays, What reaction did the poet expect to arouse in the different sections of his audience? What dramatic use was he making of this idea for an audience whose confused and contradictory feelings he observed and understood? He has in fact given us, in one of the plays most concerned with this topic, a picture of such emotional confusion ascribed specifically to Athenians (*Hecabe* 116–29):

> Then in the council of Greek spearmen
> Two factions clashed in a fierce dispute;
> These cried 'Sacrifice!' and those cried 'No!'
> The one who took your part was Agamemnon,
> Faithful to his love for the frenzied prophetess;
> But the two Athenians, the sons of Theseus,
> Though making two different proposals,
> Were united in this opinion,
> That Achilles' tomb should be crowned with living blood.
> It was wrong, they said, to give more consideration
> To Cassandra's bed than to Achilles' spear.

Although human sacrifice as a religious formality was no longer a living issue, yet all the emotional elements underlying it were still operant, especially in time of war. If scholars today, in comparable confusion, can approve Demophon for piety, censure Creon for want of patriotism, abhor Odysseus but sympathize with Agamemnon, then certainly Euripides could expect in his audience every variety of anomalous reaction. No less certainly his own attitude was as clear and consistent as the ironic method which rendered it articulate to the few, an enigma to the many. I shall therefore examine the proposition that the interest which Euripides shows in the subject of human sacrifice is related less to its historical, religious, and anthropological significance, than to the poet's overriding concern with his audience and their immediate predicament — which in the case of the plays we are now considering was first and always the war; and not only with his audience, but with the whole life of the men, women, and children, slave or free, both of his own city and of the wide Hellenic world.

One question needs to be asked at the outset. Did Euripides himself have any clear judgement upon the human sacrifices which he treats of in his plays? It has been held by many that Agamemnon is only speaking the plain truth when in *Iphigenia in Aulis* 1258 he says to Iphigenia, 'I must do this, I have no choice'; that Macaria's offering of herself was not only heroic but admirably pious, and that piety was what prompted Demophon's action; that though Odysseus in *Hecabe* is heartless, his plea for the necessity of honouring those fallen in battle is legitimate; that Praxithea is what Lycurgus took her to be, a heroic example of unselfish patriotism; and that Creon in *The Phoenician Women* demotes himself from heroic status by urging Menoeceus to escape. Each of these five propositions is based on the assumption that we are to take at their face-value — as most fifth- and fourth-century readers evidently did —the speeches made by those characters who promote or accept these sacrifices. This means that the horrified repudiation expressed by Demophon himself in *Children of Heracles* 411—14, the indignant condemnation voiced by Hecabe in *Hecabe*, by Andromache and Hecabe in *Women of Troy*, by Creon in *The Phoenician Women*, and by the chorus in *Iphigenia in Aulis* —that all this merely represents a variant opinion on an issue which is no longer controversial, since human sacrifice had no part in fifth-century religious ritual. If this is so, then the emotional power which gained Euripides the name of 'the most tragic of the poets' was little more than an academic or artistic exercise; he is rather to be praised for versatility than censured for moral self-contradiction; and he is open to the charge of sensationalism. This conclusion I find unacceptable; I do not believe that so cool an approach could produce such passionate writing, any more than that Bacon could have written *Hamlet*. An alternative conclusion is offered by that view of the poet's ironic method which has been set forth in Chapters 1—6, which alone, I believe, makes it possible to credit Euripides with both consistency and humanity.

A. P. Burnett, in *Catastrophe Survived*, page 22, says: 'The action in a sacrifice play is, like the action in a play of divine punishment, openly identified with the concerned will of god.' This statement has some validity in the critical context in which it is made; but it is important to notice that Euripides, in dealing with, for example, the punishment divinely appointed for Clytemnestra, takes a radically different moral position from that adopted by either Aeschylus or Sophocles; he severely censures both divine command and human obedience. It should be no surprise, then, if we find him developing a similar attitude in presenting the five stories of human sacrifice which occur in his extant plays. Aeschylus himself had already implied a tentative censure of both Calchas and Agamemnon. Euripides in perhaps four of the five instances he deals with has left open the possibility, however remote, of identifying sacrifice 'with the concerned will of god'; but equally, in all five cases — and sometimes with inescapable directness — he invites the opposite interpretation of his drama as ironic and significant censure.

Before proceeding to test this in detail, we should observe how these dramatic instances of 'sacrifice for victory' are connected with the two principal themes of Euripides' whole work. First, all the instances show that, once the necessity for a sacrifice has been claimed by military interests, there is no hope of overriding that claim. (It is just possible, though unlikely, that the missing part of *The Children of Heracles* told of Macaria's reprieve.) Ares is abhorred by other gods simply for this reason, that he claims priority over all the values they patronize; war is an excuse for the disregard of every sanctity, and 'Artemis detests the eagles' feast' (*Agamemnon* 138). Secondly, four of the five victims are women. This further illustrates the general readiness, voiced by many of Euripides' characters both male and female, to regard women as expendable, especially in a world where the continual slaughter of men in battle must have resulted in an excess of women over men. Thus it appears that Euripides presented the act of sacrifice, in both these aspects, as an epitome of man's *hybris*, of his misrule of the world and of his own society; and it seems at least possible that he presented it, at the same time, as an instinctive expression of guilt incurred by that *hybris*, and an attempt to expiate it.

This leads to a further point. If the act of sacrifice is a symptom of guilt, it is an easy shift from expiation —the desire to expunge a moral debt —to a more hysterical indulgence, a kind of ecstasy of slaughter, the total and final erasure of a former enemy whose blood might still have cried from the ground. A nation of hunters does not need to have this ecstasy explained (Artemis, who loved the young of all wild animals (*Agamemnon* 140–3), was herself the huntress); nor does a race accustomed to the ritual silence of a gathering before an altar, and the sight of a bull felled, flayed, and gutted, as described in the Messenger's speech in Euripides' *Electra*. Though public feeling in fifth-century Greek cities was sensitive enough to rule out the ritual killing of human beings as a religious act, it was still callous enough to order wholesale massacre and enslavement as an act of political expediency. The connexion of *The Children of Heracles* with the Spartan massacre of the Plataeans, and of *The Women of Troy* with the Athenian massacre of the Melians, plainly suggests that the judgement passed in these plays on human sacrifice was intended to prompt a parallel judgement on political massacre and on the slaughter of war in general. Since formal human sacrifice at an altar was no longer an issue, the only rational and artistic point of including it in a play (there are, regrettably, those who seem to regard these scenes as mere sensationalism) must be to suggest an analogy and to invite interpretation. In our own day the use of the imagery of 'sacrifice' has become banal beyond redemption; but in Euripides' day it held enough religious content to convey to thoughtful listeners a specific message related to their own political concerns and judgements. The central idea conveyed by the ritual of sacrifice is that one life is destroyed for the preservation of other lives. The first of the seven plays we are now to examine, *The Children of Heracles*, offers a clear analogy of this very situation; and it illustrates with special clarity both the ironic method and the poet's use of a well-known story to deliver an incisive message to those who could receive it. More than this, there is no other extant play so closely and poignantly linked with a contemporary political situation. For these reasons a fairly full exposition will be necessary.

The Children of Heracles was produced probably in 427 or 426 B.C., the fourth or fifth year of the Peloponnesian war. The first half of the play is about the proper treatment of refugees according to the Hellenic code of political behaviour (e.g. 329—30); and the final scene, of which a considerable part is missing, is about the proper treatment of a prisoner of war. At the opening of the action Iolaus, the nephew and comrade of Heracles, comes in his old age as guardian of a group of the dead hero's sons and his only daughter Macaria, seeking asylum at Marathon, in Athenian territory, from the persecution of Heracles' life-long enemy Eurystheus. The Herald sent from Argos by Eurystheus arrives with a few attendants, molests Iolaus and prepares to abduct the boys. The chorus, Elders of Marathon, intervene on behalf of the suppliants, and presently the king of Athens appears. He is Demophon, son of Theseus, and to him the Argive Herald states his case (139ff.).

'These refugees,' he says, 'are Argives. The law of Argos has condemned them to death; and Argos has a right to take them. They have sought asylum in many other cities, and no city has been foolish enough to offend Argos by harbouring them. Hand them over to me, and Argos is your ally; shelter them, and the Argive army is ready to attack you.'

Next Iolaus appeals to the king of Athens, speaking of a city's obligation to protect suppliants, and of the noble tradition of Athens as defender of the helpless. Demophon replies that he is bound by religion and tradition to protect the refugees, and promises that 'No man shall ever drag you and the children from this altar.' In the ensuing dialogue he tells the Herald, 'You are a fool to think you can quibble with a god'; and concludes the argument with 'Athens is a free city'. Iolaus responds with words of fervent praise for Athens and for Demophon (327—8):

> You are no less
> A man than Theseus! It's a rare thing nowadays
> When quality begets its like; you'd hardly find
> One in a score who's not a worse man than his father.

Then Demophon hurries off to the city to 'muster all our citizens in arms', and to 'send for prophets and make sacrifice'.

In the next scene Demophon returns, downcast and hesitant. 'I have assembled,' he says, 'all the chanters of oracles, and questioned them

> About ancient predictions, whether publicly
> Delivered, or in secret, which might indicate
> A course of safety for this country; and the experts,
> Differing in many other points, are all agreed
> On this one clear pronouncement: they insist that I
> Must sacrifice to Persephone, Demeter's Maid,
> The virgin daughter of a royal family.

Here we must pause and ask ourselves, What was the reaction of the Athenian audience to this unexpected turn? The answer will be a fairly complex one; and in this instance we will enquire first what relation this play may have had to current issues, and then whether the text offers us any reason to suspect irony.

The course of the war hitherto had tested the Athenian spirit severely. There had been both victories and defeats; but above all the onslaught of the plague had reduced and weakened the city physically and morally. It is reasonable to guess that during this period, when Athens was embarking on her most serious military undertaking since the Persian wars, one memorable name had been invoked more frequently and fervently than others: Marathon, a name symbolic of all that Athens was proudest of. Three generations later, Demosthenes still hoped to rally Athenian courage by speaking of Marathon. The chorus in this play are men of Marathon, the scene is before the temple of Zeus at Marathon. This in itself brings forward the emotional atmosphere from the twelfth century to the fifth, to events of sixty years ago, a period already established as a kind of recent heroic age, in which the new Athens was born. But there is another name, closely connected with Marathon, hardly less well known to the audience, yet never spoken by anyone on the stage, which is brought to mind again and again as the action proceeds: Plataea.

The play opens with a group of refugees sitting round an altar of Zeus, the guardian of suppliants. The Athenian audience had been familiar for the past two years with a community of three thousand or more refugees, women and children and old men from Plataea, who had been evacuated before the Spartans began the siege of that city in 429. In 428 about two hundred of the starved defenders had broken out of Plataea and joined their families in Athens; and the siege continued. There is no record to tell us what efforts these Plataeans made to persuade the Athenians to send a force thirty-five miles to try to save their menfolk from death and their city from annihilation; but it is unlikely that the refugees were not also suppliants. It is clear too that Athens, ravaged by plague for two years, could ill spare the energy for such an expedition; and in any event Athenians recognized that they could not face Spartan hoplites in the field unless they had strong numerical advantage. The exceptionally full detail, however, in which Thucydides tells the whole story of Plataea from 431 on, suggests that the matter was much in the thoughts of Athenians. Some uneasiness of conscience is reflected in his final comment, after he has recounted the surrender of the city followed by the judicial slaughter of the entire garrison (III.68): 'Such was the end of Plataea, in the ninety-third year after she became the ally of Athens.'

There are two other factors in this play which seem to turn the thoughts of the audience to Plataea, confirming the notion that the poet is using all the indirect means available to plant in their minds the name which was as disconcerting as the name of Marathon was inspiriting. First, it was universal knowledge (cf. 'This all Hellas knows', 219) that in the Battle of Marathon the only city which came to help Athens was Plataea, whose entire fighting force of a thousand men arrived just before the battle and held the left wing under Miltiades. Secondly, there is a passage in Herodotus (IX.26, 27) describing a council of war held by the commanders of another Greek army eleven years after Marathon, on the eve of the Battle of Plataea. The Tegeans and the Athenians were disputing for the place of honour in the front line on the left of the Spartan centre. The spokesman for each of these two cities, in arguing his case, re-told the legend from seven and a half centuries earlier, of how the children of Heracles came as suppliants to Athens. In the event, the Athenians were awarded the left wing; and in this play, when Hyllus arrives just before the battle with a supporting force, he and his men are placed on the left wing (671). In addition to all this, the story of Plataea as Thucydides gives it hinges upon two crimes: the slaughter of Theban prisoners of war in 431 by the Plataeans, and the slaughter of the Plataean prisoners of war by the Spartans in 427. The latter part of this play is concerned with the moral question whether or not a prisoner of war, Eurystheus, is to be killed.

There is no known evidence that a topical political meaning was perceived in this play either by the first audience or by subsequent readers. Neither have we evidence that any of the passages discussed in this book was read as ironic by anyone in ancient Athens. But the facts detailed in the last two pages form a coherent pattern unlikely to emerge except from conscious design. Even if there were only one or two among the thousands in the theatre who, when the play opened with a group of refugees seeking Athenian help, turned their thoughts to Plataea, to the memory of the debt Athens owed to her ally who fought at Marathon, to the loyalty to Athens which had led the Plataeans to defy Sparta, and to the desperate position which the two hundred defenders were in at that moment as a result of their loyalty — that fact is more significant than the blindness of the rest. But there was another crcumstance which makes it not only probable but as nearly certain as anything can be, that at the time this play was acted there was intense feeling in Athens about the obligation of the city towards Plataea. It is found in a sentence of Thucydides (III.36) which is separate from the four main instalments in which he recounts the progress of the Plataean saga. In June 427 an Athenian force captured the revolted city of Mytilene; and among the prisoners was a Spartan general called Salaethus. The heat of popular feeling in the case of Mitylene is indicated by Thucydides in his account of the long speeches of Cleon and Diodotus (III.36—52) and their dramatic outcome; and one effect of this excitement is seen in the Athenians' treatment of Salaethus. He had been sent by Sparta to lead the Mytileneans to revolt against Athens. Pleading with the Athenian government, dominated by Cleon, for his life, Salaethus undertook to persuade Sparta to raise the siege of Plataea. If he used this as a bargaining-point for his life, he knew that the issue was an urgent one, that many Athenians were anxious to save Plataea. The Athenians in their fury executed him at once. This act turned their failure to help Plataea from an excusable incapacity to a crime of monstrous ingratitude and cruelty committed for the sake of revenge on an enemy.

The siege of Plataea began in the summer of 429. The Spartans had invaded Attica in 431 and 430, and they came again in 428; in 429 they were fully occupied at Plataea (Thucydides II.71). This was a year when the Athenians, decimated and demoralized by the plague which first appeared in 430, had to face a defeat by the Chalcidians in the north, the revolt of Mytilene, and a surprise attack on Peiraeus. It is true that the year was also notable for Phormio's naval victories; but the fact that a large Spartan force was tied down at Plataea must have helped Athens to survive one of the most critical summers in the war. Loyalty to Athens cost the Plataeans the total destruction of their city and the massacre of the two hundred men who defended it for the last year of its existence. The analogy between the sacrifice of Macaria and that of Plataea, both heroically offered in the cause of Athenian victory, provides the first and most concrete example of the interpretation of 'sacrifice' which Euripides placed before his audience. The probable date of this play was 427 or 426. If it was 427, Euripides wrote it soon after the two hundred Plataeans who escaped reached Athens; if 426, he wrote it soon after the execution of Salaethus had removed the last hope that Plataea could be saved. Bearing in mind this emotional atmosphere, let us now look at some of the lines in the first two episodes. The analogy between the legendary and the immediate situation is kept from being too obvious by the fact that Eurystheus demanded that his victims be handed over, while there was no question of the Athenians' handing over the Plataean refugees to anyone. In other respects the parallel is painfully exact.

The refugees are without any home in Hellas (31). In Iolaus' appeal to Demophon comes this passage (214–19):

> But now I tell you, ties of blood apart, how great
> Your debt is to them. For their father claims to have sailed
> With Theseus when he went to get that blood-bought belt,
> And borne his shield; he brought your father up to the light
> From the dread keep of Hades. This all Hellas knows . . .

Marathon was named in line 32; and in subsequent dialogue, especially in Iolaus' appeal, 191ff., Marathon is politically identified with Athens; so that this passage alludes to the day when Plataea 'bore the shield' of Athens by holding the left wing against the invading Persians. Iolaus ends his speech with words which again recall the Plataean garrison still holding out, less than two days' march to the north:

Be their kinsman, be their friend,
Their father, brother — even their master; better that,
Or anything, than to fall into Argive hands!

The statement that 'the land of Athens is free' is made by Iolaus (62), by the chorus (113), by Iolaus again (198), and twice by Demophon (244, 287). Demophon in promising protection gives three reasons for his decision: the sanctity of Zeus' altar, kinship, and (242)

The third, which weighs most heavily, is my fear of shame . . .

When the Herald has gone, Iolaus' speech expressing gratitude touches eloquently every thought, every memory and feeling which could make the betrayal of Demophon's promise intolerable. Its chief theme is the honouring of a debt incurred by an earlier generation; and the promise itself is repeated by Demophon in proud and unconditional terms.

Then, after the first stasimon, Demophon comes back with his story of 'ancient predictions' demanding a sacrifice. It is usually assumed that his readiness to fulfil his promise and fight with Argos is now in conflict with his piety; that he is in a position somewhat like that of Agamemnon when faced at Aulis with Calchas' pronouncement;[1] and that Macaria's nobility enables him to save both honour and piety. But I believe that the truth of this scene is very different. There are at least four points which it seems that Euripides, had he meant us so to interpret it, might have managed better. First, the lack of dignity in 410—11:

Now, for myself, I am most anxious, as you see,
To help you, but . . .

This is an embarrassed man feeling his way to the breaking of a promise. The reason is soon revealed (415—19):

At this moment there are angry gatherings to be seen,
Where some say I was right to promise sanctuary
To foreign suppliants, others hold this was an act
Of folly. I have only to carry out this promise,
And civil war is on us.

This is a king confessing that he has no authority, that his subjects' opinion weighs more with him than his own judgement of right. What indeed is the function of a king if not to make a firm decision when some of his subjects want to break the Hellenic code because it involves risks, and are ready to resort to civil war to get their own way? To throw the decision back to the refugees is no less than shameful. Demophon's excuse (423—4),

> I hold my throne not as a Persian king holds his;
> I win fair dealing as I give it, deed for deed,

can perhaps be made, by a good actor, to sound impressive, but can also mean little more than 'I know I shall be obeyed as long as I please everybody.'

A second point where Euripides could surely have made the usual interpretation easier — if that was what he meant — lies in the two remarks made by the Elders of Marathon, 425–6 and 461–3:

> Can this be true? When strangers are in need, and Athens
> Is willing, does a god forbid us to give help?

They seem sure that the city is willing, and apparently are unconvinced by Demophon's report of opposition. When Iolaus has replied accepting the king's new decision and the refugees' doom, the Elders say

> Iolaus, do not lay the blame upon this city.
> To say we gave up strangers to their enemies
> Might be false rumour, yet would bring us deep disgrace.

Though they cannot say it in so many words, they are ashamed of their king. Thirdly, in 472–3 Demophon confesses

> These oracles
> Terrify me; I cannot think what's best to do.

This makes a lamentable contrast to his earlier tone, when he replied to the Herald. And finally, if we are to accept the usual view of the sacrifice as an act of pious obedience to divine command, we have to be sure that Euripides was capable of so presenting it. Every play we have so far studied in this book points to the opposite view. It is not a critic's business to speculate how Euripides, if he had wanted to show Demophon as a brave and pious hero, would have written this scene; but if with that intention he wrote it as we have it, the play deserves all the adverse comment it has received. And if the author of *Hippolytus* could a year or two later descend to this — while still capable of writing *Hecabe* soon after — we may wonder if even his usually acknowledged masterpieces are not partly flukes. I propose to abandon that hypothesis and assume that the scenes we have studied are ironical throughout; and that in interpreting the irony we should bear in mind the immediate preoccupations of the first audience, who knew that Plataean refugees were sitting with them in the theatre.

Let us return for a moment to the end of the first scene, where Demophon says to Iolaus

Your words I welcome; and these boys, I am confident,
Will keep your bidding, and remember what we have done.
I'll go and muster all our citizens in arms
And take the field . . . I'll send for prophets . . .

These words initiate the ironic design, which thenceforward develops by
its own impetus. Since our attention has been so firmly directed to memories
of Marathon, we have not far to look for an indication of the dramatist's
attitude to the 'piety' of Demophon in hesitating to commit himself to battle;
for the same piety was displayed by the Spartans when the Athenian runner
came to ask for their help at Marathon, and they replied that they would
come when the feast of the new moon was over. Euripides' attitude to the
directions given by 'oracles' is seen in all the plays which treat of human
sacrifice and in a number of others. In *The Suppliant Women* Theseus tells
Adrastus that he ought to have performed the routine sacrifices before setting
out to attack Thebes; but calls him a fool for heeding the oracle which told
him to marry his daughters to a lion and a boar. In the present scene we are
told that Demophon has sacrificed sheep or cattle on all the altars of the city,
as was proper. If these sacrifices had produced unfavourable omens he would
have been quick to tell us;[2] we must conclude that the omens were favourable. (These considerations are not irrelevant or fanciful. Every man in the
audience was familiar with routine sacrifice on military service, and no doubt
with the different attitudes to omens or oracles taken by different commanders. Listeners would apply their own experience to the situation in the
play.) If Demophon's offer of help to the refugees had been honest, he would
thereupon have led his army out to battle; for he says nothing of any need to
consult his people, as Theseus does in *The Suppliant Women*. If some special
urgent message from temple or oracle had warned him not to fight, he would
have done well to heed it; but he speaks of no such warning. Instead he says
that he 'assembled all the chanters of oracles and questioned them about
ancient predictions public or secret . . . ' By such a method of enquiry he
could find oracular support for doing, or for not doing, anything or everything. There is a passage in Euripides' *Helen*, 753—4, which shows the exact
distinction drawn between formal, routine sacrifice and listening to 'prophets'. The First Messenger, a model of common sense, says:

Better to ask the gods for blessing, after due sacrifice,
and leave prophets alone.

Even in the case of oracles directed to named persons on particular occasions,
Euripides everywhere in his plays insists that men have, and always have
had, a duty to decide for themselves whether to obey or disobey. Even
Aeschylus, in the *parodos* of *Agamemnon*, presents Calchas' oracles as con-

ditional, as a test in which Agamemnon was found wanting; and in Euripides this view is overt — as Agamemnon ought to have ignored Calchas, so Orestes ought to have disobeyed Apollo. Yet Demophon's piety rakes up anonymous, out-of-date predictions and makes them the excuse for a neglect of duty which is suggested to him by fear, but which the men of Marathon find shocking — for evading a battle in a just cause.

We now recall the words of praise with which Iolaus greeted Demophon's first promise (325–8):

> It's a rare thing nowadays
> When quality begets its like; you'd hardly find
> One in a score who's not a worse man than his father.

We recall his phrase at the beginning of the prologue (5) about the selfish man who is 'a valued friend chiefly to himself'; and his faith in the country he has come to — the Athenians 'will die sooner than betray us . . . they prize honour above life itself' (200–1); and the positive pledge that the king gave, 'No man shall ever drag you from this altar' (249). We will proceed, with one further general comment, to the entry of Macaria.

For Athenians at the beginning of the war the heroic age was the age of Marathon, when liberty and democracy were still holy ideals one could die for. In the play this period is represented by the memory of Theseus and the presence of the Elders. The new, degenerate age, Athens corrupted by power and demoralized by the plague, is represented by Demophon. (For a similar parallel used in *Orestes*, see Chapter 3, page 74.) Corruption, however, is in an early stage; Demophon has flaws but, as we shall see, is not beyond redemption. For at this moment the door of the temple opens and a young girl appears. Macaria, the only daughter Heracles ever had, has been waiting inside with Alcmene. Iolaus explains the situation to her (488–97):

> Chanters of oracles, the king says, all command
> The sacrifice to Persephone — not of a bull
> Or calf, but the virgin daughter of a royal house,
> If we, and Athens, are to live . . .
> He does not say in plain words, but says none the less,
> If we can't find some way to untie this knot ourselves,
> Then we must seek some other land to shelter in,
> Since his own first concern is to keep Athens safe.

What exactly is the situation? Iolaus sees part of it, as he shows by his judgement of Demophon's behaviour implied in the phrase, 'He does not say in plain words . . .' But Macaria understands at once what is happening. She sees that Demophon mistrusts his own authority, that he does not want to risk ordering his army to fight for a moral principle; that he is confident that no royal virgin will be forthcoming. Demophon hopes that he can thus gently push the refugees outside the temple gates, wishing them good luck. Macaria perceives that here is a cowardly king who must be made to fight. Her response is a gesture not of piety but of contemptuous challenge. Unhesitatingly she calls his bluff – but speaking past Demophon to Iolaus (500ff.):

> Before you bid me, Iolaus, I am myself
> Ready to die and give my blood for sacrifice . . .
> We should invite not sympathy but scorn,
> If we, who sat here weeping as suppliants to the gods,
> Demonstrate that a father such as Heracles
> Can beget cowards. We think better of ourselves.

She achieves her object – Demophon agrees to fight; and she must pay the price. Her speech contains several daggers to reach Demophon's heart: she refers twice to 'cowards', and observes that 'many in such ways have betrayed their friends'; her pride in her father and in herself is unlimited, as it should be; she both accepts the position that a woman's life is expendable for the life of her brothers, and condemns as unworthy of her attachment a world in which so cruel a fate crushes her, hoping to find no shadow of it below the earth (593–6). Her one request to the king is made through Iolaus (565); but even Iolaus has not the firmness to stand beside her at the altar. Her desire 'to die in the hands of women' is pointedly not a gesture of maiden modesty, since she asked first for the support of Iolaus; it is a final despair of meeting nobility, as she understands it, in any man. In bidding farewell to the young brothers for whose future she will die, she tells them (584–6) to honour Iolaus, and the Elders of Marathon, and Alcmene; Demophon she ignores, though he has just spoken to her. She asks her brothers to give her a glorious tomb, which

> Shall be, for babes unborn, maidenhood unfulfilled,
> My recompense and treasure – if there is a world
> Below the earth; I hope there is none.   (588–93)

I doubt if there is any figure in Euripides who in so few lines establishes a heroism so vivid, relentless, and clear-eyed, so perfectly embodying the ironic vision of the poet. For those whose eyes were open to the imagery of the scene, her blazing, defiant courage symbolized the spirit of the garrison of Plataea, still tying down a Spartan force which might otherwise be harassing Athens. The reality of human sacrifice can seldom have been clearer. As Macaria leaves the stage, Iolaus gives a second indication that heroic irony is beyond him, that he is old and worn out (600–1):

Farewell! Reverence forbids that I should speak ill of divine Persephone, to whom your blood is dedicated.

Characters elsewhere in Euripides are not afraid to condemn bloodthirsty gods; and this picture of pious submission is as ironic as the similar picture of Peleus at the end of *Andromache* or of Theseus at the end of *The Suppliant Women.*

The second sacrifice-play is *Hecabe*, first acted about 424. We have already studied (Chapter 6, pages 162–3) one of this play's themes, the manifold corruptions engendered by war; and in Chapter 8 we shall trace another, the meaning of freedom. But the first half of *Hecabe* is built around the sacrifice of Polyxena; and here the barbarous procedure is invested with all the decency possible —a solemn ritual, respectful participants, a sincere officiator, a superbly noble victim. What, then, is Euripides intending to say? It is clear that many among his audience would feel they had witnessed a moving and solemn occasion whose cruelty was redeemed by Polyxena's heroism. The poet has made every possible concession to religion, to the ancient, intangible compulsions which surround and sanction sacrifice; and to the feelings of a son, and of comrades-in-arms, about the honour due to a dead hero. For those who look at the figures behind the ceremony, these concessions show only that the most moving ritual, the most noble suffering, do not redeem the guilt, dishonesty, and inhumanity which together produce this compulsive act — an act in itself epitomizing the self-deception, false sentiment, and ineffectiveness of the war-mentality that demands it. Guilt and dishonesty dictate every word and motion of Agamemnon; smooth inhumanity is the prominent feature of Odysseus; and these two are in charge of the proceedings.

The sacrifice of Polyxena is first foretold by the ghost of Polydorus in the prologue. The Greeks will grant Achilles' request 'because they were his friends' and must not leave him without a gift. This laudable feeling on the part of the chiefs is enlarged upon by Odysseus when he comes to fetch the victim; but it reads like a cover for that same guilt — born of indiscriminate bloodshed and desecration of temples —which after the killing made the soldiers bring gifts for Polyxena's corpse. When the chorus first tell Hecabe that sacrifice is demanded (107–9) they indicate how decisions of this kind are made. It is an impersonal majority decision (see Chapter 6, page 165), so that even those who advocate it can deny responsibility. The chorus retail to Hecabe the account they have heard (130–5):

> And the argument pulled equally both ways,
> Till that cunning, honey-tongued quibbler,
> That pleaser of the mob, Odysseus, urged them
> Not to dishonour the bravest of all the Greeks
> For the sake of a slave's throat.

There had been a similar debate in the Athenian Assembly two or three years earlier, in 427, over the sentence passed on Mytilene, when the decision was revoked the following day. Another such debate took place in the year after this play, to decide the fate of Scione; and then the sentence of massacre and enslavement was carried out. The advocate of death on that occasion was Cleon, who doubtless would be unmoved by the words Euripides gave to Hecabe (254–7):

> You are a low and loathsome breed, all you who grasp
> At popular honours, who without a thought betray
> Your friends, for one phrase that will gratify a mob.
> Let me not know you!

Polyxena's position is different from Macaria's, and her spirit is gentler; but her clear vision and absolute resolve are the same. Her time on stage was brief; but Talthybius' report of the scene at the altar gives us the only full account in Euripides of such an occasion. Talthybius' tears are genuine enough; so is the pride with which he recounts his own part in the ritual (531–3):

> I stood up and called,
> 'Silence, Achaeans! Let neither voice nor sound be heard
> In the whole army!' I had them hushed and motionless.

So is the feeling of Neoptolemus' prayer before the sacrifice (538–41):

> Grant that we may unmoor our ships
> And with a prosperous voyage come safe to our own land –

words whose unconscious irony would be evident to even the less alert listener, since the disasters of the voyage and of the homecoming were as well known as the story of the siege. The pathos of the ritual killing is so complete that it makes an audience accept as honourable the emotion of the Greek soldiers, their punctiliousness towards their victim (575–80). After this narrative, Hecabe's reflections on the ingrained quality of human nature offer a further comment on what has been done: the life of unchangeable nobility is destroyed, and the survivors who destroyed it are unchangeably ignoble (592–602). The final thought on Polyxena's fate came nine years later in *The Women of Troy* 636–8. There Andromache brings Hecabe news of her daughter's death, and tells her:

> To be dead is the same as never to have been born ...
> The dead feel nothing; evil then can cause no pain.

The realism of such lines should help us to judge correctly what the author meant, in the play we are to study next, by Praxithea's phrases about the glory her daughter will enjoy after death.

Erechtheus is a play of which only some 175 lines survive in various fragments. Euripides produced it in 422. There is of course very much that we do
not know about its content; but the fragments available appear to be a fortunate selection, and what they tell us provides corroborative evidence both for
Euripides' purpose in taking human sacrifice as a frequent theme and for
his ironic method. The most important fragment gives us a speech of fifty-
five lines spoken by Praxithea, wife of Erechtheus, together with an outline of
the plot. The speech comes to us complete because it was quoted by the
distinguished lawyer and politician Lycurgus in 333 B.C. in the course of an
address to a jury, calling for the conviction of a certain Leocrates on a
charge of treason. This Leocrates, on learning of the defeat of Athens at
Chaeronea in 338, had decamped from the city with all his assets and effects;
returning after a few years when things seemed safe, he was brought to trial
for his unpatriotic behaviour. The speech is a flourishy performance, presenting with decorous tedium all the well-worn tropes and stances of patriotic
sentiment.

Our ancestors [says Lycurgus] set themselves a high standard in devotion to their
city. When the founder of Athens, Erechtheus, was told by the Delphic oracle that he
would overcome the invading Thracians if he sacrificed his daughter, his wife
Praxithea nobly agreed to the proposal. The daughter was sacrificed, and Athens
defeated the invader. Listen now to Praxithea's speech; you will perceive in these
lines a greatness of soul and a nobility worthy of Athens . . . How grateful we should
be to Euripides for choosing this subject for a play. He did so in the conviction that
this fine example would implant in citizens' hearts a devoted love of their country.

Here is the speech (line-numbers refer to the Greek text):

> A generous act is the more welcome when performed
> With noble readiness. Those who act, but act only
> After delay, fall short, I think, in nobleness.
> I, then, will give my daughter to be killed. My thought
> Offers me many reasons. First, no one could find   5
> Another city of more precious worth than this.
> We are a race not gathered out of foreign lands,
> But born from this soil — unlike other cities which
> Are composite of different elements brought in,
> As if by a game of chance, from various origins.   10
> The man who from another city settles here
> Resembles an ill-fitting mortice in a beam —
> A citizen in name, in fact an alien.
> Secondly, we bear children to this end, that we
> May rescue the altars of the gods and our home-land.   15
> An entire city has one name, but many souls
> Live in her: is it right I should destroy the many
> When I can give, for all their lives, one girl to die?

If I can count, and tell the greater from the less,
The fall of one man's house is not of greater moment   20
Than a whole city's fall, nor even equal. If
The children I have raised were boys instead of girls,
And flames of war enclosed us, would I then refuse,
In fear for my sons' lives, to send them out to war?
No; I would wish to have children who will fight and take   25
Their glorious place as soldiers, not mere ciphers who
People the city with their uselessness. Mothers
Who shed tears as their sons go forth to war destroy
Their manhood. I hate women who choose for their sons   30
Life before glory, and train them up to cowardice.
When soldiers die in battle flanked by all their peers,
The city gives them their reward, an honoured grave
And fame; and when my daughter gives her single life
To save this city, she alone shall win the crown.   35
She shall preserve her mother, you, her two sisters;
Why, then, is it not noble to receive this gift?
I will give up this girl, who is mine only by birth,
To be offered for her country. Should this city of ours
Be captured, what joy in my children have I then?   40
What power I have shall not betray our common cause;
The part of others is to govern; mine, to save.
Our city's health will prosper by this firm resolve:
That no man living shall, with my consent, ever
Annul the ancient customs of our ancestors;   45
Nor shall Eumolpus and his Thracian troops set up
Their trident decked with garlands on the city's steps
To oust Athena's olive and the Gorgon's gold
And leave the Maiden's shrine unhonoured. Citizens,
Take for your use the child I bore! Deliverance   50
And victory be yours; for I shall never shrink,
To spare one life, from saving Athens. O my land,
May all who live within you love you as I do!
Then we should live at ease, and you be safe from harm.   55

It is hard to believe that Lycurgus, in reciting these lines to the jury, really
thought that they showed nobility and greatness of soul; but it is still harder
to see what purpose he could have served by mocking the men he wanted
to persuade.

There are other scenes in Euripides where a parent contemplates the
imminent slaughter of a child, sometimes where the consent of the parent is
in question, sometimes when compulsion is absolute. Of the latter kind, we
have Hecabe in *Hecabe*, Andromache in *The Women of Troy*, Iolaus (a guardian,
not a parent) in *The Children of Heracles*; of the former, Medea in *Medea*, Creon

in *The Phoenician Women*, Agamemnon and Clytemnestra in *Iphigenia in Aulis*. In none of these cases is there any room for doubt that parental affection and tenderness exist; in some – pre-eminently in *Medea* – there is an exquisitely expressed tension between this feeling and the opposite call of duty or resolve. Why does Euripides allow Praxithea not one passing allusion to any such inward struggle, to any natural humanity? We can accept 'My thought offers me many reasons' (line 5); and in so poignant a case we expect the first reason to be one that will touch the heart. Instead we are given a formal political platitude – an honourable patriotic sentiment, if you will – but followed by reasons which, being of a kind to rouse heated political dispute and bitter feeling, are curiously, indeed horribly, out of place. Praxithea's second reason could sound acceptable in certain terms; but the terms employed show that to this mother her child is an *arithmos*, a cipher. This woman has so completely adopted what she conceives to be the masculine attitude, that she has become a monster. Next she presents a picture of the soldier's death, met shield to shield in the excitement of battle among his fellows; and is evidently unaware of the contrast between this and the cold cruelty and loneliness of ritual throat-cutting before an altar. She spends eleven lines in saying how she would send her sons to battle – if she had sons. Compared with her, Medea was a sane and warm-hearted person. Finally we observe with embarrassment that a dominant theme in the speech is the speaker's own present heroism and future glory.

Of all the Euripidean speeches advocating or deprecating human sacrifice, this alone presents, in a posture of self-denying nobility, arguments favouring a proposed sacrifice as a patriotic action. We must therefore ask, What proportion of the audience – which included both men and women – would accept this speech as an admirable patriotic utterance? For an answer to this our first evidence must be the fact that Lycurgus himself appears to have so accepted it,[3] and to have assumed the same attitude in the large jury he was addressing. But we must remember that he was speaking in a city where tragic drama had become largely a matter of 'revivals', a 'period' entertainment; and we should give proper weight to the second line of evidence, which is our own experience in the study of Euripides' method, and of his character as a writer. I believe that we can know enough of Euripides to say, even of so isolated a fragment, that here we have his irony in its most combative vein. The special interest of this example lies in the fact that we have Lycurgus' speech to demonstrate how unshakable, how impervious to reasoned attack, was the belief of most Athenians that death before an altar could be accepted as an appropriate fate for a young woman if war or religion required it – or at least that it had been appropriate in the not-so-remote past. As Demophon and several other characters show, the idea was found repulsive only by those whose immediate family was threatened. It thus becomes clear, first, why Euripides felt it necessary to return so persistently to this theme; and secondly, that irony, of a kind perceptible to very few, was the only kind of attack possible for a poet who did not intend to be silenced.

Our knowledge of the action of *Erechtheus* is largely conjecture; but the later fragments reveal that the sacrifice was carried out, and the battle fought; that Athens gained the victory, but Erechtheus was engulfed in a chasm of the earth by Poseidon, who favoured the Thracians; and that the two sisters of the slaughtered girl Otionia killed themselves in fidelity to a death-pact made by all three; this shows the ironic import of line 36 above. Another point to be noted is that, whereas the legend of Erechtheus in its usual form ma e him the father of Cecrops and three other sons, Euripides establishes (line 22) that the daughters of Erechtheus and Praxithea are their only children. Therefore in the final scene we find Athens safe indeed from invasion, but without either a king or a direct heir to the throne; and Praxithea, self-styled 'saviour of her country', a desolate and childless widow drowned in tears — confirming the impression that her speech was not meant for our applause.[4]

Finally, it is fair to ask, What is here the alternative to ironic interpretation? It is to say, for example with Webster,[5] 'Praxithea's speech to the modern ear is unforgivable, but we do not really know how it was counterpoised in the economy of the play.' (There are other unforgivable speeches, such as that of Clytemnestra in *Iphigenia in Aulis* which we examined in Chapter 2, pages 46—8, to guide us in interpretation.) It is to suppose that the creator of Macaria and Polyxena was, in writing this play, as insensitive as Lycurgus and his jury; that he could compose Praxithea's peroration of self-praise with the purpose of rousing honourable emotion —to which we could only reply in the poet's own words from *Orestes* 819, *to kalon ou kalon*, 'that noble deed was not noble'; that in this play alone he abandoned the scorn and indignation which he pours upon those characters in other plays who advocate sacrifice. It is against this general background that we should consider the meaning of Praxithea's speech.

The case of Menoeceus in *The Phoenician Women* is somewhat different in detail, but the same in substance. Instead of a maiden, the victim is a youth; but emphasis is still laid in his innocence and immaturity — unlike his brother Haemon he is a virgin (944—8). The play would in fact be structurally complete without this third episode; but the dramatic presentation of war in its essence which this play undertakes would be incomplete without a picture of sacrifice — its morbid compulsion and its noble generosity. The scene follows a stasimon (quoted in part in Chapter 6, pages 171—2) in which the evil and monstrous powers wielded by the Sphinx and the dragon are allied to the power of Ares and contrasted with the life-giving joy of Bacchus, the god native to Thebes. At the end of the scene the innocent

Menoeceus calls Ares to witness that he dedicates himself to the dragon. The issue between the two worlds of joy and of hate, of life and of death, is presented here in legendary terms; and the pathos of Menoeceus is that, since he naturally accepts the authority of Teiresias, his selfless courage is claimed and consumed by the urgency of war, and to no purpose. The question whether his sacrifice brought any good to his country is as obscure, and as disregarded, as in every one of the plays we are studying in this chapter.

Teiresias initiates the theme of sacrifice; and though in his first speech he warns Creon that disaster is near and 'evil holds advantage over good' (889), yet his second speech offers no valid hope of life or joy. The only gain promised from the sacrifice is the favour of Ares (936) and of the earth which bore the sons of the dragon's teeth. His reasons (930—48) are dragged out of childish legends from the incredible monstrous past, and his business is entirely with the evil powers antagonistic to life and joy. He speaks an ominous word when he first enters (825—5):

I have come here from the people of Erechtheus; there was war there too, against Eumolpus, and I made the sons of Cecrops victorious.

This seems (in spite of the anachronistic mention of Cecrops) to carry an allusion to *Erechtheus*, produced thirteen years earlier, and to that victory which had such sinister consequences (see above, page 197); and it seems natural to infer that Teiresias here claims to have delivered, or interpreted, the oracle prescribing the sacrifice of Otionia. The point of the reference is not to contrast Erechtheus' pious obedience with Creon's impious reluctance, though that interpretation remains open to those who can see no further; rather it is to remind us that in the earlier play the sacrifice, an antique barbarity initiated from the same suspect source, proved deceptive and ineffectual. This significance is ironically emphasized in 856—8:

> TEIRESIAS: This golden garland which I wear
>   They gave me, from their spoils captured in war.
> CREON: I take your garland as an omen of victory.

The Theban victory, like the Athenian, will cost the life of the king.

Teiresias' earlier speech contains several veiled allusions to the imminent peril of Athens and to previous warnings which the poet has uttered unheeded (878—9); but here we are concerned rather with Creon's attitude to the sacrifice which Teiresias commands. Having at once rejected the idea (919) and defied Teiresias, he is suddenly pierced with terror — not of the supernatural, but of the all too natural use which political or military power will make of such terror (973—5). He kneels before the prophet, knowing that once such a dangerously powerful ceremony has been authorized by 'religion' the citizens will insist on its execution (925—6). Agamemnon faces the same situation in *Iphigenia in Aulis* 516—26 (see below, pages 201—2); both cases remind us of the compelling fascination, half religious, half erotic, which such a spectacle could exert on a mass of unruly soldiers. To make matters worse, the petulant complaint with which Teiresias departs (954—9) suggests that he is merely doing his job, asserting his position in order to preserve it, and repeating without conviction a traditional rigmarole; that he is as much the victim of mantic mumbo-jumbo as his credulous clients:

> To practise divination by burnt sacrifice
> Is folly. Offer unwelcome words, and those for whom
> You practise hate you. If you speak falsely, in compassion
> For your enquirers, you offend the gods. Phoebus
> Fears no one; he should speak his oracles himself.

When Teiresias has gone, Creon speaks of the sacrifice in the same terms as Demophon used in *Children of Heracles* 411—14: no man in his senses would agree to such a thing. Commentators on this play call Creon's reaction 'un-heroic' — perhaps comparing him with the heroic Praxithea. But Creon is a man who trusts his natural instinct as a human being — as Agamemnon and Orestes should have trusted theirs when challenged by oracles; in this matter, as in others, Euripides' attitude is consistent from play to play. However, Creon's intuitive decision for humanity and common sense is powerless against Ares, who engrosses to his own ends the heroism of innocence. When Creon has gone, Menoeceus echoes (999—1005) the response of Macaria — though her eyes were open, while his are blind. Then he calls Zeus and Ares to witness that he is no traitor; that he will kill himself and 'purge our country from her sickness'. The rest of the play shows that this hope is empty; that once more, though victory is gained, the royal house is destroyed. Irony touches his exit (1015—18):

> If each man
> Would take the noblest gift of which he's capable,
> Reckon it fully, and offer it for his country's need,
> Our Hellene cities would be less experienced
> In sorrow, and the future would be bright with hope.

One man's 'noblest gift' may be his life offered, not in sacrifice but in battle; another's, the truth offered in a tragic play. The First Messenger (1090ff.) refers perfunctorily to Menoeceus' suicide — 'the deadly sword which brought deliverance to Thebes'; Creon mourns (1313) for the son 'who gave his life for Thebes'; but the sublimity of the self-sacrifice, for the necessity of which there is no evidence whatever, is swallowed in the flood of despair and death which covers Thebes after the invading army has dispersed.

Iphigenia in Tauris is a strange play, always popular, and one which draws widely different comments from different readers. Some find the tone light-hearted even in the earlier scenes, and are content to know that the oppressive gloom is designed to enhance the joy of recognition in the second episode. Yet in successive scenes every lighter touch is at once balanced with a sombre thought. During the lyric rejoicing of the recognition both Orestes and Iphigenia break in with bitter recollection (850–66). The only really light-hearted passage is the bogus procession (1152–1233). Even the moment of strongest hope, when the chorus have promised their silence, sounds like a cry from the depths to a distant light (1075ff.); and the 'Halcyon Ode' which follows blends nostalgia with bitterness. And, since the occasion which Iphigenia never forgets was a sacrifice for victory, it is natural to suppose that the author was investing this ancient story with the same analogous meaning for the war-oppressed world of 413 B.C. as we find in his other sacrifice-plays. Orestes' replies to his sister's questions show how disastrous was the victory bought with her blood. The chorus too are sacrificial victims of war, survivors from the horror of their captured town, which they describe in their second stasimon; and now condemned to assist at the bloody rituals of Artemis, and in the last scene saved from impalement only by the poet's device of breaking the nightmare and substituting a charade. Orestes is a casualty of the same war, destroyed by Apollo as his sister was by Artemis; indeed, in *Orestes* 191–3 Electra uses the word 'sacrifice' in exactly this sense (*exethuse*):

Phoebus sacrificed us, laying upon us the murder of our mother.

At the end of a play haunted by the mental and physical sordidness of ritual murder, it is a relief to hear Athena in the epilogue (1459–61) firmly assert the proper function of ritual — to recall by a harmless symbol man's escape from barbaric darkness and cruelty:

> The priest shall with his sword touch a man's throat
> And draw one drop of blood, as ransom for
> Your blood now spared . . .

Iphigenia is a complex character drawn in great detail. She has endured the whole ordeal of sacrifice except the final stroke, and twenty years of loneliness and deprivation. She has an instinctive love of family life in all its intimacy and stability; and she, like Alcestis, is a priestess as well as a victim. In particular she loves her father; who, as head of her family, had struck a deadly blow at family piety and love, when he led her to the altar. A number of Euripides' earlier plays arraigned the cruelty of fathers to their daughters (e.g. *Protesilaus, The Cretan Women, Danae*); this is the first of the complete plays to show in full the psychological effect of such cruelty: a noble nature perverted by ever-burning resentment. When she is told of the subsequent murders committed in her family, pity and grief at last liberate her from resentment. Having learnt from her experience in the Tauric temple that it is for her, as a mortal, to decide whether human sacrifice is right or wrong, and not for Artemis to instruct her, she understands the enormity of the wrong her father did to her; and she weeps for him. She does not speak entirely with the voice of Euripides, because she still clings, like many of the author's intelligent contemporaries, to the belief that gods must be good, or they are not gods (391), which was certainly not the creed of Euripides. Her criticism of Artemis, though somewhat naïve, is a natural attitude for a sensitive and non-intellectual woman. There is nothing specially attractive about Iphigenia, despite her readiness to die if it should prove necessary for Orestes' escape. We notice the selfishness which makes her ask the chorus to endanger their lives in her cause (1056ff.). But she is, perhaps more than any other figure in Euripides, a fully-drawn portrait of a woman whose life has been sacrificed to men's warlike ambition, who has survived many years and in some degree come to terms with her fate. This may be part of the reason why the play is popular.

Iphigenia in Aulis does not add any particular detail to the comment on society made through the other sacrifice-plays; but it uses the story to point, with equal clarity, to both those aspects of male *hybris* which have occupied the stage in most of the dramas. The single cruelty which ends the action is here, as it was in Aeschylus' *Agamemnon*, a foreshadowing of the multiple cruelty which the Greek army set out to accomplish at Troy. In lines 773–92 the chorus of girls from Chalcis identify themselves in sympathy with their counterparts in Troy who will be sacrificed when the city falls. The killing at Aulis was an act characteristic of the pursuit of war, which is exclusively a male pursuit and a burden imposed by men upon populations of which they constitute only one half; and it was an act characteristic of men's attitude towards women in a society where the confused and warped Clytemnestra is as expendable, as much a victim, as her daughter. One notable concept is made explicit here, which has been hinted at in earlier plays (see above, page 174, and *Phoenician Women* 973). The idea of human sacrifice is presented as something which, once proposed and set in motion, bears an evil life of its own, and rouses mysterious impulses that can be quenched only by the shedding of blood. It is in fact, like Dionysiac possession, an aspect of the unconscious revolt of the primitive human spirit against the restraints made necessary by living in families and in organized communities, a resurgence of the irrational desire to kill and to witness killing.

This process is first seen operating in Agamemnon himself. Once the sacrifice has been spoken of by Calchas, he neither questions its efficacy or morality, nor orders the fleet to get out oars and row (see Chapter 2, page 43), but acts like a man in a dream, pursuing against his will a course he is ashamed of. After Iphigenia's arrival, when even now it is perhaps not too late, when he evidently believes in Menelaus' 'repentance' as genuine (473ff.), he even argues against Menelaus that the sacrifice is now inevitable. Even when he contemplates escaping with his family to Argos, he despairs of holding out behind his Cyclopian walls, which in any other circumstances he would have trusted till the last moment. It is the mere idea of sacrifice, backed by the unreasoning savagery of a large and undisciplined army, which takes possession of his will and becomes a *mania*, an insanity over which he has no control. Further, both Achilles and Clytemnestra, who make many motions as if to oppose the sacrifice, seem at the same time to commit every blunder which must lead towards its execution, as though they were mesmerized into accepting and even promoting it. Clytemnestra, in fact, for all her protesting, seems less concerned with her daughter as a real person than Agamemnon is. Her attitude is not much preferable to Praxithea's.[6] In the background always is the sinister figure of Odysseus, whose power lies in his knowledge that the idea of sacrifice will give a commander a hold over his men that nothing else will.

The three choral odes of this play contain one curious puzzle. The girls from Chalcis were present all through the quarrel over the intercepted letter; and they commented approvingly (402—3) on the speech in which Agamemnon defied Menelaus and said he would not sacrifice his daughter. Yet, after the reported arrival of Iphigenia has entirely changed the situation, and Agamemnon, now resolute to proceed with the sacrifice, has forbidden the chorus to reveal anything (542), their first stasimon, in which they are alone and perfectly free to express their feelings, contains no reference to all this. It is a cool, if deeply felt, reflection on the conflict between love and virtue, showing appreciation of both, and concerned not with Iphigenia but with Helen and Paris, whose love they picture in lyrical phrases free of censure; and ending with a welcome to Iphigenia which endorses Agamemnon's deceit to an uncalled-for degree. We must, I think, conclude that we have here another consequence of the lack of revision which is evident in the unsatisfactory text of the prologue; the only alternative is the unwarranted supposition that the horror of what is being planned has numbed their minds, so that as soon as Agamemnon disappears they cease to believe it. After the first scene between Agamemnon and Clytemnestra the chorus move a step nearer to reality; they contemplate, not the killing which will take place today in the grove of Artemis, but the still distant massacre and holocaust of which it is the prefigurement. Their picture of the death-agony of Troy lacks nothing of vividness, and seems to take the chorus half-way from the incomprehension of the first ode (if that is what the first ode expressed) towards the horrified condemnation of the third. And in the third ode even this condemnation has to struggle forward, as it were, out of incredulous darkness into the cruel light of plain statement. The ode begins with a lovely description of the marriage of Peleus and Thetis, and the prophecy of the greatness of their son Achilles – whose distressing hollowness the chorus have just witnessed; and then (1080):

> Your wedding-day, Iphigenia, will be different ...

and at last they have to believe the immediate truth, and speak of blood that pours from a throat. Once they have looked at the physical truth, the spiritual truth bursts forth (1098ff.):

> Where now can the clear face of goodness,
> Where can virtue itself live by its own strength? –
> When ruthless disregard holds power,
> When men, forgetting they are mortal,
> Tread down goodness and ignore it,
> When lawlessness overrules law,
> When the terror of God no longer draws men together
> Trembling at the reward of wickedness?

The chorus, like Iphigenia and her mother, and like the Trojan girls they pictured in their second ode, are women helpless in a world of armed men – men whom the livery of Ares has rendered impervious to reason, beauty, truth, or quietness. Euripides has concentrated all that he can express of the insanity of Hellas in 406 B.C. into the symbolism of this play's words and action, culminating in a murder which was the crime not merely of a weak king or a corrupt prophet or a pompous athlete, but of a vast army of ignorant and unruly men whose mutinous shouts are heard off-stage when Achilles enters in the fourth episode.

To conclude: Euripides' interest in the theme of human sacrifice was not primarily historical or speculative; and he had no more need to resort to this theme for its melodramatic possibilities than had Aeschylus or Sophocles. Rather he chose it as a vehicle for his comment on the assumption made by states and individuals that war justifies every crime; to point out that patriotic emotion too often gives a quasi-religious authority to dark and barbaric impulses; and to show that here, as elsewhere, woman is usually the victim. I put forward this purely speculative suggestion: that Euripides in 427 was distressed to observe how many Athenians saw Macaria's self-offering as an act of religious dedication and Demophon's shiftiness as commendable piety; that in 424 he was again shocked to find his audience as susceptible to the religious aura surrounding the murder of Polyxena as the sentimental Talthybius himself; and that in 422 he tried a third time in vain, with Praxithea's horrifying speech, to shake their acceptance of traditional barbarity.

Be that as it may, Euripides used these stories of sacrifice because they offered a symbol of the two most important truths he had to express: the two guilty failures of mankind in learning how to live in a society of two sexes and in a world of independent city-states. The consciousness of these failures is summarized by Agamemnon in his exit speech in the play we have just studied. The one unquestionable necessity, he says, is that he and his army destroy a nation and its home (1261–3). Not to love his children would be mad (1256); but he is resolved to kill his child. He is acting, he says, for the freedom of Hellas; yet he himself is not free, but a slave of Hellas, and this slavery is a shameful compulsion to pervert his own nature and his own sanity. This is no less true of the whole army; and the army and its leaders together are Hellas; so the slavery is self-imposed. Therefore it begets the act of sacrifice, which is without reason and ultimately self-destructive. Agamemnon's claim that he is the slave of Hellas appears as a noble posture; but when he makes it he feels more shame than nobility. Is slavery ever noble, or freedom ever real? This question runs from beginning to end of Euripides' work, and it requires a separate chapter.

8

FREEDOM

We have looked in Chapter 4 at the picture Euripides gives of the life accorded to women by the society of his day. It is clear that he saw the antagonism between the two halves of humanity as an ever-present evil and the cause of infinite suffering; and his plays set forth the whole problem impartially from many different points of view. But there was a second antagonism and division in humanity which deeply occupied his mind: the mutually exclusive worlds of the slave and the free. The barrier between these could ⚡ sometimes be crossed. When a city was destroyed its free men had the privilege of dying, while the free women were enslaved and might conceivably regain freedom later, or at least bear sons who were not slaves; and we saw in several plays how in moments of crisis a bond would be felt between a slave of either sex and an oppressed free woman (as in *Medea, Ion, Iphigenia in Aulis, Alcestis, Andromache*). But in general it was true that to a man his free status was likely to be as dear as his life. Homer's Achilles, when appearing as a ghost to Odysseus, said (*Odyssey* XI.489–91) that it was better to be a living slave than to be king of all the dead; but the living Achilles would never have acted on that belief. Fifth-century Athenians might be forced, like those captured at Syracuse, to accept slavery; but freedom, for those who possessed it, was more worth dying for than anything else they knew.

The patriotism of Euripides, as of most Athenians, was based on the conviction that Athens ensured for its citizens a greater measure of freedom than other cities. There is no irony in Phaedra's lines (*Hippolytus* 421–3):

I want my sons to live in glorious Athens, and hold up their heads and speak like free men there . . .

nor in Demophon's repeated statement in his first scene (*Children of Heracles* 244, 287) that 'this city is free'. The claim was justified; but political freedom can only survive as the collective product of personal moral freedom; and this is a quality not guaranteed by any constitution, but one which, for all citizens male or female, may be threatened, lost, or won, at any time from unexpected causes. This truth is admitted in an unguarded moment by Hippolytus at the beginning of his tirade against women (*Hippolytus* 616–24). Why, he asks, must women be necessary for procreation? It would be better that men should 'buy their sons in embryo, at a suitable price; then they could live at

home like free men [literally, in free homes], without women'. Thus he
reveals that he regards marriage as slavery not for the woman but for the man;
that he lacks confidence in his power to preserve his own freedom in a
sexual relationship. The fact that Athenian marriage so often meant slavery
for the woman indicated a weakness in the whole concept of freedom: its
privileges were being enjoyed on credit, without payment of the true price.
Hippolytus' words illuminate a confession, and become a political comment;
and the same is true of many passages we shall look at in this chapter. Two
plays, *Hecabe* and *Iphigenia in Aulis*, show Euripides particularly aware of the
question, Who is free? and both are plays about war —which is natural, since
in most wars new freedom is sought and old freedom tested. The theme occurs
also in a striking passage in *Orestes*; and for most free characters in the plays,
as for the citizens in the theatre, the consciousness of free status is, in every
word and act, a part of the essential person.

This consciousness was kept alive and sensitive by the constant presence
of slaves. In Aeschylus and Sophocles we find a number of parts given to
slaves: the Watchman in *Agamemnon*, the Nurse in *Choephori*, the Guard in
Antigone, the two Shepherds in *Oedipus Tyrannus*. Their function as slaves
provides contrast, colour, humour; but they are there as persons attached to
one or other of the free characters. In Euripides the slaves are not only
individuals, they are also representatives of that other world whose pulse
and passion flowed always within arm's reach of the free man, was at his
disposal or at his mercy, yet was to him for ever an unknown life. In at least
twelve plays of Euripides a significant part in the action, or something
significant to say, is given to slaves — sometimes to three slaves in one play.
The Fragments too contain frequent expression of strong opinions about the
character and position of slaves. All these considerations show freedom, or
the want of it, as an element in Euripides' thought which is worth study.

In the Hellenic world from the Homeric age to the age of Euripides it was
generally assumed that anything like a complete human life was available
only to that small proportion of the race — something between one-fifth
and one-tenth — who could claim to be free males, with the privilege of lord-
ship over women and slaves. Stated in this way, the situation appears at
first, to the modern mind, outrageous — until we reflect that in the modern
world, with its infinitely enlarged resources, the privilege of having enough
food to eat and enough comfort to sustain health is still confined to a scarcely
larger proportion of human beings. And just as in the modern world the
hope of a better future seems to depend largely on the intellectual, moral,
and technical activities of the privileged minority, so in the ancient world the
unjust distribution of freedom was to some degree justified by the fact that it
made possible the development of that heroic ideal which we meet in the
Iliad, and especially in the dominating figure of Achilles.[1] Euripides, I
surmise, saw that in the fifth century this justification had ceased to exist.

In the nine plays which we studied in Chapter 6 he took stories of war from the vanished heroic world and filled their roles with men and women of his own day. In these plays the heroic ideal is realized, though in suffering rather than in action, by three or four women; in one episode of one play, *The Suppliant Women*, the heroic ideal is partially achieved by Theseus, whose behaviour before and after that episode reveals serious flaws; while every other male character in these plays exhibits in painful variety the loss of the heroic tradition, the partial and flawed nature of accepted virtue; and reports of battles show the bravery of ordinary soldiers dishonoured by the disregard and corruption of their leaders. The ideal once lost, the social inequity upon which it had formerly been founded was no longer justified. Not only does Euripides condemn the subjection of women as an affront to humanity, and the arrogance of enslavement as vulgar pretension, but he scrutinizes the freedom for which men value their lives, probes the performance of the free man among his fellows; and finds, not a virtue but a slogan, a word without substance, a self-deception which is wearing thin and exposing its wearer to self-contempt.

There was, indeed, an obvious reason why Euripides in his later work invited reflection about freedom. There can be no doubt that from the beginning of the war freedom was the principle more often invoked than any other to stimulate the patriotic effort of citizens. It was Athens that had won from Persia the freedom of Hellas at Marathon and Salamis, and founded the Delian League to preserve it. When Athens turned the League into an oppressive empire, Sparta rallied other states to liberate Hellas from Athens. The routine appeal to the love of freedom, which on both sides raised the temperature of every peroration, made common and meaningless a term covering a variety of issues in which great numbers of confused individuals were confident that they knew what the word meant. The political freedom of states, the personal freedom of citizens, and the spiritual or moral freedom of men and women in their thoughts and actions, were all described as *eleutheria*. Those who were thought not to possess *eleutheria* were despised; those who claimed it based their claim on contradictory grounds. Euripides has no definition to offer; his intention seems to be to present a variety of situations where freedom is in question, in a way that will induce self-searching in the listener or reader.

It may perhaps be helpful to compare the experience of reading Euripides with that of reading a modern work such as Solzhenitsyn's *The First Circle*, which has for its theme the same axis of freedom and necessity around which the motions of Euripides' figures revolve. In that novel freedom is the unquestioned desire of every character to whom the sympathy of the reader is drawn; but of the seventy men and women presented the great majority know that they have not achieved more than a distant glimpse of freedom. Spiritual freedom has been achieved, at an agonizing emotional and physical cost, by those prisoners who have suffered most, and by no one who is not a prisoner. The value of such a book lies largely in its power to make the reader examine and revalue his own life and freedom, and those of his neighbours and his society, against the experience of the people in the story. In looking to see whether we can find anything like this kind of value in Euripides, we will begin with *Hecabe*, first acted in 425 or 424. The play is about cruelty, suffering, and revenge; but a more contemplative consideration of the meaning of slavery and freedom lies close to its centre.

Hecabe in her first sentence introduces herself as a slave. The stiff joints and feeble muscles which a queen can wear with dignity now make the old slave a pathetic sight. The chorus too, once noblewomen of Troy, are now slaves. They enter with the news that the Greek leaders have resolved to sacrifice Polyxena at Achilles' tomb; and they report how Odysseus had urged the others (135)

> Not to dishonour the bravest of the Greeks
> For the sake of a slave's throat.

Hecabe calls Polyxena out and tells her. Polyxena in her single scene is presented as the full embodiment of *eugeneia*, aristocratic nobility, the ideal product of *eleutheria*. Her first reaction to the news is horror at the barbarity of the notion; her second, grief for her mother's distress; her third, to welcome death in preference to the slavery which has been forced on her. When Odysseus comes, Polyxena keeps silence for a hundred and twenty-five lines while her mother pleads and argues. 'If a slave may question a free man,' says Hecabe, she will remind him of a former occasion when he knelt before her begging for his life; 'that day you were my slave' (249) — and Odysseus confesses it. Hecabe's passionate reasons range from contempt for superstition, through the vindictive plea that Helen should be the one to have her throat cut, to pitiful supplication (291–2):

> In your country's law
> Killing is killing — there is no distinction made
> Of slave or free man.

This was only partly true of Athenian civil law; but in war whole populations were regarded as enemies, and denied all rights against death or enslavement. In Odysseus' reply the chief point is, 'We must deny no honour to those who fall in battle'; which begs the only question worth asking — whether the ritual taking of human life is a suitable honour for the dead. The speech is an insulting prevarication; and the chorus comment (332–3):

> O gods! How wretched is the condition of a slave,
> Forced to endure the wickedness of conquerors!

The measured clarity of Polyxena's speech is a contrast both to the painfulness of Hecabe's plea and to the falsity of Odysseus. Freedom can recognize
Necessity, and Polyxena will come with him not only because she must, but
because to die is her wish. What is life worth to her? When my life began,
she says (349ff.),

> My father ruled all Phrygia . . . Rival thrones
> And palaces contended, which should call me queen . . .
>   I was a god, in all
> Except mortality. Now I am a slave. That name
> Alone, being new to me, makes me in love with death.
> Then, chance might give me a harsh-minded master, who,
> Having paid money for me, would send me to his kitchen —
> Sister of Hector and many others royally born —
> To make bread, sweep the house, stand weaving at the loom:
> Day after day of bitterness! And some bought slave
> Would claim my bed, soiling what kings once sued to have.
> Never! I will yield up this daylight from free eyes;
> Hades shall have my body.

When Hecabe makes a last despairing protest, Polyxena answers her with
a cool realism full of contempt for Odysseus (404ff.):

> Dear mother, don't fight with him; force is on his side.
> Do you want to be thrown prostrate on the ground, wounded,
> Dragged, hustled, pushed? dishonour done to your old age
> By a young man? That is how he will treat you. So,
> Don't struggle. It is not worthy of you.

There is no place in this scene for that questioning of the social order which
for brief moments in other plays sets master and slave side by side as human
beings; here freedom is the simple essential glory of life, and now that Troy
is gone, (420)

> Born free, of a free father, I shall die a slave.

When Talthybius comes, moved and shocked, to report the sacrifice, it is
this simple view of the matter that fills his thoughts as he contemplates the
prostrate Hecabe (497—8):

> I'm an old man; but I would pray for death
> Sooner than come to anything like this.

His narrative depicts a scene in which the pure nobility and free courage
of the central figure diffuses over a vast and silent assembly the light of a

religious experience, strong enough to transcend the physical barbarity
enacted, and momentarily clothe alike ignorant superstition and callous
policy in a seemly robe of ritual. Here is the ideal and traditional spiritual
magnificence of mortal freedom in the presence of the unseen world. When
Neoptolemus drew his gold-hilted sword, he gave a sign (544ff.)

> To the young men appointed, to take hold of her.
> Polyxena saw, and this is what she said: 'You Greeks,
> Who laid my city in ruins, I die willingly.
> Let no one lay hands on me; I will give my neck
> Steadfastly to the sword. So, in the name of God,
> Let me stand free, and kill me; then I shall die free.
> Since I am royal, to be called slave among the dead
> Would be dishonour.' The whole army roared consent;
> And Agamemnon told the youths to set her free.

Even Hecabe is in some degree soothed from wild rebellion to philosophical
despair, knowing that Polyxena died royally (592ff.):

> How strange, that bad soil, if the gods send rain and sun,
> Bears a rich crop, while good soil, starved of what it needs,
> Is barren; but *man's* nature is ingrained — the bad
> Is never anything but bad, and the good man
> Is good; misfortune cannot warp his character,
> His goodness will endure.

But the significance of this reflection is not on the surface; the philosophical
despair of the poet is deeper than Hecabe's. For this drama shows, in its
treatment of the theme of freedom and slavery, a pattern somewhat similar
to that of *The Children of Heracles*; after a first half exhibiting a heroic ideal,
the second half turns a harsh contemporary light on the same concept to show
what has become of it in democratic Athens at war. I think it is only part
of the truth to say that in this play we are shown Hecabe reaching the limit of
her endurance and then breaking under the last straw. This quiet and philosophical speech invites also another interpretation: that the time-sequence
is irrelevant, that we are not to consider any relation between the painful
loss of Polyxena and the painful loss of Polydorus; that rather we should
contemplate the same person, Hecabe, in similar circumstances confronting
a similar assault of Fate or human cruelty, but now playing out the action in a
world where the name of freedom has lost the ennobling aura with which
it once surrounded and redeemed the struggles of mortal passion, has
become debased by vulgar use and perverted to sordid ends — in fact, in the
world of the Peloponnesian war; a time when we may be sure that few
speeches in the Athenian Assembly failed to belabour hearers with the

freedom for which Athens had fought at Marathon, and the slavery which Sparta wished to impose on Hellas.

The first half of the play has shown us the achievement of spiritual freedom by Polyxena; and she is dead. Now Hecabe is confronted with the murdered body of the last of her sons; and Agamemnon, who, though reluctantly, has just witnessed Polyxena's death, has come, consumed with self-conscious guilt, to bid her perform burial rites (733—8):

> AGAMEMNON: What is this dead body doing near my tent?
> HECABE: Hecabe, my own most wretched self, what shall I do?
> Kneel before Agamemnon? Or bear all in silence?

Just before Agamemnon entered she described Polymestor's murder of her son as

> A crime without a name; a sacrilege; an act
> Outstripping speech, or wonder, or endurance.

The killing of Polyxena had been becomingly decked with religious ritual; yet it was performed to gain a desired end, and was in itself the same act — but carried out by men with pretensions to civilized values, and in that aspect an even more heinous crime. For what purpose does Hecabe now consider kneeling before the commander-in-chief who bowed to other men's wishes for her daughter's death? For revenge, Endurance, strengthened by Polyxena's nobility, completed the first tableau and exhausted its possibilities. The second crime, not having religion to disguise it, provokes a response as savage as itself. Agamemnon's guilt makes him patient (729ff.):

> AGAMEMNON: Why do you stand there mourning, with your back to me,
> Instead of saying what has happened? Who is this?
> HECABE: He may regard me as a slave and enemy,
> And push me from him; so I shall add pain to pain.
> AGAMEMNON: What's in your mind? I am no soothsayer, to trace
> The path your thoughts are following, unless you tell me.

Twice more Hecabe takes counsel with her own soul, speaking of Agamemnon as if he were not there. The effect of these fourteen lines is to establish the relative positions of the two: for the free and victorious king, guilt and dependence; for the enslaved queen, authority and the freedom bestowed by suffering. Suddenly authority kneels before weakness, and Agamemnon's guilt asks Hecabe (754—5)

> Do you beg for freedom? That is readily granted.

The first sign of what has happened to Hecabe since she saw her son's body is given in her answer:

> Not freedom, no; but vengeance on a murderer.
> To gain that, I'll accept an age of slavery.

If this part of the play is understood as a sequel to the first half, then Hecabe here betrays Polyxena in devaluing that freedom for which her daughter welcomed death, and counting it second to revenge; and in so doing Hecabe, unlike Polyxena, has 'warped her character under stress of misfortune' (597—8). On the other interpretation a further, complementary meaning is added; what we witness here is not only an accountable moral weakening but a change of scene from the sublime to the real world where a fifth-century Demophon (123—7) has replaced the Theseus who died when Priam was young; the transference of a noble character, Hecabe, from the heroic age to an age where the ignoble erodes and corrupts the heroic.

Since Agamemnon entered, Hecabe has not spoken of Polydorus; it is even possible to infer that when he hears her speak of 'vengeance on a murderer' he can think only of the murder of Polyxena:

> Then what help is it that you beg me for?

Hecabe soothes his uneasiness:

> Not, Agamemnon,
> Such help as you think I would ask. — You see this body
> That I was weeping over?

Then the story of Polymestor and the gold is detailed in *stichomythia*. Why has Hecabe, in her ascendancy over her captor, apparently forgotten this man's part in Polyxena's death? She has not forgotten it; her revenge on Agamemnon will be to enslave him as he has enslaved her, to make him betray his ally, quake before his army, obey his prisoner's orders (e.g. 889), become a tool for her revenge, and live to remember it. When Agamemnon exclaims in horror (775) at Polymestor's crime, does he succeed in forgetting any of his own guilt? No; for he ends the dialogue with (785)

> Was ever any woman so misused by Chance?

and Hecabe, instead of rejoining, 'Misused by *you*', cryptically flatters his self-excuse:

> None, unless it is Chance herself that you speak of.

She then goes on to ask his help in punishing Polymestor. It is true that

Euripides seldom showed an act of revenge that was not plain folly, and usually disastrous; but there are times when, unless Law inflicts punishment, Justice must seem to be dead — and it is for such a moment that Hecabe now speaks (798—805):

> I am a slave; I may be feeble; but the gods
> Are strong, and strong is the great Law that governs them.
> It is by Law that we believe the gods exist;
> By Law we live, by Law distinguish right and wrong.
> If Law stands at your bar and is dishonoured there,
> If men kill guests, rob temples, and are not condemned
> And punished, there is no more justice on the earth.

It is a tableau which will be repeated in *The Women of Troy*. The magnificent cadences pour forth — and all to gain an end which, when later it becomes visible to us, shames with its sordid success the serene despair of Polyxena and mocks the divinity of Law. An elusive but haunting irony underlies the whole speech, as the eloquence intensifies to include even Cassandra's humiliation (824—30), and appeals to 'my master, great light of Hellas' (841); till the passion in Hecabe's words, and her adulation of the man who has destroyed her, strike the chorus as strangely perverse, so that they comment (846—9) on the way love and hate, friend and foe, may change places. But Hecabe's eloquence pales before the explicitness of Agamemnon's reply. He would like to satisfy both justice and the gods,

> If we could find some way to carry out your wish
> Without letting the army think I have connived
> At killing Polymestor for Cassandra's love . . . (850—6)

The issue of slavery and freedom here reaches its crux. Hecabe has already stated (756—7) that freedom is of no concern to her in comparison with revenge; she has appealed to the king to uphold law and justice, in the name of her daughter now enslaved to the king's bed; and the king has replied, in effect, that his upholding of law and justice must depend on either deceiving, or gaining the approval of, 'the army' and 'the Greeks' who are his masters. Hecabe replies (864ff.):

> A free man? There is no such thing! All men are slaves . . .
> Since you're afraid . . . I will set you free from fear . . .
> Know what I do, but take no hand in it.

All she asks is that he will prevent the Achaeans from interfering with her project. Three times Agamemnon incredulously questions her power to do anything; she reminds him of two legends which record the rebellion of female against male in earlier generations, the marriage of the Danaids, and the Lemnian massacre; and her words cast before them the shadow of Clytemnestra's axe, to which Polymestor will give substance in the last scene. Then she dismisses him, with orders which he accepts without protest. Hecabe has shown that freedom is a quality not bestowed by the chance of sex or the hazard of war; Agamemnon has illustrated what Hecabe said when thinking of Polyxena (595ff.):

In human beings, character is ingrained; the bad is never anything but bad, and the good is good.

Yet Hecabe herself now casts doubt upon her own dictum. She had appealed to Law in the hands of a king; but since the king has declined to uphold Law and has declared himself a slave, Hecabe too, having renounced freedom, turns to the slave's resource, violence outside the law; she has no alternative way to reach her vengeance, and 'The king — the king's to blame.' With the whole power of the Lemnian tradition behind her, the slave-heroine prepares and carries through her plan. When bloody revenge has been executed, when Polymestor has pled his cause to Agamemnon and Hecabe has answered him, she concludes her cold legalistic rhetoric with this address to the judge (1232–7):

> Agamemnon, if you help this man,
> You help an impious, perjured, and polluted traitor,
> And by upholding evil soil your own fair name.
> Yet — you're my master, and I'll moderate my words.

Agamemnon submits, as he must, gives judgement against Polymestor and acquits Hecabe.

Next we must study some of Euripides' numerous portraits of men and women who have learnt perforce to live without freedom. We shall look carefully at four of those most clearly characterized: the Old Slave and the Nurse in *Hippolytus*, the Old Slave in *Ion*, and the Servant, *therapōn*, in *The Children of Heracles*. In ten other plays parts of some interest are given to slaves; and these we shall consider as a group. Since it is obvious both from the surviving plays and from the Fragments that Euripides was deeply interested in the whole situation which slavery presented, there are two questions to be asked: first, What did he take to be the effect of slavery upon their moral judgement in general, and upon the particular quality of freedom or independence in their attitudes? and secondly, Was there any justification for the feeling (expressed, for example, in several Fragments from *Alexandros*, where the slave who challenges free men proves to have been born free) that a population of slaves was an enemy race within the city walls — the feeling which in Sparta led to a periodic official massacre of Helots?

First, the Slave in the prologue of *Hippolytus*. He opens the action by offering to his young master, with gentleness and tact, pious and sensible advice which if heeded might have averted or softened the tragedy. He knows his advice will be unwelcome, but gives it out of his own sense of responsibility. (Near the end of the play, 1263—4, another slave gives similar advice to Theseus, who, already shaken by the catastrophe, does not reject it.) When the warning goes unheeded, the Old Slave's response is to pray to Aphrodite to forgive Hippolytus for his foolishness. In this he illustrates the perennial fact that good men impute their own goodness to their gods; and in this respect he does not understand the nature of gods as the Nurse does. (The significance of his prayer that Aphrodite may forgive Hippolytus will be considered in the next chapter.) But he understands human nature, and knows that Aphrodite is a part of it, and that she cannot be ignored without peril. His error in theology is one that will have no worse effect than his own disappointment; his dialogue with Hippolytus gives a picture of humane and simple piety rare among Euripides' characters.

Phaedra's Nurse is the most fully and dramatically developed of all the anonymous persons in these plays. She is unmistakably a slave; but any homeliness or vulgarity in her outlook — and it is hard to be sure that we know how to recognize such qualities — is to be found only in the surface of her expression, not in the things she says. She is vividly aware of death as the end of life, as the other world always invisibly present. She is aware of the cost of sympathy and kindness, and of the never-silent question whether the thankless tasks of affection are worth undertaking (186, 253—60); yet she does not hesitate to undertake them far beyond her simple duty — unlike the chorus of Trozenian noblewomen who remember (785) that 'it is never safe to interfere'. To her Phaedra is a motherless child for whom she is responsible, and Phaedra is dying; to probe her trouble, then, is not curiosity but devotion. There is no need to extend the same defence to her ill-judged action in telling Hippolytus; but her ill judgement is no more discreditable and disastrous than Hippolytus' narrowness and cruelty or Theseus' rash fury. Her single error was fatal; but when in excusing it to Phaedra she says (701), 'After all, wisdom is only happening to guess right', she speaks part of the truth.

But slavery has allowed this old woman more than a kind heart and an honest, practical, fallible judgement; she also has a theology soundly based on knowledge of the world. The Slave in the prologue recognized the existence and power of Aphrodite but knew little of her nature; the Nurse knows her well. Love 'is the sweetest of all things, yet full of pain' (348). The clarity of her perception, which equals that of the chorus in the first stasimon, flows from her lips in poetry (447–50):

Love rides on clouds and strides through the swollen sea. The whole world was born from Love; she sows every seed; every creature on earth sprang from that desire which is her gift to us.

She understands two paradoxical opposites — the absoluteness of gods and the independence of humans, and knows that for the most part we make our own moral laws and we alone can uphold them; and she expresses this (453–8) in terms closely echoed by Theseus in a passage in *Heracles* (1316–19) which may be ironic but has never been thought vulgar or flippant. What she does not understand — though she had opportunity to observe it — is a certain effect of *eleutheria* and still more of *eugeneia*: that free men and women make for themselves out of their freedom laws whose restrictive power is sharper and more far-reaching than that of rules sanctioned by punishments, and purchase at this cost certain exquisite personal and social values which only a few even of the free learn to inherit. Among such values are Phaedra's ideal of chastity in marriage and Hippolytus' ideal of chastity by renunciation of sex. It is not the fact that she is a slave that prevents the Nurse from understanding these values; this is her nature, which, like the opposite, passionate nature shared by Phaedra and Hippolytus, is found among both slave and free.

These values would have been understood by the Old Slave in the prologue, who did not understand Aphrodite. But the Nurse shares with him his other knowledge, that the only alleviation for human error and suffering is pardon. (The particular meaning of *syngnōmē* and its distinction from the Christian concept of 'forgiveness' are discussed in the next chapter.) She asks Hippolytus (615) to forgive her:

Forgive! We are human, lad; it's natural to do wrong —

and she confesses to Phaedra that she is to blame (695). Pardon is something Aphrodite is incapable of bestowing; but Phaedra, who is not incapable, will pardon neither the Nurse nor Hippolytus; Hippolytus will not pardon Phaedra; Theseus will not pardon Hippolytus; while Hippolytus, whose unforgiving hatred of woman destroyed them all, is unaware of any guilt, forgets Phaedra, and absolves his father as a fellow-victim, not as a fellow-sinner. The 'palace slave' who comes as Messenger is wiser than Theseus (1263–4). The people in this play who understand the necessity and the purity of pardon are the three slaves.

We come now to *Ion*. The third episode opens with the entry of Creusa supporting an aged man who had looked after her as a child. The portrait of this slave is second in fullness only to that of Phaedra's Nurse. Like her, he has intelligence, and up to a point sound judgement; beyond that point he is reckless. Like the Nurse, he fails to understand that in the free world there are restraints from which the world of slaves feels free; while at the same time both freely obey the binding laws of loyalty without expecting any reward. The warmth of mutual affection and trust between Creusa and her slave offers a contrast to the relation between Creusa and her husband. The slave knows better than Creusa what Xuthus' selfishness is capable of, and asks the right questions (768ff.). He is wholly identified with the house of Erechtheus, and has always shared that hatred for Xuthus as a foreigner which the chorus too, Creusa's slaves, expressed in the second stasimon just before this scene. This is his undoing.

His first speech, 808–31, shows acuteness and imagination, but since both are inspired by malevolence towards Xuthus, the picture he gives of his supposed villainy is unfair and untrue; Xuthus is selfish and cruel and deceitful, but he is an average man and not a wholly unscrupulous schemer. The Slave's second speech, 836–56, displays an ironic unselfconsciousness of his own behaviour as a slave. Just as Euripides shows women, like the chorus in *Andromache*, accepting and defending the subservient status which men give them, so here the slave is jealous for the honour of his free mistress when it is threatened by the intrusion of 'this nobody, this slave's brat' (837–8):

Why, it would at least have been only a single insult if he had got himself a son and heir from a free-born woman — after asking your permission, and in view of your barrenness.

To an alert listener the multiple irony of this is high comedy, as well as trenchant comment on a disease in the heart of society. The point of the probe is reached in the last sentence (854–6):

Yes, it's only the name of slave that carries disgrace with it; in every other point a loyal slave is as good as a free man.

The slave carries his loyalty to the point of attempting murder, and when the accepted risk materializes, of suffering torture; and though the play is a comedy and even its serious themes are not profound in feeling, yet this anonymous chattel bears a much longer and more interesting part than the only other adult male in the story, and leaves the audience to ask the question implied in 855–6, Is a free man as good a man as a loyal slave? After all, the murder he attempted was sponsored by a queen.

The Servant in *The Children of Heracles* is unlike any of the others. As a person he does not affect the working-out of the plot, but plays a key-role in setting the tone of the second half of the play, of which indeed he becomes, from line 630 on, a sort of stage-manager. He shows less subservience than any other slave in Euripides, is assured and facetious, patronizes and mocks Iolaus, knows how to manage Alcmene, and claims from her the freedom she had promised him. But his function in the dramatic pattern is to corrode, by his mocking realism, the atmosphere of heroic idealism which introduced the first half of the action, and so to transfer the situation bodily into the disillusioned world of 427 B.C. What the audience actually saw when the Servant brought Iolaus, too superhuman to utter a word, on to the stage after the battle (793–6) is anyone's guess; but the respect due to the 'miracle' of rejuvenation is measured by Alcmene's dry 'Quite remarkable!' (798) – after which she passes quickly to more important matters; so that when, a little later, the Servant reaches this point in his messenger-speech (857–8), the sardonic understanding between him and Alcmene is as clear in relation to the 'miracle' as it is later (1020–5)[2] in relation to the execution of Eurystheus. However, fascinating as the Servant is, both in character and in function, he is really a comedy slave, a *scapino*, who is here to unmask tragedy; the only thing he says about freedom is that he means to have it (see 789, 890), and he adds little or nothing to Euripides' analysis of freedom as a quality of life.

A quick review of other slaves in Euripides reveals a remarkable consistency. The two slaves, male and female, in *Alcestis* are the only two characters who do not regard the death of Alcestis as a calamity falling primarily on Admetus. In *Medea* the Nurse, the Tutor, and the Messenger are the only characters (other than the chorus) who are humane and balanced in their judgement of Medea; for Creon and Jason are her enemies, and Aegeus knows nothing. In *Andromache* the Female Slave and the Nurse are perfect in devotion and common sense, and the Messenger condemns vengefulness as the mark of 'an evil-hearted man' (1164). The chorus of women slaves in *Ion* risk the threat of death for loyalty and truth. The Old Man in *Electra* is loyal, gentle, and sympathetic to Electra, and in Orestes' cause will abet murder; he and the Peasant are the only characters that could be called aimiable. In *The Phoenician Women* Antigone's Tutor is given one of the few messages in the play that is not ironic (154–5):

> Our enemies come with a just cause.
> My fear is that the gods may see this all too well.

In *Helen* the Messenger is given a 'true word spoken in jest' – a thoroughgoing denunciation of prophecies and oracles, which the chorus endorse heartily. To the Phrygian in *Orestes* is entrusted, both in his unique narrative and in his dialogue with the insane Orestes, an important key to the understanding of the play – the perception of the symbolism of Helen. In *The Bacchae* the Guard, the Herdsman, and the Messenger are the only persons who in a bewildering world keep their heads and their integrity. Finally the Old Slave in *Iphigenia in Aulis*, torn between two loyalties, decides for humanity against deception and cruelty. To summarize: the slaves in Euripides, more than twenty individuals and a chorus, are loyal, honest, brave, sympathetic, shrewd, and in only two cases unscrupulous; though their problems cannot be the centre of dramatic interest, their behaviour and moral judgement are clearly on a higher level than that of most of the free men and women. Therefore the generalizing condemnation of slaves found in the mouth of some characters is offered for our criticism rather than approval; and a general conclusion can be drawn that Euripides' characterization of slaves was meant to direct men's thoughts to their own freedom and bid them criticize their use of it.

In studying *Hecabe* we found Agamemnon exposed by his prisoner as a slave to the will of the army which called him commander. This situation was the inevitable echo of the more famous situation at Aulis ten years earlier, which Euripides took as the subject of his last play. The characters here are Agamemnon, Menelaus, Clytemnestra, Achilles; Iphigenia as a child of perhaps thirteen; and Agamemnon's Old Slave. Of these six the last two alone show any sign of spiritual freedom. Agamemnon is enslaved by fear of his army, his brother, and his wife. Menelaus, having no principles at all, is enslaved to the expediency of the moment (e.g. 519). Clytemnestra cannot escape from the emotional effects of many years of marital discord. Achilles is the prisoner of his own shallow self-esteem. The theme is worked out in considerable detail.

Early in the prologue Agamemnon says to his slave (16)

> I envy you, friend;
> And I envy any man who has reached
> The end of his life safe, humble, obscure.

At the end of the prologue indecision and guilt overwhelm him (136—7):

> I am out of my mind, God help me!
> I sink in ruin and madness.

When Menelaus has intercepted the letter and is quarrelling with Agamemnon he tells him (330)

> ... and I'm not your slave.

He then gives a long and detailed account of Agamemnon's enslavement to ambition —

> Your politeness then, your universal handshake, open house
> For the common soldier, ready audience to all ... (339—41)

When Agamemnon learns that Iphigenia has arrived — and he has delayed sending his second letter until a day when he must have known she would arrive at any moment — he complains that some *daimōn* has tricked him, and pities himself for being a king (448):

> the demand
> For dignity governs our life, and we are slaves
> To the masses.

After Menelaus' false repentance Agamemnon claims as irresistible the Fate he himself has precipitated (511—12):

> We are in Fate's grip,
> We are forced to go on; we must shed my daughter's blood.

What forces him? The truculence of the army, the stubbornness of Calchas, the ambition of Odysseus — these are not Necessity, any more than his own cowardice is. At the end of the second episode another slavery suddenly rises up and fetters him: he commands his wife to go home, and she refuses point-blank, leaving him balked and furious.

In the second stasimon the chorus picture the coming day when the Greek army will achieve their object in this great expedition: the capture of Troy, with the slaughter of men and enslavement of women and children (784—5):

> God grant that neither I nor my children's children
> Ever face such a prospect! —

and as these words were written this prospect was an imminent one for Athens. After this ode Achilles appears, and at once explains the compulsion which already irks him, and which will in the last scene enslave him (813—15):

> I have to keep the Myrmidons quiet. They're always at me:
> 'What are we waiting for, Achilles?' . . .

When Clytemnestra and Achilles have together discovered how they have both been deceived, the Old Slave enters, and reveals how Agamemnon is caught like a slave in his own shackles; which inspires Achilles first to declare that he intends to 'show himself a free man', and next to bind himself with great oaths to prevent the death of Iphigenia. At the end of the scene, as an afterthought, Achilles remembers (1019—20) that it will be wise, if possible, to continue in favour both with Agamemnon and with the army, and try words before actions. The chorus in their ensuing ode show that they recognize Achilles as no less a slave than Agamemnon. They know (1080ff.) that the sacrifice will take place.

At the end of the fourth episode Agamemnon, after listening first to Clytemnestra's painful rhetoric, then to Iphigenia's touching truth, proclaims the slavery he has accepted (1257–75):

> I shrink in dread from carrying out this act, my wife;
> Yet if I do not, dread remains. I must do this.
> Look at this fleet of war-ships marshalled here, this huge
> Army of bronze-mailed warriors from the Hellene states,
> Who cannot sail against the walls of Troy, or raze
> That famous city to its foundations, unless I
> First sacrifice you, as the prophet Calchas commands.
> A strange lust rages with demonic power throughout
> The Hellene army, to set sail immediately
> And stop barbarians from raping Hellene wives.
> If I refuse to obey the oracle, they'll come
> To Argos, and kill me, you, the whole family.
> Menelaus has not made a slave of me, my child;
> I came to Aulis not to serve his purposes;
> I am slave to Hellas; for her, whether I will or not
> I am bound to kill you. Against this I have no power.
> So far as lies in you, child, and in me, to ensure,
> Hellas must be free, and her citizens must not
> Have their wives stolen forcibly by Phrygians.

(Certainly nothing that could be called 'the freedom of Hellas' was menaced by the liberty Helen took in leaving her husband.) Finally, when the shouts of the rioting army have been heard approaching, and Iphigenia offers herself willingly for sacrifice, she ends her speech thus (1400–1):

> Greeks were born to rule barbarians, mother, not barbarians
> To rule Greeks. They are slaves by nature; we have freedom
>   in our blood.[3]

The chorus's comment on this is restrained but clear (1402–3):

> Your nature, princess, is indeed noble and true;
> But events fester, and divinity is sick.

The poet has not attempted to tell his hearers what freedom is, in any of its aspects. He has suggested that what people readily call Necessity is in many cases not *anankē* at all, but their own weak selfishness. He shows us people, who would certainly claim to be free members of a free society, fettered in their practical decisions and confused in their thoughts about their personal freedom and the freedom of Hellas. The conclusion is the same as that reached in earlier plays about other moral values, that we must make each discovery for ourselves and expect no help from gods either in attaining or in practising freedom or any other virtue.

The case of Agamemnon raises the particular question of man's freedom to obey or disobey divine injunctions. This was a question which, in the centuries following Euripides, lost nothing of its relevance either in personal matters or in political issues. We have already noted (Chapter 2 page 48 and note 12) how Aeschylus presented the choice which faced Agamemnon, showing that he first asked the wrong question, and even then could and should have disobeyed the oracle of Calchas. This interpretation, recently clarified by modern critics, was probably missed by most ancient readers; but Euripides seems to be emphasizing just this point when in *Iphigenia in Aulis* 1259—68 he makes Agamemnon say:

> Look at . . . this huge army of bronze-mailed warriors . . .
> Who cannot sail against the walls of Troy, or raze
> That famous city to its foundations, unless I
> First sacrifice you, as the prophet Calchas commands.

Here the first thing that is assumed is, as in the parodos of *Agamemnon*, the necessity of annihilating a whole city and nation; the second is the validity of Calchas' clairvoyance; the third is the urgent need to 'stop barbarians from raping Hellene wives'. Doubtless these assumptions seemed acceptable enough to many people in the original audience; but there is no reason to suppose that to Euripides they seemed any less irrational, even ridiculous, than they do to thoughtful people today. Indeed I would question whether a critic to whom these assumptions do not seem irrational and false has any hope of understanding Euripides. The acceptance of these assumptions, says Agamemnon, is begetting 'a strange lust' (literally the phrase is 'a sort of Aphrodite', 1264) which 'rages with demonic power throughout the Hellene army'. Euripides makes it as clear as Aeschylus did, that Agamemnon had both the power and the duty to disobey Calchas, just as Orestes had the power and the duty to disobey Apollo's command to kill his mother; just as Admetus had, at some point, the opportunity to accept 'imminent death' and refuse the escape Apollo offered — it was only when the escape had been accepted in principle that Admetus found he 'must endure the gift of the gods'. In all these cases Euripides shows his heroes as free to accept or to refuse freedom.

This brings us to one further significant passage designed to appeal for clear thinking about freedom, *Orestes* 1163—71. In 408, with defeat drawing closer every month, there must have been many desperate speeches in the Athenian Assembly whose echoes would be recognized in these words of Orestes:

> Since I am now at my last gasp in any case,
> I want to hurt my enemies before I die,

To pay back those who have betrayed me in their own coin,
And hear them howling who brought misery on me.
I am the son of Agamemnon, whom Hellas
Chose for command by merit — no despot, but one
Who had a god's strength in him; whom I will not shame
By a slave's death, but breathe my last like a free man,
Getting revenge on Menelaus.

The prime cause of Orestes' downfall had been his enslavement to an out-
worn tradition of personal revenge, supported by religious authority, but
condemned in specific terms by Tyndareos (*Orestes* 494—506):

> ... his duty was to take
> Lawful proceedings, prosecute for murder, and
> Expel his mother from the palace.

Orestes, his revenge once executed on the old principle, was enclosed by the
further slavery of guilt and insanity. Now he recalls Agamemnon as an
example of a free ruler over free men, and promises to emulate his father's
freedom — 'by getting revenge'. The irony is powerful enough merely in the
context of the story; but still more trenchant when felt as related to the
position of the Athenians at a moment when they were persuading themselves that their recent success in the Bosphorus outweighed the Spartan
force occupying the Attic fortress of Decelea.

Human freedom, physical and spiritual, always presents insoluble
paradoxes. As an absolute it is self-destructive; it can be bought only by
self-restraints; it can never be secured, must always be won by 'eternal
vigilance'. People need no poet to tell them to love freedom; but only a
poet can teach them how to recognize and renew it. When Euripides after
producing *Orestes* left Athens for the northern mountains, he may have been
in search of freedom — there is no record of his motives; but *The Bacchae*,
completed by 407, is a play about freedom, its elusive and ambiguous nature,
its delights, dangers, and deceptions. Pentheus rejects freedom because of its
dangers and deceptions, and opposes them with chains and prison doors,
but is privately enslaved to what he thinks are its delights. Cadmus and
Teiresias are exploiters and manipulators of the idea of freedom, but are themselves devoid of its spontaneous quality. The chorus have a spontaneous love of
freedom, but think of it as an absolute, to be claimed by instinct; whereas the
creative balancing of freedom with restraint demands reason. They possess a
part of the truth, but cannot work out a complete view; so that after the catastrophe their attitude to Agaue is ambivalent. Again, it is the Herdsman and the
Messenger, both slaves, who alone are free from error in their perception of
the ambiguous value of freedom. They take no sides, they watch, escape, and

report; and this indeed was Euripides' own role in his quiet exile. Freedom, when worshipped as an absolute and formulated in ideologies, proves to be a god with all the incalculable, terrifying, and unforgiving properties of divinity; to bring life and not destruction, freedom must be blended with law, Dionysus must share the sanctuary with Apollo.[4] But whether any such message was received by any but the smallest proportion of those who first saw or read *The Bacchae*, is more than we can tell. There are many words in the play for 'prison' and 'fetters'; the words *eleutheros, eleutheria,* do not occur; yet not only is this play, more clearly than any other, a dramatic meditation on the ineradicable instinct for freedom, but this is the theme which relates it closely to *Iphigenia in Aulis,* written within the same fifteen months. *The Bacchae* deals with freedom as a primitive instinct, and explores its anthropological and psychological implications; *Iphigenia in Aulis* (like *Hecabe* twenty years earlier) examines the social, moral, and emotional patterns which man has constructed on the basis of this instinct, the conventions of law, of slavery, of military practice; and shows how far they have slipped away from any connexion with that inexpressible urge of the soul which myth embodied in the divinity of Dionysus. The two plays together give, from their two different angles, a stereoscopic view of the most elusive and insoluble of all the questions which baffle the spirit of man in its attempts at self-comprehension; a realm of uncertainties whose substance can be caught only in poetry such as this from the third stasimon (*Bacchae* 866–76):

> O for long nights of worship, gay
> With the pale gleam of dancing feet,
> With head tossed high to the dewy air –
> Pleasure mysterious and sweet!
> O for the joy of a fawn at play
> In the fragrant meadow's green delight,
> Who has leapt out free from the woven snare,
> Away from the terror of chase and flight,
> And the huntsman's shout, and the straining pack,
> And skims the sand by the river's brim
> With the speed of wind in each aching limb,
> To the blessed lonely forest where
> The soil's unmarked by a human track,
> And leaves hang thick and the shades are dim.

9

THE CURE OF ANGER

The first word in European literature is 'anger': the *Iliad* begins with the quarrel between Achilles and Agamemnon.[1] Three centuries later, a dozen and more words meaning or implying anger chime incessantly through Aeschylus' *Oresteian Trilogy*. Anger is the most prevalent of human emotions. From the beginning, as Medea says (*Medea* 1079–80; she is speaking of her own *thymos* roused by Jason's desertion), anger 'has been the cause of greatest evils to mortals'. In every age anger has most often arisen from a sense that justice has been ignored or challenged. Anger is the mainspring of tragedy, and a theme of most serious narrative whether epic or dramatic.

Though the function of anger in the motivation of the *Iliad* is clear, the nobility of this passion is not immediately evident to modern readers. The quarrel in the *Iliad* is staged in a cosmic setting and expressed with superb force and eloquence; but it is a quarrel which on the surface involves little more than the disputed possession of a concubine. Its deeper essence needs imaginative interpretation of a rare quality, such as is found in C. H. Whitman's *Homer and the Heroic Tradition* (Harvard 1958), Chapter 9; here the anger of Achilles is convincingly shown as a supreme assertion of identity by one who is content with no less than the absolute in his own behaviour as a man, and who in the course of this pursuit learns and accepts the cost of the absolute — the lives of his friend, his enemy, and himself. Meanwhile on the battlefield the storm of mortal evil, of pain, grief, loss, hate, and death, is fiercely intensified, until in the final scene Achilles and Priam sit talking together in the quiet of Achilles' tent, and the thousand separate anguishes recede and fade, and human life knows itself and its end, and anger withdraws.

It is reasonable to suppose that the sublimity of Achilles' anger was more readily apprehended by Euripides than it is by us; and that the various kinds of anger which, void of any such dimension, rage through his plays reflect his awareness that the heroic world is as dead as Achilles, that an absolute standard in human living (did he perhaps recognize it in Socrates?) must be found intolerable by society; but that the evils caused by unheroic resentment, by the anger of miserable or deluded persons, are no less disastrous, and the needed answer is still to be sought. The work of his first twenty years as a tragic poet is almost entirely lost to us; fifteen of the seventeen surviving plays

were produced during twenty-four years of the Peloponnesian war. From
studying the fragments it is possible to infer in general terms that in the plays
of the early period anger, and the response to it, are personal; in the later
plays war is often the setting, and the context political. In all the extant plays
except *Alcestis* and *Helen* revenge is either the central theme or an important
element in the plot (and *Helen* too contains in the first stasimon, 1155–7, a
brief but clear condemnation of revenge as self-defeating folly). That is to
say, these plays continue the search for justice, and for a remedy for anger
caused by the neglect of justice, which Aeschylus began in the *Oresteian
Trilogy.*

Clearly, after lawless revenge has been condemned,[2] the next step towards
a civilized response to anger is legal redress; this is advocated in practical terms
by, for example, Tyndareos in *Orestes* 500–11; and it had already been set
forth formally as an ideal by Aeschylus in *Eumenides*, with the added
humanity of a bias for mercy 'when the votes were equal'. But in many
human disputes legal redress is out of reach; in any case it cancels anger only
on one side of the quarrel; and, as Aeschylus repeated many times, no redress
can restore blood once spilt. Beyond legal redress a further measure is possible, the act of pardon, *syngnōmē*. The act of voluntarily renouncing anger
and reprisal for injury received is logically the only act which can terminate
the vicious cycle of revenge. At the same time the grace of pardon bears a
strange and indefinable quality. In its real and reciprocal operation, which
can occur only between one mortal and another, it is subtle, complex, and as
variable as humans themselves; it is simple only in its unreal aspect when
men cry to gods for pardon, as Cadmus does to Dionysus – because this is an
impossible request. The word *syngnōmē* does not occur in any serious sense of
'pardon' before the time when Euripides was writing his later plays. The
growth of the idea, one would surmise, received a setback during the generation of the Peloponnesian War and the troubled period which followed.
Then after three generations more we find Menander, the admirer and fol-
lower of Euripides, making pardon the central issue in the three comedies of
his mature period of which the largest fragments have survived to our day,
and in his treatment of it showing a subtlety no less sensitive than that of
Euripides. But before going any further we must look more closely at the
meaning of the word.

The account in *Iliad* XXIV of Achilles' remission of anger, of Priam's kissing
of the hands that had killed his son, does not contain the verb *syngignōskein*,
for neither it nor its cognates were in Homer's vocabulary; but that memorable scene undoubtedly shows for the first time a poet's answer to the most
painful and eternal of life's questions, How can anger reach an end? Aeschylus, though absorbed in probing the same question, still has no word for
'pardon'. In the second half of the fifth century this verb meant 'to have a

fellow-feeling' with someone, 'to agree in judgement', and so 'to make allowance'. The notion differs from that of Christian 'forgiveness' in two ways. First, Christian 'forgiveness' (the New Testament word is not *syngnōmē* but *aphesis*, 'remission') is an extension of Christian 'love' to cover and cancel a particular wrong that has been committed, and involves a positive emotional attitude of forgiver to forgiven; usually, though not always, it involves also a mutual relationship because it acts in response to repentance. *Syngnōmē*, on the contrary, is much less an emotional initiative; it is simply the decision to cease anger and renounce reprisal; a rational and civilized attitude towards unpleasant facts. The second difference is, that Christian 'forgiveness' is a debt owed by every believer to those who injure him, because he knows himself indebted to God for the forgiveness of his own sins; thus the emotion involved is twofold, that of receiving and that of bestowing forgiveness — bestowing on one's neighbour what one receives from God. Whether any but the rarest human spirit is capable of conceiving and sustaining such a relation with the Infinite, is a question the ancient Greek did not have to answer, since, though he might on occasion, like Hippolytus' slave, or Cadmus, beg a god to forgive, such a prayer was never granted; gods could not forgive, it was not their function. The Christian notion of forgiveness, then, is a complex one and essentially religious; the notion of *syngnōmē* which began to be current in the late fifth century is simple and without religious implications; and this is the 'pardon' which we find in Euripides, though the context sometimes makes the word 'forgiveness' preferable. It is perhaps a less creative idea than Christian 'forgiveness'; yet it is a quality, an attitude, more within the compass of ordinary men and women, and valid as an available answer to some of the many evils which afflict human life as a consequence of anger. We first find it subtly and tentatively suggested in *Alcestis*; it is a theme running through *Hippolytus* from beginning to end; it is referred to significantly in *The Women of Troy* and *Electra*; and in other plays its absence or refusal is noted in the disasters arising from revenge.

In our study of *Alcestis* in Chapter 4 (pages 99–105) we saw the central figure, Admetus, grow steadily into the recognition of his own guilt. His situation is one which in the actual world can have no solution, since the dead do not live again; but the story provided by legend makes it possible to explore his predicament more deeply by contemplating the imagined miracle. His guilt, which he shares with all other men, is that of unthinking selfish assumption; like every free male, he lives his life at another's expense. In addition to this, Heracles, on returning from his fight with Death, reproaches Admetus with a wrong done to a friend (1009–13):

> I think I might have been trusted as your friend . . .
> You never told me that your wife was dead.

This latter wrong, however, was not a serious one; and by readily pardoning it Heracles prepares the feeling on stage for a more profound experience. What Admetus had done to Alcestis was not recognized, in the first half of the play, by either husband or wife as a wrong; they both assigned all blame to the selfishness of Pheres and his wife. The truth of the situation is first expressed by the female Slave (197–8), and her perception is later shared by the male Slave (769–71). Indeed, the wrong committed was (see pages 101–3) so much an accepted element in society that Euripides can have had little hope of its being recognized as a wrong by any except those few who could penetrate his irony. Therefore the communication of repentance and pardon in this case demanded a delicacy of treatment beyond the capacity even of Euripides to express in words; and even the face of Alcestis, whether with or without a mask, is veiled until after pardon has been bestowed by a touch (1119–20). Heracles may or may not understand just what is going on; but by warm-hearted instinct he knows it is his task not merely to bring Alcestis back to life, but also to restore communication of a kind for which words are in-adequate (1114–19):

> ADMETUS: I will not touch her; but – there is the house.
> HERACLES: Your own right hand! No less will satisfy me.
> ADMETUS: My lord, I do not wish it. You are forcing me.
> HERACLES: Come, your hand! Now, take her hand in yours.
> ADMETUS: Here, then. I would as soon cut off the Gorgon's head.
> HERACLES: You have her?
> ADMETUS: I have, yes.
> HERACLES: Hold her for ever, then!

That Admetus, having suffered the fullness of guilt and repentance, now knows he is forgiven, is made clear by his words (1157–8),

> Now we have changed to a better life than that we had before.

In a good modern performance the emotion which this last scene can arouse may spring partly from the simple surprise of a happy ending; but its real power lies in the recognition of forgiveness.

Irony is usually the weapon of the cynic. To advocate forgiveness is the opposite of cynicism; yet irony conveys the gentleness as well as the harsh-ness of *Alcestis*. Harshness is felt in the following fragment from an unknown play (no. 1030) which seems to reflect a comparable situation:

> So you imagine that the gods are likely to forgive, when a man wants to escape death by making a vow, or . . . ? If so, then the gods are even more stupid than mortals, if they regard generosity as more important than getting one's rights.

Medea, the next surviving play after *Alcestis*, is a play about the unforgiving world. It is a bitter play, but hardly cynical; even the treatment of Jason is just. While Admetus is the unusually perceptive man, who can through painful struggle recognize guilt, Jason is the average man, who cannot. Appreciation of the moral balance of this play has sometimes suffered through failure to see fully what Medea was doing when she killed their sons. She loved them with a mother's love raised to the rare power of her passionate nature; but she knew, first, that society allowed her to claim little or no right in them — they were Jason's property by law, hers by allowance. Secondly, she knew that Jason's love for them was entirely different from hers. He loved them, not for themselves, but because they were his life. A king without a son was rootless and insecure. Jason had cherished Medea because she gave him sons. With the prospect of sons of greater value —royal Corinthians — from Glauce, Jason could risk losing the two he had; when Glauce was dead, his two sons were his life. Early in the play Medea tells the chorus (374—5)

> Today three of my enemies I shall strike dead:
> Father, and daughter; and my husband.

The plan to kill Jason by the sword (379, 393) is rejected for the more effective plan, the living death which a childless man will feel for years. If, then, revenge is a blow to be struck for justice, this is the death which must be inflicted, though its cost to the avenger is infinitely greater.

As if to emphasize the rigidity of anger which fills the air of this play and makes pardon impossible, there is a small episode which is designed to exhibit the pattern of repentance and pardon as a grim mockery. Medea decides to ask Jason to come to her, and then to 'give him soft talk' (776). When he comes she begs him to 'forgive the things she said' (869—70), and presents a detailed imitation of repentance. In response Jason (see page 109) easily bestows on Medea a pardon which arises partly from guilt but chiefly from patronising folly, a general contempt for women, and obtuse confidence. Only a man himself incapable of repentance could be so fatally deceived by its counterfeit.

So Euripides here goes to the root of the question, Is revenge right or wrong? Philosophers had already asked this question and were to ask it increasingly; and certain kinds of revenge, such as refusal of burial, were generally admitted to be wrong; but the principle of revenge was unassailed. Medea's indignation, *thymos* (1079—80) told her that Jason's injustice to her was wrong. Not to condemn, attack, and destroy the doer of wrong is to betray right. So Medea, at unimaginable cost to herself, strikes for the right. The poet's comment may be perceived by asking, at the end of the play, what in fact has revenge achieved on behalf of right? Restitution is out of the question. Jason has recognized nothing of the wrong he did to Medea; he pities, not Creon or even Glauce, but himself; and Medea he curses. In other words, revenge has accomplished nothing. This is the relevance of the play to the broad theme of pardon, and this gives *Medea* its place between *Alcestis* and *Hippolytus*.

Hippolytus as we know it was a recension; Euripides produced the first version of it perhaps about 435. The earlier play apparently presented Phaedra as a shameless lecherous woman and Hippolytus as a blameless hero. The second version, produced in 428, maintains instead a subtle moral balance, and a touching sympathy of experience, between these two characters. Both are young idealists; each remembers a mother who had felt the cruelty of Aphrodite. Since the remains of the first *Hippolytus* comprise only forty-five lines in nineteen fragments, it is idle to try to compare the plays; the point of referring to the earlier version is to suggest that, though the surviving play was produced in the fourth year of the war, its theme really belongs to the pre-war period; the war-time plays begin the following year with *The Children of Heracles*. The first half of *Hippolytus* is the climax of a long series of plays about the misery inflicted on women by the unjust position which society gave them, and by the contempt and hate which men felt and expressed towards them – perhaps not a majority of men, but enough to constitute a problem; and about the desperation and crime to which, in extremity, this attitude could drive a woman of heroic temper. The dramatic pattern of *Hippolytus* shows a family group of which each member in turn suffers from the anger of another, each loves, and each destroys. In the first half of the play we see the self-contained world of women – Phaedra, the Nurse, and the chorus; in the second half, the self-contained world of men – and between the two worlds there is no communication. The healing power of pardon fails to gain any entrance to the first world; it operates not at all between the two worlds, where it is most needed; but it penetrates at last, in a strictly limited application, into the man's world, to reconcile the dying Hippolytus with his father.

There are two other separate worlds shown in this play. Nowhere else in Euripides, except in *The Bacchae*, is the operation of the supernatural world made so visible as a force directing human events. The mortal world is warm, passionate, anguished; the immortal world cold, self-concerned, invulnerable. Aphrodite and Artemis demonstrate the nature of the universe in which fallible mortals strive for their integrity. They, as gods, know neither justice nor pity; neither consistency nor logic, and only a negative harmony; they are glory and power, the imperviousness of natural law, and the harshness of truth disclosed. They are neither good nor bad; their beauty is incommunicable; but mortals, whether slave or prince, project their own goodness upon the heartless face of the cosmos. It is the curse of heroes that they desire to be as gods; and the world of the gods, as Aphrodite describes it in her prologue speech, reveals itself as the model upon which the free males of the Hellenic world have built for themselves a human cosmos to serve their pleasure. Aphrodite shows at the outset that statement needs to be seemly and symmetrical rather than true (5–6):

> To those who reverence my powers I show favour,
> And throw to the earth those I find arrogant and proud.

Legend said that in a long life Theseus had shown continual devotion to Aphrodite; the play shows Phaedra outwardly resisting, inwardly yielding; yet Aphrodite, so far from showing favour, uses both as tools for her revenge on Hippolytus, and destroys both (47–50):

> Phaedra shall save her honour, but must lose her life;
> For I will not yield my rights through regard for her misfortunes,
> But my enemies shall pay what they owe till I am satisfied.

In Olympus there is neither mercy nor pardon; and as we have seen (above, page 216), heroic mortals tend to emulate gods.

Hippolytus enters. He knows that, being a hero and a prince, he is as a god among his fellow-humans. He feels that he knows Artemis well, because his father's mortal cosmos gives him the glory and power of the gods, as it has given him their cruelty. But it has not given him their invulnerability; he will suffer first grief, then death. As an athlete and hunter he is devoted to Artemis and to chastity; he is very young, and, like some young men, does not want women yet. He has seen among his fellows those who, to his judgement, have lost their wits, lost half their manhood and all their free dignity, for the pleasures of sex. The religious contemplation of Artemis satisfies his romantic mind and does not enslave his body; he is not yet sure enough of his freedom to endanger it with love. This unsureness is subtly reinforced by the knowledge that his mother, born royal and free, had become his father's war-captive (1082–3):

> O my unhappy mother! The bitterness of my begetting!
> May no one that I love ever be called bastard!

He combats his unsureness first with the thought of his uniqueness, then with the resolve never to put his uniqueness to the test (84–7):

> I alone of mortals enjoy this honour ...
> And may the end of my life's course be as the beginning!

The Old Slave who warns him against 'aloofness' — his words are the essence of both piety and tact — evokes from his master two lines (98, 104) which show Hippolytus, whether consciously or not, claiming the life of a god. When the prince and his huntsmen have gone, the Slave prays to Aphrodite (114–20):

You must show forgiveness, if anyone through youth or a bold spirit utters foolish words against you. Think that you did not hear them. Gods ought to be wiser than mortals.

Being a good man, he associates wisdom with forbearance and pardon. His piety rests on mistaken belief, for he did not hear Aphrodite speak.

When the chorus enter and talk of Phaedra's sickness, they surmise that the queen may have offended Artemis, either in Athens or years ago in Crete, and that unforgiving anger has crossed the sea to afflict her. They do not share the Slave's pious error; they know that gods are unalterable fact and do not forgive. But now enters Phaedra, dazed with starvation and her secret guilt; and, supporting her, the Nurse, alert with the knowledge that a woman's life is a losing battle which must be fought to the last ditch; full of sympathy, resilience, and fallible judgement. The whole of her long and splendid sequence finds its apex in her last word to Hippolytus in 615. She understands the real world, including the gods, better than any other character; the one thing she does not understand is the strange quality of those to whom the ideal is as important as the real — the quality which Phaedra and Hippolytus share. The sorrows and the brevity of life, the special afflictions of women, the intractability of men, the beauty and terror of love, the urgency of compromise, the helpless dilemma of the girl she has to care for — all these are her data; and they converge to one conclusion (615):

Forgive! We are human; we cannot help doing wrong.

This is the second prayer for pardon. The first (117) was addressed to a god; this is addressed to a young man who makes an unpardonable presumption of divinity. Hippolytus ignores the plea for pardon, and ends with his *credo*, which is its opposite (664–6):

My curse on you all! I shall never become weary of hating women, even if people say I always repeat the same thing[3]. Well, women, it seems, always are evil.

The often expressed attitude of hatred towards women (see Chapter 4, pages 98, 114) has already been mentioned by Phaedra (407); and a little later (413) she expressed her own hatred for women whose standard of conduct differed from her own. Nowhere in Euripides' extant work is there an instance of a woman expressing in words forgiveness for the cruelties which male hostility inflicted on her[4]; the nearest approach to it is the final scene of *Alcestis*, discussed above. In *Hippolytus* the prince spurns the Nurse's plea; and the cruelty of his tirade (616–68), delivered pointedly to the Nurse in Phaedra's presence, is outrageous enough to ensure her vengeance as well as her death. The Nurse's part is now over; she creeps away, and Phaedra's blazing refusal to forgive her is the more poignant because it matters so little. We do not expect Phaedra to forgive Hippolytus. What she says of him is significant (728—31):

He shall have an equal share in my suffering, and learn to be gentle.

'To be gentle' is *sōphronein*, 'to be moderate'; but it also means 'to be chaste'; and the word rebukes not only the hatred and cruelty he has shown to Phaedra, but the whole attitude of which this was a part, the arrogance which chose one god and spurned another (104), ignored good advice, prized his own unique sanctity, and condemned half the human race as unfit for his company. Yet when Hippolytus, cursed and banished by his father, says farewell to his friends, his last word is this (1100—1):

Whatever my father thinks, you will never see another man more *sōphrōn* than I.

The obvious meaning here is 'more chaste'; but Hippolytus' exit line echoes Phaedra's exit line. The narrow truth of his word is contradicted by the broad truth of hers; and the event will demonstrate this.

When Theseus finds Phaedra dead, he sees the disaster to his house as 'a harvest gathered from far off', as the result of 'sins of someone in time past' (831—3). He is living for a year of exile in Trozen, to purchase pardon for a specific sin (34—7); but unatoned sins, his own and his ancestors', are countless, and the debt is not pardoned. Then he reads Phaedra's letter; anger bursts in him, drowning all thought of pardon, and he takes to himself the action of a god (887—9):

Poseidon, my father, you promised me three curses: with one of them strike down my son!

When told that Hippolytus is dying, he thanks Poseidon (1169—70) for implementing his curse 'like a true father to me'; the will to revenge is stronger than pity or paternal love. Once again, where freedom and royal power have crippled humanity, the slave speaks the truth (1263—4):

Consider: your son is struck down. Listen to my advice and do not be harsh to him.

Then Artemis appears, and all the facts are told.

When Artemis has used the facts to lash the abject misery of Theseus, she adds (1325—6):

Yet even you may still find pardon for what you have done.

By this she chiefly means that Theseus, unlike his wife and his son, will survive to suffer; that Fate will let him off any further punishment, since

Aphrodite's plotting had made his action 'pardonable' (1326). For Artemis pardon is a legalistic concept and has none of what we know as its humane quality. It is most unlikely that this line is meant to refer to Hippolytus' forgiveness of his father; for the goddess shows how she fails to comprehend any such relationship when in 1435 she advises Hippolytus 'not to hate his father' — after Hippolytus has already (1405–9) shown his spontaneous desire to forgive. Further, when Hippolytus (1415) wishes that his curse could reach a god, Artemis reassures him that she has no intention of pardoning Aphrodite, but will kill Adonis to compensate her loss of her own favourite (1420–2). In spite of this Hippolytus says that he pardons his father 'at her request' (1442); like his old slave, he cannot bear to know that gods are amoral, so attributes to divinity virtue which belongs only to humanity — his own; and after the goddess has gone, the reconciliation between father and son is complete and touching. The two are now alone together in a male world. Theseus acknowledges his fatal fault and receives pardon; he will bring up Phaedra's sons to be noble like Hippolytus (1455). This line points to an aspect of the play's irony which has not often been noted.

Hippolytus dies deeply convinced of his own innocence and nobility. This conviction, which fills his lyric lines, 1347–88, is confirmed three times by Artemis, and is shared by Theseus and the chorus. His earlier scene, the quarrel with his father, leaves no doubt that he regarded his own character as being near perfection. The chorus in the fourth stasimon reflect the feeling of ordinary people about a young man like Hippolytus: he was a glorious figure whose ascetic purity was accepted as an ornament of fleeting youth soon to be replaced by the full life of maturity — hence 'the jealous rivalry of girls who longed to be your bride' (1140–1). The noblewomen of Trozen, moved by the pathos of splendid youth cut off untimely, forget that earlier they grieved no less for Phaedra's untimely death precipitated by Hippolytus' cruel words. The contemporary rituals which Artemis describes in 1423–7 give the same picture of Hippolytus as a romantic hero; but there is a curious point to notice here. In all the plays concerned with the Trojan war, blame for each subsequent death or disaster is laid on Helen as its ultimate, remote 'cause'; but here no condemning reference is made to Phaedra either for her unlawful love or for her lying letter. Artemis is objective and fair (1300–12, 1429–30); Hippolytus mentions her only once, in 1403 — 'Aphrodite has destroyed us all three.' The whole blame is cast on Theseus as the immediate cause; and Theseus receives his son's forgiveness. In other words, the author has taken care at the end of the play to prevent the audience from recalling that world of women in which the long first episode took place — that wrestling between truth and desire, those exquisite subtleties of fear, resolution, passion, despair, and honour, which in that scene engaged the rapt sympathy of the audience; all that is, in the final scene, entirely forgotten.

Why is this so? We should assume that the author knew what he was doing, and that by composing his play thus he wished to produce a certain effect. We can see the effect produced, by referring again to Aristophanes, *Frogs* 1045, where it is demonstrated that the Athenian public knew Phaedra was a whore and would never have any other opinion, however often they listened to the first episode of *Hippolytus*. We can, in fact, see here the same device we observed in *Medea* (see pages 108—9): the unacceptable truth is exposed early in the action, so that later events may cover the memory of it. Here the unacceptable truth is, that a woman like Phaedra is not necessarily a whore deserving the abuse Hippolytus hurled at her. This, Euripides knew, was not a matter about which you could argue with the Athenian public. You could win their attention and instinctive sympathy for the twenty minutes of the scene; and then you had to let them go away and say they had seen a play about a whore — because they would certainly never admit to anything else. If most male listeners had been capable of appreciating the touching idealism and honest subtlety of Phaedra's self-searching, they might have been even more scandalized. The truth of Phaedra's position, and the Nurse's cry for pardon, were unlikely to reach more than a handful of those present; but the text was there for the reader.

And the text has more to reveal. Both Phaedra and Hippolytus speak at some length about their own attitude to ethical questions. Phaedra's words go straight to the point and are painfully honest (380—1):

We know and see what is right, yet fail to carry it out.

Not trusting her own tongue, she had resolved on silence; finding her self-mastery incomplete, she had resolved on death (393—402). But her isolation is too much for her, and she speaks, and thus opens a door to the hope of living. Her part in the scene is a vivid mixture of intelligence and passion, self-knowledge and self-deception. By contrast, Hippolytus' words in his first scene with Theseus contain no self-searching; he is not aware of any problem in the situation itself, still less of any flaw in his own behaviour. He knows he is honest (1001); he knows he is *sōphrōn*, self-controlled; but in the sphere which most sharply tests the self-control of most men, the experience of sex, he has shirked the whole issue; being afraid of the power of love, he has put hatred in its place (664—5). He will keep his oath, even to a slave, at any cost; but this decision is a simple one. For him goodness involves, and can afford, no complexities; he is good, and knows it. At the end of the play all the sorrow, sympathy, and music go to this beautiful, dull prig; the intelligent, sensitive, real anguish of Phaedra is forgotten as though it had never been. Hippolytus, unaware of any fault in himself, bestows forgiveness on his father for behaviour no more vicious than his own. Phaedra, whom half the audience are, for the brief minutes while the spell of her truth binds them, willing to forgive — Phaedra will forgive neither herself, nor the Nurse, nor Hippolytus.

It is perhaps not an accident that this, the last of the plays belonging to the pre-war series (see above, p. 230), was also the last in which Euripides looked squarely at *syngnōmē* as the rational alternative to *dikē* in its punitive aspect. If Hippolytus had shown to Theseus the same spirit he showed Phaedra, he would have cursed his father and so ensured further calamity. The *sōphrosynē* he showed in the face of death was a degree of achievement, even if in the exuberance of life he could not forgive a woman. Once the outbreak of war had intensified the fighting passions of Athenians, repentance and pardon were no longer an acceptable theme. Before 431 *Philoctetes* was perhaps the only play in which Euripides used a plot connected with the Trojan war; beginning with *Andromache* (426?) we have from the Trojan cycle eight complete plays and two known from fragments. The war at Troy was a fertile source of examples of the destructiveness of revenge. In these plays repentance and pardon are seen only in distant and fleeting glimpses. We will look first at *Electra* (413).

While Clytemnestra in her carriage approaches Electra's cottage, there is a dialogue (962—87) between Orestes and his sister in which he, in effect, begs her to let him off the task of killing his mother, and she remains obdurate. The killing of Aegisthus has been more than enough for Orestes; so far from hardening him, the sight of his own kill has made him see more clearly what further he has resolved to do; he now repents of his resolve, knowing (as the Dioscori twice confirm in the epilogue) that Apollo was wrong; but he is afraid to face Electra when she calls him 'coward' (982). When Electra too has shared in murder, her sight becomes as clear as her brother's; and in all Greek drama there is no more poignant scene of despairing penitence than this antiphony of horror (1177—1232); for there is no one left to forgive them. The dispassionate words of the Dioscori, however, hold out to them a hope which is also the implicit message of the end of *Heracles*. Pardon from a wronged victim, as in *Hippolytus*, is a healing act; but more important, and more often the only healing available, is self-pardon, which Orestes will eventually achieve, after torment by Furies and trial by a foreign court (1317). That this final and spiritual dealing with the source of evil is intended by the poet, becomes clear from the closing words of the Dioscori (1290—1):

> When you have fulfilled the appointed period of blood-guilt,
> You shall find happiness, and be freed from these troubles.

The word for 'find happiness' is *eudaimonēseis*, which means a deeper well-being than that of *eutychia*; and the same idea is suggested by the following phrase, *tōnd' apallachtheis ponōn*; for this is an echo of the opening line of

Agamemnon, where the Watchman prays for ultimate 'deliverance from troubles', *tōnd' apallagēn ponōn*. Thus the whole passage in Euripides implies a hope, a possibility, that the recurrent curse may end in release and pardon. Electra, indeed, though shown as a miserable and warped person, is treated by the poet with a gentleness far removed from the harsh condemnation we find five years later in *Orestes*, where Pylades' future bliss as her husband is among Apollo's caustic speculations. Here in *Electra* her discharge from all further punishment suggests appropriate pity for a woman sick in mind.

The theme of pardon forms a part also of the scene between Electra and Clytemnestra. Only after Clytemnestra has entered the cottage does the chorus give us the traditional picture of the relentless, invincible queen as a grim agent of justice (1163—4):

Like a lioness from the mountains roaming through meadows and orchards she carried out her purpose.

This image is incredibly unlike the woman who has been on stage for the last ten minutes; Clytemnestra is more pathetic than formidable. Her first speech, it is true, can be played in several very diverse tones; but the scene as a whole is decisive. This Clytemnestra is a mere shadow of the vengeful Fury who single-handed overcame the King of Men. In eight years of guilt she has become weary, lonely, frightened, apologetic; she has in fact repented, but can hope for no pardon from herself or from anyone else.

Twice she mentions forgiveness. If Agamemnon had sacrificed Iphigenia to avert

The capture of his city, or to exalt his house;
Or if, to save his other children, he had taken
One life for many, he could be forgiven.

She could not and did not forgive him. Her foolish ramblings (1035—48) are a realistic mixture, representing the self-deceptive justifications she has comforted herself with since she killed her husband, implying — as if hoping to convince herself — that she took Aegisthus for a lover because Agamemnon brought home Cassandra. She is self-hypnotized with the mere convention of reprisal, which leads to her childish conclusion (1047—8),

Well, what could I do?
None of your father's friends would have helped me kill him.

The pathos of this speech is that her unsuspecting words 'but teach bloody instructions' to the daughter who is as fast bound to a pretence of 'necessity' as she was herself, and who after the killing will experience not this sad and hopeless repentance but a violent revulsion of self-loathing. Electra in her reply seizes on this point, and tries to enrich her coming triumph by adding to death the fear of death (1093—6):

> And if death
> In justice demands death, why then, I and your son
> Orestes must kill you to avenge our father's death;
> For if the one revenge is just, so is the other.

But Clytemnestra in her heartfelt remorse is now — strangely yet credibly — too innocent to see the shadow. Her answer to thirty-seven lines of concentrated hate is to speak of love (1102—10):

> My child, your nature has always been to love your father.
> It is natural; some children love their fathers best,
> And some their mothers. I'll forgive you. I do not,
> In fact, exult unduly over what I did.
> With what insensate fury I drove myself to take
> My grand revenge! How bitterly I regret it now!

The genuineness of both her repentance and her pardon is not impaired, rather confirmed, by the fact that it springs from dread of Orestes' return (1114). These lines are unexpected and free from irony; nothing could state more convincingly that in this once fierce spirit the fire of retaliation is dead and is replaced by reason and readiness to meet hatred with forbearance. Here once again significant truth is heard from the lips one would least expect to utter it. In any other context the notion of Clytemnestra pardoning Electra would be ironic; here, since we know what will happen in the house, it provides beforehand both the cause and the cure of Electra's purging tears (1230) —

> We love you, though we hated you!

In *Iphigenia in Tauris* (412?) the theme of anger and pardon is muted but persistent. The central figure tells at the very beginning the story of a monstrous and unforgettable wrong done to her by one whom she loved. Iphigenia's chief anger is against Agamemnon; but in her prologue narrative she mentions also Helen, Menelaus, Calchas, and Odysseus — and later in the play she wishes death upon all four by name (356—7, 525, 531—5). It is her indignation and thirst for revenge that have enabled her for so many years to carry out her sacrificial duties in the temple of Artemis. At the same time she knows that they have degraded her from what she still thinks of as the proper kind of life for a Hellene (378—9, 452—5, 1143—51 etc.). She hates both Artemis and herself (380—91); she longs to be free of her resentment; and the play shows the progress of her liberation. A. P. Burnett has pointed out (*Catastrophe Survived* 52) that at 565 Iphigenia, having learnt of her father's death, can now think of him with pity; and that after this, having put aside vengeful feelings, she can ask for news of her beloved brother – the withdrawal of anger leads towards recognition. In her soliloquy 344–91 Iphigenia herself expresses a similar process. She begins with vicious bitterness, first against Greeks in general (350), then against Helen (354–8); but the picture of her imagined revenge, with Helen as her victim, recalls the picture of herself as victim at Aulis, with her father officiating as priest; and the thoughts of home with which she then appealed to him (365–71) lead finally to memories of family love, and these in turn bring her to attribute, erroneously, her own innate humanity to Artemis, and the Taurian ritual to the barbarity of the natives. So at last (992–3) she reaches the point of 'renouncing indignation against the father who killed her'. Though *syngnōmē* is not mentioned here, this play gives the fullest picture in Euripides of a heart struggling to free itself from the anger which demands revenge.

We should mention briefly four other passages dealing with the refusal of pardon, and one passage where it is spontaneously offered. The first of these we have already studied in sufficient detail in Chapter 5, pages 147–8 *et al.* – Helen's request to Menelaus for pardon. Here the only further remark to be made is, that when Menelaus and Helen next appear on Euripides' stage, in *Orestes* (408 B.C.), Menelaus is a different man, reasonable and humane, and it becomes evident that he has pardoned Helen. The second is in the last scene of *The Children of Heracles*, where Eurystheus, captured in battle, kneels bound before Alcmene. There is here no question of forgiveness, or of any reciprocal emotion except hate and fear; but pardon, the renouncing of reprisal, is possible – is in fact not only possible but prescribed in such circumstances by Athenian usage (966):

> Those taken alive in battle we do not put to death.

Since Hyllus was an ally, in charge only of his own contingent, he must obey the Athenian code in the treatment of his prisoner (967–8). The familiar resolve for revenge is stated by Alcmene, the plea of the victim of revenge by Eurystheus (989ff.):

> Whether I wished
> To be his enemy or not, our enmity
> Was a plague sent by Hera – yes, a god's to blame;
> This was a sickness . . .

Here is an example of an issue in which we may either say that we can perceive the poet's mind, or on the other hand insist that any such assumption is mere conjecture. Even if the Elders of Marathon had not already given their judgement, the text here provides ground for decision. Line 1019, 'Since this is the city's wish', indicates that in the preceding lacuna a message came from the Athenian Assembly confirming the Elders' principle that a prisoner's life must be spared. But Alcmene is not easily opposed.

> SERVANT: Let the man go unharmed. This is the city's wish.
> ALCMENE: What if I obey the city's wish, and still he dies?
> SERVANT: That would be excellent. How can it be arranged?
> ALCMENE: A simple matter — listen: I will kill the man,
>   Then give his corpse back to his friends who come for him.
>   Thus I fulfil the letter of the Athenians' wish . . . (1020—5)

To suggest that the speaker of these lines is not under the poet's condemnation is to carry academic detachment to absurdity. Alcmene's words are a quibble[5] which, coming from a suppliant and a foreigner, is little short of an insult to the city which has protected her. The passage implies that the rational solution to the issue of this scene — the fate of Eurystheus — though probably rejected in the lost dénouement, is pardon.

Thirdly, there is the Messenger in *Andromache*. This play is a pattern of revenges — Neoptolemus, Hermione, Menelaus, Orestes, are all avengers; and at the climax of the story, at the end of the Messenger's narrative, come these lines (1161—5):

> This is what
> Apollo, the divine dispenser of oracles . . .
> Did to the prince who came to make his peace with him.
> This god, like any evil-hearted man, remembered
> An ancient grievance: how can he be wise and good?

The real point of these lines is not the simple man's discovery that gods are not wise and good; rather they remind the listener that, though many will agree in condemning vindictiveness, few are ready to practise pardon.

The fourth passage is in the final scene of *The Bacchae*, where Cadmus, punished by Dionysus for his daughters' impiety, begs to be pardoned. Here there is no hope, since gods are unalterable fact and incapable of mercy. The fifth passage, in which pardon is spontaneously offered, is found in *The Phoenician Women* 1444—6. Here Iocasta kneels beside her two dying sons. Eteocles is already speechless; but Polyneices with his last breath says of him,

> He became my enemy; but he was still my dear brother.

However, in human affairs it happens most often that there is no one from whom pardon for a violent wrong can be asked. Agamemnon could not seek pardon from Iphigenia, nor Clytemnestra from Agamemnon, nor Orestes from Clytemnestra. Each had to make terms with his own guilt. There are cases where the one person upon whom devolves responsibility to pardon bloodshed is the repentant killer himself. This situation is illustrated in the last scene of *Heracles*.

After returning from his descent into the lower world Heracles reaches his palace in Thebes just in time to rescue his wife and three sons from death at the hand of the usurper Lycus; and he promptly takes his revenge by killing Lycus — an act which, to an audience that has witnessed the usurper's cruelty and knows the innocence of his victims, seems laudable and satisfying. Immediately after, Iris and Madness enter the palace. Madness herself pleads in vain on behalf of goodness (856) against the action — or reaction — of implacable cosmic forces personalized as the malevolence of Hera; and Heracles kills Megara and the three boys. When he returns to sanity, and is dissuaded by Theseus from ending his own life, the question of where to find pardon presents itself to him in a concrete form. As he prepares to depart with Theseus for Athens he picks up his bow (1377–85):

> My bow! which I have loved, and lived with; and now loathe.
> What shall I do — keep it, or let it go? This bow,
> Hung at my side, will talk: 'With me you killed your wife
> And children; keep me, and you keep their murderer!'
> Shall I then keep and carry it? With what excuse?
> And yet — disarmed of this, with which I did such deeds
> As none in Hellas equalled, must I shamefully
> Yield to my enemies and die?

Theseus, to whom the gods count for little, and who sees man's life as solely man's concern, has counselled him to live and suffer; his view is merely fatalistic, and he acquits Heracles of all guilt. Heracles on the other hand clings to the old belief that there is a moral element in divinity — a belief of which he would have been cured if he had listened to the talk between Iris and Madness. Yet from his false belief Heracles has learnt a certain truth about himself. Theseus regards him as not morally guilty, only unfortunate. Heracles, over and above his ritual pollution by the shedding of kindred blood, feels guilt in himself, while at the same time knowing himself 'a slave to Fortune' (1357). The bow is a symbol of his essential nature, and of the life he has lived. He has been a man of constant violence. His strength has on the whole been used in the cause of humanity; but only on the whole. Heracles was no Buddha, no Jesus; he destroyed dangerous beasts; he also sacked peaceful cities. He is a man of war, of blood, of revenge. He has never denied this; but now his wife and sons lie dead before him, and at last he sees, from the victim's view, the face of violence. What is he to do?

Must he disown the activity of so many years – disown himself now, because of the violence which at other times he has gloried in exercising? Shall he leave his bow behind?

> Never! This bow
> Is anguish to me, yet I cannot part with it.

To deny and condemn his own character and career would have been as abject as to take his own life. What he has done, only he can forgive. He knows he is Heracles, and will never be anything other than he is; this knowledge qualifies him to expiate his own guilt. In response to the friendship of Theseus he decides to live, and to keep his bow.

The subject of this chapter is the incomplete conclusion of the long search for 'justice' which began with the *Iliad*, absorbed the tragedians, was commented on by Thucydides and analysed by Plato, and is still found, at the end of the fourth century, as Menander's theme in three comedies of his mature period. Here at last Justice has stepped down from the Areopagus, where Athena is President, to the streets where slave and master both exercise free speech – from the heroic to the domestic level; but the subject has in no sense become a trivial one. Menander knew that justice, the universal preoccupation of human society, is not exclusively a matter of blood-feuds between royal houses. He had studied Aristotle's *Ethics*, had distinguished the types and degrees of wrong-doing, of punishment, of reward, as a student under Aristotle's successor Theophrastus. He had learnt that justice is a matter of neighbours and relatives, of fidelity and consideration, of money and hot temper. He did not attempt, so far as we know, to deal seriously with the wrong-doer whose problem is *self*-forgiveness – that is properly a tragic theme; but forgiveness, its earning and its bestowal, as a mutual relationship between imperfect human beings, is the subject of *The Arbitration*, *The Shorn Hair*, and *The Samian Woman*. In all these plays, as in others, Menander refers to, quotes, and imitates Euripides. It is natural to suppose that in choosing this central interest he was consciously continuing where Euripides had left off, and within his narrower limits bringing one aspect of the perpetual issue of life, and of drama, to its logical conclusion.

It may well seem to some readers that some of the interpretations of Euripides' thought offered in this book, and especially the analysis contained in this last chapter, reflect a desire to find support in an ancient author for moralistic views on the problems of today's society. It is true that a critic who is not deeply and imaginatively concerned about such problems is unlikely to see far into the mind of such a writer as Euripides; but the proper answer to this comment is found in a passage of Thucydides to which I have referred several times, III.82–4. He is describing the effect of the war between Athens and Sparta upon the struggle between the democratic and oligarchic parties which polarized politics in most cities of the Hellenic world.

The whole Hellenic world was convulsed ... Opportunities for bringing in the foreigner were never wanting to the revolutionary parties. The sufferings which revolution entailed upon the cities were many and terrible, such as have occurred and always will occur, as long as the nature of mankind remains the same ... Revolution thus ran its course from city to city, and the places which it arrived at last, from having heard what had been done before, carried to a still greater excess the refinement of their inventions, as manifested in the cunning of their enterprises and the atrocity of their reprisals. (Crawley's translation)

The relevance of this well-known passage to today's news-headlines is now a commonplace; but we are less often reminded that this was the world — and it was a small one — in which Euripides lived; and it seems unlikely that the tragic poet saw and felt the stresses of life, the hopeless agony of feud and reprisal, less clearly and intensely than the historian. The very fact that the word for 'pardon' was only then coming into use for the first time suggests that some people were at last beginning to express their weariness of the obligation to inflict cruelty for cruelty. But in the matter of reprisal, as in other human errors, Euripides propounded no doctrine, advocated no specific reform. His function as a dramatist was to hold up a mirror; and among artists the dramatist was unique in that his function was to mirror the ugly, the banal, the false, along with the true and the beautiful. Euripides showed men and women enslaving each other, fearing, punishing, hating; sometimes asking for pardon, rarely granting it; looking to gods for a solution instead of to themselves. He invited his audience to contemplate what they saw, knowing that his picture of them would be viewed by nearly everyone with either blindness or hostility; and he veiled it in an irony so consistent that only those few who would learn his language could find for themselves his full meaning. Thucydides did not have to read aloud his History, by permission of a committee, before the assembled *dēmos* at a religious festival; he was writing in exile, for those who would take the trouble to read; so he needed no veil of irony. Few who read the History today would question the aptness of his perceptions to twentieth-century humanity. It is time that the same claim should be established for Euripides' plays.

In this book I have not attempted a comprehensive appraisal of Euripides' work, but have confined my enquiry to two aspects of it: his dramatic method and his social message. To write creatively about Euripides the timeless artist — about his poetic power, his skill in structural and emotional design, his psychological perceptiveness, his seasoning of sublimity with sardonic humour, his radical vision of the broad human scene, his hope, despair, and patience — these are undertakings to be justified only by the ability to perform them superbly well. In my reading of his plays I have broken some of those pointless rules which tend to become encrusted about professional studies when they have allowed themselves to be led into a defensive posture; and I have asked some questions of a kind often censured as unscholarly. Both are, I believe, things worth doing, as a limited contribution. What we still await, and have awaited too long, is a great book, written by one who is both a scholar and a man or woman of our own time and of a culture wider than the classical field, who can present to the contemporary world of letters, on a level worthy of such a theme, the mind of Euripides.

NOTES

CHAPTER 1   THE CLAIM TO INTERPRET

1. The Preface to *Troilus and Cressida*, Quarto 1609.
2. H. Lloyd-Jones, *The Justice of Zeus* (California U. P. 1971) 147.
3. See e.g. H. D. F. Kitto, *Greek Tragedy* (Methuen 1950, 2nd edn) 230. And J. H. Finley, *Three Essays on Thucydides* (Harvard 1967) 20, says in reference to Euripides' *Andromache*, 'it is true that, writing war-plays for popular hearing, Euripides is often led to blacken Sparta . . .'
4. Kitto, *Greek Tragedy* 362.
5. J. Jones, *On Aristotle and Greek Tragedy* (Chatto and Windus 1971) 266.
6. See note 37 below.
7. See A. W. Verrall, *Euripides The Rationalist* (Cambridge 1895) and *Four Plays of Euripides* (Cambridge 1905).
8. E.g. L. H. G. Greenwood, *Aspects of Euripidean Tragedy* (Cambridge 1953), the chapter on *The Suppliant Women*; and Wesley D. Smith, 'The Ironic Structure in *Alcestis*', *Phoenix* xiv (1960) 127—45.
9. See P. H. Vellacott, *Sophocles and Oedipus* (Macmillan 1971).
10. Clearly most of those meanings which Euripides committed to ironic expression would be available only to readers. If in using the ironic method his prophetic sense anticipated the world of libraries which began to develop in the next few centuries, he can hardly have foreseen how shallow popular sentiment such as Lycurgus exhibits, and the academic formalism initiated by Aristotle, would obliterate his living message.
11. G. Steiner, *In Bluebeard's Castle* (Eliot Memorial Lectures, Faber 1971).
12. *The Justice of Zeus* 145—55.
13. E.g. Jones, *On Aristotle and Greek Tragedy* 250.
14. D. Barrett's translation from *The Frogs and Other Plays* (Penguin 1964).
15. Did Aristophanes understand and admire Euripides enough to imitate him in this way? There is little evidence. Certainly he is likely to have been among the few who realized how Euripides worked. And there is the curious verb *euripidaristophanizein*, used by Cratinus in a fragment of an unidentified play (see Meineke, *Fragm. Com. Graec.*, vol. 2, 225): '"And who are you?" some clever spectator may ask — a rather too subtle user of words, one who *euripidaristophanizes*.' A scholiast explains that 'Aristophanes was presented in [a] comedy as one who made fun of Euripides and yet imitated him.' If I have correctly interpreted the significance of Dionysus' choice of Aeschylus at the end of *The Frogs*, the ironic twist which Aristophanes gives to that scene could well be described by this compound word, which in that case would mean 'to

treat Euripides as Aristophanes did', i.e. to make fun of him, but to do so by using the kind of irony which was characteristic of Euripides; so that the meaning of the passage would be, to the discerning, complimentary to him and not derisory.

16. *Poetics* 53 a.

17. *On Aristotle and Greek Tragedy* 242.

18. *On Aristotle and Greek Tragedy* 241.

19. See Chapter 8, pages 219—21.

20. Of Aeschylus Aristotle mentions only *Prometheus* and *Choephori*; of Sophocles only *Oedipus Tyrannus* and *Antigone*.

21. *Poetics* 54 a 28—9. In this and subsequent references I have used T. S. Dorsch's translation (Penguin 1965).

22. For the traditional view of Menelaus in *Orestes* see e.g. A. P. Burnett, *Catastrophe Survived* (Oxford 1971), Chapters 8 and 9, and Finley, *Three Essays on Thucydides* 41. See Chapter 3.

23. Just as Electra's judgement on Helen in the same play (lines 126—9) has always been accepted. See pages 62—3.

24. *Poetics* 54 a 32.

25. *Poetics* 54 a 37—54 b 2.

26. *Poetics* 54 b 31—5.

27. *Poetics* 56 a 25—7.

28. E. g. R. D. Laing, *The Politics of Experience* (Penguin 1967).

29. I do not here wish to assume that Thucydides' and Euripides' reactions to events of the war were necessarily similar. The question is a large one; there are certain consonances in the two writers, and from these we may draw suggestions which if otherwise supported, may help our understanding of both.

30. Compare Aristotle, *Poetics* 54 a: 'There can be goodness in every class of person; for instance, a woman or a slave may be good, though the one is possibly an inferior being and the other in general an insignificant one.' This is Dorsch's translation; Jones (*On Aristotle and Greek Tragedy* 42) translates, 'although no doubt one of these types is inferior and the other wholly worthless'.

31. For Euripides' use of this image see Chapter 3, e.g. pages 58, 74, and Chapter 6, page 173.

32. For an entirely different interpretation of Apollo's role in *Orestes* see Burnett, *Catastrophe Survived*, Chapter 9. See also pages 78—9.

33. For a different view see Lloyd-Jones, *The Justice of Zeus* 154—5.

34. See Aristophanes, *Thesmophoriazusae* 445—50.

35. E. g. Hecabe's address to Zeus, *Women of Troy* 884—8.

36. An exceptional passage is Amphitryon's address to Zeus in *Heracles* 339—47. It can hardly be called ironic; it expresses the despair of a mortal in extremity. Nor, I think, is there irony in *Bacchae* 1349, 'Zeus my father ordained all this from the beginning.' Does a 'religious' outlook necessarily involve crediting gods with moral values which we recognize? I doubt if an answer to this can be found in Euripides.

37. See e.g. P. T. Stevens' edition of *Andromache* (Oxford 1971), where the editor, not

regarding this epilogue as ironic, is led to apology in his commentary on lines 1235 and 1279, and to censure in his Introduction, pages 14–15.

38. See C. H. Whitman, *Euripides and the Full Circle of Myth* (Harvard 1974), page 114: 'Co-existent contrarieties, maintained by a detached, unfaltering self-consciousness, unconcealedly timing and managing all, hold the key to the art of the ironic mode.' This book, a group of essays on Euripides, is full of the author's characteristic illumination.

CHAPTER 2   THE IRONIC METHOD 1

1. For a more summary presentation of the special nature of Euripides' irony see my Introduction to *Orestes and Other Plays* (Penguin 1972) 9–14.

2. See R. B. Gamble, 'Euripides' *Supplices*; Decision and Ambivalence', *Hermes* XCVIII (1970).

3. See e.g. Kitto, *Greek Tragedy* 230ff.; Stevens' edition of *Andromache* 9–15; and my Introduction to *Orestes and Other Plays* 26–43.

4. Important features of this interpretation of *Andromache* were first expounded by A. W. Verrall, *Four Plays of Euripides*.

5. For two reflections on the fairy-tale quality of popular legends, both spoken by the chorus, see *Electra* 737–44, *Iphigenia in Aulis* 797–9.

6. For the date of this play see Stevens' edition, Introduction, pages 15–19.

7. The question, What city is meant? is of no importance, even if we could be fairly sure of the answer. The question here is, Why did Euripides make Menelaus suddenly change his behaviour? Stevens, page 183, says, 'It seems to be the intention of Euripides to present the Spartan Menelaus first as a bully, then as a weakling'; but does not suggest any dramatic purpose behind such an intention.

8. See e.g. Stevens' edition, note on 547.

9. I have found in discussion that other critics sometimes deprecate the kind of argument I have used here as 'detective work'. What is legitimate argument in literary criticism, and what is not, must be left to the judgement of the reader; but much valuable Shakespearean criticism of the last fifty years could be called 'detective work' with equal aptness. Especially when a writer employs irony as Euripides does, he invites 'detective work' from those for whom his more important meaning is intended. The essential safeguards in such study are taste, imagination, and a true conception of the author's general outlook. For further lines of enquiry in connexion with this play see my Introduction to *Orestes and Other Plays*, pages 31–2.

10. There is a good deal of interpolation in the text of this play. Anyone wishing to study it seriously should read D. L. Page, *Actors' Interpolations in Greek Tragedy* (Oxford 1934). Even the most sceptical view of the text, however, should not substantially affect the argument of this chapter.

11. The text of this play mentions oars very frequently, e.g. 174, 765, 1388; and sails only in one doubtful passage.

12. See Kitto, *Form and Meaning in Drama* (Methuen 1964) 4–5.

CHAPTER 3 THE IRONIC METHOD 2

1. Two other plays, *Augē* and *Oedipus*, now surviving only in fragments, were probably produced in 408 with *Orestes*. It is not possible to say what was the chief theme of either; though the former seems to have told the story of yet another cruelly-treated woman, while the latter provided Stobaeus with four more comments on the nature and place of woman. If, as the present chapter maintains, the interest of *Orestes* is primarily political, and its symbolic theme the insanity of war, and if the other two plays were both concerned with the man—woman relationship, then the whole programme may well have been offered as a kind of 'last testament'. The possibility that Euripides intended to go to Macedon only for a limited visit need not, I think, be considered.

2. See Burnett, *Catastrophe Survived*, Chapters 8 and 9, for an account of this play which is stimulating and thorough, but with which I disagree at almost every point.

3. W. D. Smith, 'Disease in Euripides' *Orestes*', *Hermes* xcv (1967).

4. W. Arrowsmith, Introduction to translation of *Orestes* (Chicago 1958).

5. Burnett, *Catastrophe Survived* 186. Similarly Finley, *Three Essays on Thucydides* 41: 'The Spartan Menelaus ... is portrayed as quite capable of deserting the ties of blood when it is dangerous to defend them.' But the lines to which the writer refers (*Orestes* 718—24) are not spoken by Menelaus; they are the insane Orestes' abusive reply to Menelaus' offer to help him 'by diplomacy, not by force' (710).

6. '[Menelaus] minces forward branded by costume and wig as a languishing and effete prince who has spent too long in softening eastern climes' — Burnett, *Catastrophe Survived* 185, where all this is based on the chorus's phrase *pollēi habrosynēi* (349) and Tyndareos' retort (485). Menelaus has, as one would expect, put on his best tunic and cloak for his arrival in Argos. The reference to his hair (1532) is shouted by Orestes at the height of his insanity.

7. Kitto, *Greek Tragedy* 347.

8. See *Phoenician Women* 1269, 'Two heroic warriors, two brothers, are at this moment reeling towards death.' See also Chapter 6, pages 167ff.

9. The potential force in the optative verb 'endure' may be taken either as conveying a statement of future probability, as in the version given, or as expressing mere potentiality, i.e. 'is able' rather than 'is destined'. I think the future sense has more point.

10. There is another reference to *Phoenician Women* in 1555, where the image of 'two lions', often applied to Eteocles and Polyneices, is applied to Orestes and Pylades.

11. We need not press the traditional account which made Clytemnestra and Helen twins. Clytemnestra must have been nearer fifty, if Iphigenia was nubile when Agamemnon went to Troy.

12. Compare Sophocles' *Electra* 449, where Electra tells Chrysothenis to cut off the ends (*akras phobas*) of her own hair and Electra's to offer at the grave of Agamemnon.

13. See note 6 above, and page 63.

14. Thucydides II.43; Aeschylus, *Eumenides* 852.
15. At 1596ff. we have this sequence:

    ORESTES: I will kill Hermione.
    MENELAUS: Kill her — if you do you will suffer for it.
    ORESTES: I'll do it, then.
    MENELAUS: No, no, no! Stop! Do no such thing!

    In 1597 Menelaus' 'Kill her' is naturally taken as the conditional use of the imperative, since one second later, appalled by the madman's literalness, he yells a contradiction. Burnett (*Catastrophe Survived* 193) takes this 'command' as the final illustration of Menelaus' 'depraved cruelty', and says that 'Menelaus will not give up his chance at the Argive throne, just to purchase his daughter's life'; and further assumes that Menelaus' appeal to the Argives in 1621–2 indicates that he has already won the citizens to his support and that a body of them now appears armed in the orchestra to attack the palace under Menelaus' direction. I find no support for all this in the text. The result of trying to build a circumstantial account upon the frantic cries of 1608–17 is illustrated by G. A. Seeck's conclusion (quoted in Burnett's note 7 on pages 193–4) that 'the entire motif of firing the palace ... should be deleted as interpolated matter'.
16. The Oxford Classical Text (G. Murray) brackets 1631–2 as interpolated. Such an expedient illustrates the hopelessness of trying to make sense of this play on the basis of the usual interpretation of Helen's part in it.

CHAPTER 4   WOMAN

1. A. W. Gomme, essay on 'The Position of Women in Athens' in *Essays in Greek History and Literature* (Blackwell 1937).
2. See e.g. Lloyd-Jones, *The Justice of Zeus* 146–7.
3. See Burnett, *Catastrophe Survived* 127: 'It has been argued that with this play Euripides meant to reduce the spectator to a bitter atheism, or to a bitterer belief in a malignant and mocking heaven, but this essentially Victorian attitude, based upon disapproval of the seducer god, is now giving way.' The answer to this is, that if the critic who (like Ion in 341, 370, 436–44, and the chorus in 506–8) disapproves of divine rape is prejudiced, so the critic who (like Athena, 1595) approves of it is equally prejudiced. The poet includes expression of both views in his play. Creusa is ready to praise Apollo when, after seventeen years of cruel neglect, he presents her with a son. Euripides, knowing (as Ion knows) that rape is an act of men, not gods, pities both her sad life and her foolish belief. Whether compassion was 'essentially Victorian' is doubtful; but it was essentially Euripidean.
4. See e.g. *Iphigenia in Tauris* 576–7, where the chorus, after sharing sympathetically the sorrows of Orestes and Iphigenia, speak two lines asking a little sympathy for their own sorrows, and are ignored. Later in the play, however, they risk their lives to help the royal family (1075–7).
5. *The Tragedies of Euripides* (Methuen 1967) 2ff.
6. Plutarch, *Moralia* 988e.

7. There is an echo of this in Menander's *Samian Woman* 553–4, where Niceratos proposes to burn a dubious baby.

8. Loeb Library, *Select Papyri*, vol. iii (1970) ed. Page, 108ff.

9. *Classical Philology* LX no. 4 (Oct. 1965) 240–55; reprinted in *Euripides*, ed. E. Segal (Prentice-Hall 1968). I find this essay more helpful than the chapter on *Alcestis* in the same author's *Catastrophe Survived*.

10. *Phoenix* XIV (1960) 127–45; reprinted in *Euripides*, ed. Segal.

11. In *Alcestis* 180 there is a textual uncertainty. If the MSS are right, the word 'alone' refers not to the bed but to Alcestis, who recognizes that, though the ideal of marriage demands that a wife be ready to give her life for her husband, she knows no other woman who would be ready to meet this demand.

12. Euripides repeats this contradiction in *Andromache* 1253–6, 1268–72, where Thetis tells Peleus first that she will make him immortal, then that all men must die.

13. This is why Alcestis demands that he shall not replace her with another wife. Her acceptance of the probability that he will have a concubine, whose sons could not be rivals to hers, is delicately conveyed in the Servant's narrative, 181.

14. The fact that the concept of guilt — not ritual guilt but moral — so clearly emerges in this, the earliest of the extant plays, reminds us how limited is the picture we have from the lost plays — even those of which substantial fragments remain.

15. 'On Euripides' *Medea*', *Hermes* XCIV (1966).

16. A more literal version of the last three lines (428–30) is: 'The history of ages has many things to say about the parts played by women and those played by men.' The context shows the sentence as a notable *meiosis*.

17. Euripides could express the opposite feeling when it was appropriate; see e.g. *Heracles* 632–6, *Ion* 490–1.

18. Charles Segal, '*Hippolytus* 108–128', *Hermes* XCVII (1969).

19. I take the ironic view of this play to be the only one which makes dramatic sense. See Chapter 2, pages 32–42.

20. This, however, is disputed; see Stevens' edition, note on 1047.

21. See an article by Bernard Knox, 'Euripidean Comedy', contributed to *The Rarer Action* (New Brunswick 1971).

22. See e.g. Fragment 658 from *Protesilaus*: 'The man who includes all women in a general censure is not wise but a fool. Among many women you will find this one bad, that one noble.'

23. See the Nurse in *Medea* 122–7: 'To have learnt to live on the common level is better.'

24. Menander went on where Euripides stopped; forgiveness of a man by a wronged woman is the theme of several of his mature plays.

CHAPTER 5   HELEN

1. I made a first approach to it in my Introduction to *The Women of Troy* in *The Bacchae and Other Plays* (Penguin 1954).

2. *Electra* 1226. This attitude, however, is as new for the chorus as it is for Electra; all through the earlier scenes they encouraged her to vengeance. As for 479–86, if it were not for 'your adultery', *sa lechea*, in 481, we would probably assume that 484–6 must be an anticipation of the death of Clytemnestra; and it is true that at 1066ff. Electra dismisses the traditional story that Clytemnestra's motive for killing Agamemnon was revenge for Iphigenia. But in the first stasimon none of the audience either knows this or would guess that 'your adultery, evil-hearted daughter of Tyndareos' could refer to anyone but Helen. This is supported by 211–14, where the chorus show that any reference to adultery makes them think of Helen, not Clytemnestra.

3. The Greek says 'the old man'. This is usually taken to refer to Priam; but it may possibly mean the old slave whom Priam (in *Alexandros*) ordered to expose the child, and who instead preserved its life.

4. Cicero, *De Fato* 15.34 – 16.36; Clement, *Stromateis* 8.9; von Arnim, *Stoicorum Veterum Fragmenta* 2.346. I am indebted to Mr R. W. Sharples for bringing these passages to my notice.

5. *Select Papyri*, vol. iii (1970), ed. Page (Loeb Library).

6. The play on Aphrodite/*aphrosynē* may well occur before this, but I do not know of an instance. It is hard to believe that in 415 B.C. the pun had not been threadbare for a long time.

7. See the article 'Euripidean Comedy', by Bernard Knox, referred to in Chapter 4, note 21.

8. *Transactions of the American Philological Association* (1971).

9. See Frazer, *The Golden Bough* (Macmillan 1933), Part 6, 253ff.

CHAPTER 6   COMMENT ON WAR

1. Kitto, *Greek Tragedy* 362ff.

2. A. W. Gomme, *Essays in Greek History and Literature* 120.

3. See Burnett, *Catastrophe Survived* 216: 'Orestes cannot tell his friends from his enemies, his victims from his saviours, or for that matter many another thing from its opposite.'

4. This general view of the scene was put forward by Greenwood in *Aspects of Euripidean Tragedy*, Chapter 4.

5. It is uncertain in what city *Andromache* was first produced. See Stevens' edition pages 15–21.

6. See Murray's note at the beginning of *Supplices* in the Oxford Classical Text.

7. See above, Chapter 1, pages 6–8.

8. Kitto, *Greek Tragedy* 351–62.

9. Webster, *The Tragedies of Euripides* 219.

10. After Polyneices' prayer for success in killing his brother come the following lines, 1369–71: 'At this many shed tears of shame to think that such a thing could happen, and looked this way and that uneasily.' Murray, following Valckenaer, brackets these lines; they are certainly not of high quality and may be an interpolation.

11. The references to Dionysus found in the first two stasima suggest a connexion of thought with *The Bacchae*, written within the next three years and probably contemplated over a long period. There too Dionysus is the god who favours peace (416ff.) and is opposed by the man of war (780ff.); but there the god of freedom is shown by events to be dangerous and tyrannical. In interpreting *The Bacchae* we should take into account the different presentation of Dionysus in *The Phoenician Women*.

12. Aeschylus, *Agamemnon* 803–4. Agamemnon sacrificed Iphigenia in an attempt 'to create willing boldness in men who were going to their deaths', *tharsos hekousion andrasi thnēiskousi komizōn*.

13. Euripides surely had this exit-line in mind when he made Clytemnestra mention (1149) that her own marriage with Agamemnon had been a crude rape.

14. This speech of Iphigenia is referred to by Kitto, *Greek Tragedy* 365, as 'all sorts of nonsense'. A true description; but when Euripides made a serious character talk nonsense he had an ironic purpose in doing so.

CHAPTER 7   SACRIFICE FOR VICTORY

1. See Chapter 5, page 133.

2. See e.g. *Iphigenia in Tauris* 1179, *Electra* 826–8; Sophocles, *Antigone* 1001–11.

3. It is sometimes said that the critical opinions of men such as Lycurgus, or Aristotle, are not to be disputed because they, being so close in time to the author, must have understood him better than we can. We can add to the list of such opinions that of the writer of the Hypothesis to *Orestes*, who says that in this play 'all the characters are bad except Pylades'.

4. It is worth noting also that Lycurgus, Demaratus, Plutarch, and Apollodorus all give the oracle in this form: 'You will win if . . .'; not 'You will lose unless . . .'.

5. *The Tragedies of Euripides* 130.

6. An interesting passage in Jones, *On Aristotle and Greek Tragedy* 241ff., about the parody of an Euripidean monody in Aristophanes, *Frogs* 1331–63, suggests that Euripides saw the tragic reality of trivial disasters. Praxithea, and to a lesser degree Clytemnestra, both exhibit a trivial incomprehension of tragic reality.

CHAPTER 8   FREEDOM

1. See C. H. Whitman, *Homer and the Heroic Tradition* (Harvard 1958), Chapter 9.

2. I ascribe lines 1018–19, 1021, to the Servant. The only other possible ascriptions are to the chorus or to another Messenger; and the lines are out of character for both, and in character for the Servant.

3. See above, Chapter 6, page 176, and note 14.

4. See Chapter 6, note 11.

CHAPTER 9   THE CURE OF ANGER

1. *Iliad* I.1: *mēnin aeide, thea* . . .

2. The principle of condemning revenge as an unworthy and destructive motive

was not invented by the modern conscience, any more than it is followed in modern practice; nor was it invented by Christianity, nor by Plato. It is advocated in certain books of the Old Testament, where it is given divine authority; and Thucydides, writing about the Corcyrean revolution of 427 B.C. (III.84), makes it clear that he endorses this principle.

3. For the common belief that Euripides always expressed hatred of women, see Aristophanes, *Thesmophoriazusae, passim.*

4. For Clytemnestra's pardoning of Electra see page 238.

5. They are, in fact, the third such quibble in the play; the others are at 257–8 and 410–24.

INDEXES

INDEX OF CRITICS AND EDITORS CITED

Pairs of page numbers indicate the relevant page in both text and notes, together with the number(s) of the note(s) in question.

Verrall, A. W.: *Euripides the Rationalist* (Cambridge 1895), 4, 245 (n. 7); *Four Plays of Euripides* (Cambridge 1905), 4, 245 (n. 7); 35, 247 (n. 4)

Webster, T. B. L.: *The Tragedies of Euripides* (Methuen 1967), 17; 91–2, 249 (n. 5); 97; 163; 167, 251 (Ch. 6, n. 9); 197,

252 (n. 5)

Whitman, C. H.: *Euripides and the Full Circle of Myth* (Harvard 1974), 22, 247 (n. 38); *Homer and the Heroic Tradition* (Harvard 1958), 206, 252 (Ch. 8, n. 1); 225

Wilamovitz-Moellendorf, U. von: edition of *The Women of Troy*, 146

GENERAL INDEX

Plays by Euripides are entered under their titles, with the most important references first, and passing references (to the play or any of its characters) last; plays by other dramatists are entered under the dramatist's name. Individual characters in plays are in all cases entered under their names, with the plays as subheadings; parentheses denote a play in which the character is mentioned but does not appear. Euripides' attitudes to specific subjects (e.g. gods, war, women), and such topics as his irony, his use of the chorus, his epilogues and his audience, are indexed under these headings.

Italic page numbers indicate that information (other than bibliographical references, for which see Index of Critics, etc.) will be found not only in the text but also in one or more notes (pp. 245–53) signposted there. For subjects mentioned in a note but not in the corresponding text passage, the page number for the note is given, and the note itself identified within parentheses.

'Contemporary' means 'contemporary with Euripides (or whoever else is in question)'. Euripides is shortened to E. throughout, and the following abbreviations are used for certain of his plays:

CH	The Children of Heracles	PW	The Phoenician Women
IA	Iphigenia at Aulis	SW	The Suppliant Women
IT	Iphigenia at Tauris	WT	The Women of Troy

Achaean army, *see* army

Achilles, 93; in Homer, 42, 205, 206, 225, 226; (in *Hecabe*, 192, 208); in *IA*, 42–6, 83, 126, 174–6, 202–3, 219–20

Admetus: in *Alcestis*, 36, 82, 99–105, 112, 126, 222, 227–9

Adrastus: (in *PW*, 168;) in *SW*, 25–32 *passim*, 157, 159, 168, 189

adultery: significance of Helen's, 132–4, 251 (Ch. 5, n. 2); Greek view of, 135

Aegeus: in *Medea*, 25, 107, 113, 126, 218

Aegisthus: (in *Electra*, 74, 236, 237; in *Orestes*, 55, 66, 69)

Aeolus (fragment), 95

Aeolus: in *Melanippe* plays, 97

Aerope: in *Cretan Women*, 95

Aeschylus: his contemporary standing, compared with E.'s, 1; various levels of his audience, 4; in Aristophanes' *Frogs*, 9–11, 94; dramatic irony in, 23; women in, 83, 84–5, 151; slaves in, 206; anger in, 225–6; Aristotle on, 246 (n. 20); *Agamemnon*, 3, 24, 63, 83, 84, 85, 89, 132, 143, 151, 163, 182, 206, 237; —, sacrifice of Iphigenia in, 12, 13, 43, 48, 133, *174*, 178, 179, 181, 189–90, 201,

222; *Choephori*, 63, 74, 84, 108, 125, 181, 206, 246 (n. 20); *Danaides*, 134; *Eumenides*, 24, 84, 226; *Prometheus*, 246 (n. 20); *Suppliants*, 84, 85, 125, 151

Aethra: in *Suppliant Women*, 25, 27, 29

Agamemnon, 55, 58, 74, 101, 126, 134, 170, 172–3, 240–1; in the *Iliad*, 142–3, 224; in Aeschylus, 3, 12, 48, 133, 143, 181, 190, 201, 222, 252 (n. 12); (in *Electra*, 237;) in *Hecabe*, 85, 162–3, 192, 211–14, 219; in *IA*, 12, 30, 42–9 *passim*, 51, 112, 132, *174–6*, 179, 180, 187, 196, 199, 201, 203–4, 219–22; (in *IT*, 200–1, 238–9; in *Orestes*, 140, 223); in *Telephus*, 127; (in *WT*, 163, 165)

Agaue: in *Bacchae*, 84, 125, 223

agōn (contest): an element in most Greek plays, 3

Agora, the, *see* Athens

Aias (Ajax), 93; in Sophocles' play, 91

aidōs (sense of right), 79

Alcestis (438): presentation of woman in, 99–106; *syngnōmē* in, 227–9; fully comparable with later plays, 2; man's inhumanity to woman in, 18; and the world of belief, 22; and *Andromache*, 36,